VOICE INTO ACTING

Integrating voice and the Stanislavski approach

CHRISTINA GUTEKUNST AND JOHN GILLETT

Illustrations by Dany Heck

Bloomsbury Methuen Drama
An imprint of Bloomsbury Publishing Plc

BLOOMSBURY
LONDON · OXFORD · NEW YORK · NEW DELHI · SYDNEY

Bloomsbury Methuen Drama

An imprint of Bloomsbury Publishing Plc

50 Bedford Square	1385 Broadway
London	New York
WC1B 3DP	NY 10018
UK	USA

www.bloomsbury.com

Bloomsbury is a registered trade mark of Bloomsbury Publishing Plc

First published 2014
Reprinted 2014, 2017 (twice)

British Library Cataloguing-in-Publication Data
A catalogue record for this book is available from the British Library.

ISBN: PB:	978-1-4081-8356-4
	ePDF:	978-1-4081-8544-5
	ePub:	978-1-4081-8450-9

Library of Congress Cataloging-in-Publication Data
Gutekunst, Christina.
Voice into acting : Integrating voice and the Stanislavski approach / Christina Gutekunst and
John Gillett.
pages cm
Includes bibliographical references and index.
ISBN 978-1-4081-8356-4– ISBN 978-1-4081-8450-9 (epub) (print)– ISBN 978-1-4081-8544-5
(epdf) 1. Voice culture. 2. Elocution. 3. Method acting. I. Gillett, John, author. II. Title.
PN4162.G88 2013
792.02'8–dc23

Series: Performance Books

Typeset by Fakenham Prepress Solutions, Fakenham, Norfolk NR21 8NN
Printed and bound in India

CONTENTS

PART TWO THE ESSENTIAL VOCAL SIX – AND INTEGRATING ACTING INTO VOICE 29

PART THREE   INTEGRATING VOICE INTO THE ORGANIC ACTING PROCESS 169

ACKNOWLEDGEMENTS

We'd first like to thank all those inspiring voice and acting practitioners who have gone before us, and without whom this book would not exist. They are all evident within the text.

In particular we'd like to acknowledge and thank those who assisted in our personal training and growth.

For Christina, Ulle Weber, Heide and Peter Kost, Helga Mattke, Martin Porteous, Peter and Barbara Bridgmont, and David Carey; and my colleagues at East 15, especially Philip Weaver, Lucy Skilbeck, Richard Ryder, Colin Sadler, Rikke Liljenberg, Nicola Collett, Edda Sharpe and Jan Haydn Rowles – with all of whom I had passionate discussions and worked closely in order to improve the integration of voice into acting. Dearest thanks to all the members of my family, especially to my sister, mother and father for always believing in me, and to my grandparents, Wolfgang and Lotte Fischer, who helped me to get started. My deepest thanks go to all my students, past and present, for whom I developed this approach.

For John, Robert O'Neill and the Actors Workshop, who enthused me with the Stanislavski approach; Joan Paton, who introduced me to the importance of voice with kindness and skill; Nancy Diuguid and Mike Alfreds for their commitment to Stanislavski's aims; and to all the students, actors, directors and voice practitioners with whom I've been able to learn and develop and practise my work. Thanks, too, to Bryan and Andy for being around to talk.

We'd both like to thank all those who participated in our voice and acting workshops over the years, through which we clarified our ideas and practice; special thanks go to the Re:Actors Theatre Group, especially to Frances Rifkin and Michael McNulty.

Many thanks to those who read parts of the book in draft form: Andrew Leung, Louise-Mai Newberry, Dr Helen Castle, BSc, D.Clin. Psych.; but especially, Jan Haydn Rowles and Edda Sharpe, loyal, inspiring and generous friends and colleagues, who read much of the text and gave so much of their time to make many useful suggestions, and in addition supported and encouraged us through the final stages of the writing process. Finally, thanks go to Jenny Ridout and

John O'Donovan who encouraged us with their belief in the book and led the editorial team.

We'd like to thank Dany Heck with all our heart for her wonderful pictures and for her lifelong friendship with Christina!

FOREWORD

Several years ago Christina and John talked to us about an idea they had for a book. It was to be a book that would aim to provide the highest calibre of technical voice training, fully integrated with truthful, impulse and action-based acting. We were excited.

Over the course of time we have felt not just excited, but honoured to be reading this book ahead of the industry and to have been involved in the process of its creation. As voice coaches working across the industry, in TV, film and theatre, both in the UK and internationally, we are sure that actors from all levels of experience will be as excited by this book as we are and, like us, will be thankful that the authors have shared their exceptional process with us.

The vast depth of experience and an unquestionable passion for the actor's process that is shared by both practitioners is strongly evident in every exercise and every detailed description of their approach. The result is a working process that gives the actor a solid, practical approach to Voice into Acting.

We have worked with many actors in the profession who have been taught and directed by Christina and John, and we have seen the work in action at first hand: actors giving technically secure, truly connected performances, time and time again, in all sorts of contexts and in all sorts of circumstances.

It is surely every actor's desire to be 'in the moment' and to be connected and truthful to the character and the world of the play. *Voice into Acting*, with its wealth of knowledge and beautifully practical exercises, gives the actor the skills to be exactly that.

This book breathes new life, purpose and imagination into the underlying principles of voice training. It gives holistic and creative purpose to the mechanics of voice training, and connects with the vital relationship between voice work and the acting process. It will no doubt fast become an actor's bible.

Jan Haydn Rowles and Edda Sharpe
Authors of *HOW TO DO ACCENTS* and *HOW TO DO Standard English ACCENTS*

LIST OF ILLUSTRATIONS

The copyright for all illustrations is with Dany Heck, Christina Gutekunst and John Gillett.

INTRODUCTION

'All I have is a voice
To undo the folded lie ...'

September 1, 1939, W. H. AUDEN

This book is aimed predominantly at professional actors, student actors and voice teachers, but also at acting teachers and directors and anyone who wants to explore how to integrate voice work and an organic acting approach. It is our view that voice work must become acting work and acting work become voice work. For actors, we look at voice work from the viewpoint of Stanislavski's approach to acting and offer exercises to connect acting impulse with voice. For voice teachers, we show the connections between voice work and acting, as well as pointing out the traps that create a gap between them.

We came to this book from a belief that acting performance, regardless of style of writing, should express a reality, the truth of human experience, and the themes of writers and the world they create. Our voice is a key means for this expression. It needs to be well produced and flexible. It needs to express the literal meaning and formal structure of a text; and, in order to do this to the full, we believe it needs to express the imaginary circumstances of the world of the play and the characters. To achieve this, voice must be fully integrated with the acting process. So amidst the plethora of valuable books on voice, voice and text, and voice and the actor, this book is about voice and *acting*, and specifically, acting with language.

There is a continual struggle to find a balance between these three aspects of acting a script – voice production, the formal nature of language and the imaginary world – and one may often be emphasized to the detriment of the others. Performances we see from student or professional actors fall into three main categories: the connected, experienced and truthfully real, integrating voice and physicality within the acting process, and expressing both literal and subtextual meaning; the vocally proficient, producing literal meaning and sense of form and structure of the language, but technically describing the character and the action of the script, and lacking real meaning and life; and a deliberately quiet, low-key monotone, seeking to replicate the truth of everyday reality by, in effect, imitating it from the outside with a 'naturalistic' manner, and also lacking real meaning and life. So, we often see performance hit the rock of recitation or the hard place of a half-hearted 'Method'. This book is about the attempt to achieve the first example, the centred and integrated voice and performance that stand between these two modes.

To understand what the actor needs to do to create such a performance we won't develop an abstract theory, but observe what we experience as 'good' acting and try to analyze its components so that we can recreate them. Konstantin Stanislavski (1863–1938), the Russian actor, director and teacher, whose theory and practice we offer in this book, did precisely this. He learned from the actors who found a sense of truth and inspiration and drew audiences into a greater understanding of human experience: actors like Mikhail Shchepkin, the Russian 'father of realism', and the Italians, Tommaso Salvini and Eleonora Duse. How did they make the imaginary world of theatre seem real? How did they find connected feeling? How did they avoid getting stale and mechanical? How did they create the life and spirit of a role? Out of such questions came Stanislavski's 'system' or approach to acting, which has been embraced throughout the world and survives in various forms because it alone offers a thorough approach to connecting with real human experience in performance, through which we are not only entertained but moved, provoked and enlightened.

The challenge for the actor

If we consider what constitutes a good acting performance, many would agree that the following elements need to be present:

- a sense of reality and truth in the creation of circumstances and character

- awareness, ease, focus and clarity

- responsiveness and spontaneity

- engagement of the will and narrative drive

- imagination

- creation of emotional life and atmosphere

- physical and vocal embodiment of the character

- control and a sense of perspective within the role

- the sense of a whole integrated person

- communication of character and the play's story and themes to the audience
- full expression of the content and form of language.

Certainly a number of these points offer universal criteria for the art of acting through different periods and styles of theatre, from the Greeks to Brecht. Our contemporary view, of course, is strongly affected by the predominance of a realist theatre style since the nineteenth century, followed by the realism normally demanded by film, radio and television.

When we look at *how* to achieve reality, integration and communication, however, we hit some basic differences of approach and a variety of problems.

Experiencing or pretending

Stanislavski – and many others, from Bernard Shaw to Jean Benedetti and Uta Hagen – have identified two opposing forms of acting approach. He often referred to them as Representational and Organic.

Stanislavski has been the prime proponent of the Organic approach, an approach based on the natural resources and experiences of people in their everyday lives. This emphasis on the natural is not 'naturalism', which is a style of theatre, creating the outer appearance of reality through detailed settings and soundscapes. Stanislavski used this approach in his early productions of Chekhov's plays at the Moscow Art Theatre, but later rejected it as an evasion of coming to terms with the more important reality of our essential humanity and experience.

Organic acting *recreates human experience* and draws on our full human make-up – integrating mind, body, imagination, will, senses and emotions – as the raw material through which the actor can transform credibly into another character while performing. We do physical, verbal and psychological *actions* truthfully in imaginary circumstances to create what he called *the life of the human spirit of a role*. We use our imagination to probe *what* we're doing and *why* in the action of the script, to prompt *spontaneous responses* to other people and events and find that elusive quality of *being in the moment*. We start with the *text* but then explore the *subtext* and go back to the text: we start with *conscious* preparation but in order to reach the *subconscious* and our intuition and creativity. Stanislavski emphasized the importance, not just of the inner life of a role, but of using the voice and body expressively to create a fully *physicalized* character, and of communicating the themes and imaginary world created by the writer (see *An Actor Prepares, Building a Character* and *Creating a Role* (Methuen Drama); or *An Actor's Work* and *An Actor's Work on a Role* (Routledge)).

The alternative Representational approach had its chief theorist in Benoît-Constant Coquelin (1841–1909), the French actor who believed you should only experience and feel in rehearsal but not in performance, which requires *imitation* of the experience: 'The actor does not live but plays' (quoted in *An Actor's Work*: 26). At its best, as Stanislavski recognized, this approach could be artistic; but whether, even in its most skilled form, it can ever convince and affect an audience like an experienced performance is questionable. Representational acting literally *represents* a character and a reality. It *illustrates* it like holding up a picture of a real person. It will present a *manner* and an *emotional state.* We often see the outward *form* of character and an *effect* but not a living, breathing human being. It draws on conscious choices coming from the *intellect,* and is most concerned with *how* to present the character.

So, the essential difference between the two approaches is *experiencing and pretending*. It's often the case that actors and directors favour one or other of the approaches, but we aren't talking here of Representational or Organic *actors.* Actors might use bits of both approaches due to eclectic training, varied professional influences and different directors' methods. As Stanislavski pointed out, you may see elements of both within the same production or even the same actor performance (*An Actor's Work*: 35).

Examples of both approaches will be found across the globe, even in the US, home of the Method, Lee Strasberg's interpretation of Stanislavski, and in Russia, home of Stanislavski himself. Lev Dodin, the Artistic Director of St Petersburg's Maly Drama Theatre, has pointed to the dangers of commercialism in theatre, and of repetition in an actor's life, even within his own Stanislavski-influenced company: the actor does the same thing every day, rehearsing and performing continuously, and may find that he or she is 'not rehearsing and creating anything but just keeps replicating the same thing again and again' (*Journey Without End*: 68). We can represent either out of choice, or from failure to keep experiencing in each moment with freshness and spontaneity.

Between the 1920s and 1940s, Stanislavski's influence came to Britain, to rival the Representational tradition, via the productions of Theodore Komisarjevsky and the teaching of Michael Chekhov and Michel Saint-Denis. Since the 1960s, most British drama schools have included Stanislavski teaching on courses, either as one of a number of influences, or as a basic training. However, it takes time, repeated process, and absorption to develop a sure and creative acting process, and even students and actors with a grounding in Stanislavski can easily slip into clichéd forms of representationalism. So, while many actors won't aspire to an Organic approach, many do but will have problems sustaining it.

There are also a number of other personal, social and practical issues that can adversely affect both actor performance and the effectiveness of a voice teacher's intervention, which we'll look at in Chapter 1.

In this book we aim to explore what an organic acting approach means for voice work.

The challenge for the voice teacher

We can probably all agree that a good voice:

- only uses those muscles necessary to do the job economically and effortlessly
- functions through a harmonious balance between the breathing apparatus, the larynx and the whole vocal tract
- is free of unwanted noises, pressure and tension
- sounds full and supported in every pitch
- can be loud or quiet at will
- can reach far and flows full of resonance
- is clearly articulated.

Over the last century, voice training has included approaches based on scientific, physiological analysis; elocution and articulation; language and text analysis; and psycho-physical exploration. Voice teachers working in schools or the entertainment industry will most likely integrate a mixture of these. The qualities above will indeed produce a good, healthy and even beautiful voice – but this won't necessarily express an actor's impulses, their thoughts, will and feelings. A focus on the nature of our physical organism or on language and sounds alone can lead to an overly technical approach, and students and actors may well experience here a disconnection between voice work and acting process.

The voice is *essentially* a tool of communication for the human being and the actor in particular. In everyday life, it responds to imagination, impulses, wants and needs. To integrate voice and the acting process, the key question is: *what is the voice responding to?* This will depend on the circumstances in the script and the impulses the actors have created and received, as well as the initial words on the page. In this psycho-physical approach, conscious control over muscles and vocal expression 'must be diverted from muscle to impulse. The ultimate controls are imagination and emotion' (*Freeing the Natural Voice,* Kristin Linklater: 44). If we don't make this connection between word and inner life we shall still be doing two parallel processes: vocal process and acting process. The voice should respond in a fully integrated way to the experience of the actor as the character while communicating the text: as Linklater says, 'voice work must be acting work' (*Freeing the Natural Voice*: 232).

So, rather than learning about breath, alignment, pitch, resonance and articulation in isolation, the actor experiences acting, movement and voice as one, as strands of an interwoven thread that produce a unified performance: for example, alignment of the spine, breath and the driving force of the support muscles connect with the actor's will; and the intonation, accentuation, range and resonance of the voice become shaped by impulses from the imagination, feelings and given circumstances of a text.

What's in this book

* Last year was the 150th anniversary of Stanislavski's birth and he is still the most widely read, discussed and practised of acting theorists.

He is taught in most acting schools where voice teachers work.

* This book is seeking to make a specific contribution to – and not substitute for – all the varied and valuable work done on voice and speech up to this point.

* It is not meant to be a comprehensive form of training – we are assuming that the reader has a basic level of training and/or practice.

* We *are* offering a step-by-step guide to integrating voice into acting, and to enhancing the independent creativity of the actor and the effectiveness of voice teachers.

- For voice teachers, with or without actor training or understanding of Stanislavski, we offer new or alternative techniques to try out in order to harmonize with actors' creative processes and achieve richer results.
- For actors, we offer ways to integrate voice work into an acting process encountered and studied to varying degrees, which is organic and thorough and can enhance vocal identity as a character.

* **We'll explore how voice can:**

- **respond to and express creative impulse**
- **fully express language in content and form**
- **communicate human experience**
- **express the imaginary circumstances and the character**

- **transform and adapt to different roles**
- **connect with the audience and the space.**

* Each chapter may be read separately, but it is best to see it as part of a process of integration running through the book.

* The exercises are specific to this process and will help develop a unified practice of keeping the vocal connection to acting.

* We use boxes throughout to provide additional information: either extra instruction on exercises, or new insights and alternative information on a subject – these can be read sequentially or skipped until a later point.

* Also, from Part Two, we present symbols throughout the book to remind you of vocal elements that should become *Vocal Givens* in the acting process.

In Part One, we look at disconnection and integration of voice in the acting process, and the nature of the brain and how it relates to the creative process.

In Part Two, we examine the essential vocal elements and how to integrate acting.

In Part Three, we focus on an organic acting process based on Stanislavski's approach and how to integrate voice.

In Part Four, we draw all the elements together in a unified process by working on a piece of text in rehearsal and performance.

Below is a simplified 'map' of the elements in the process:

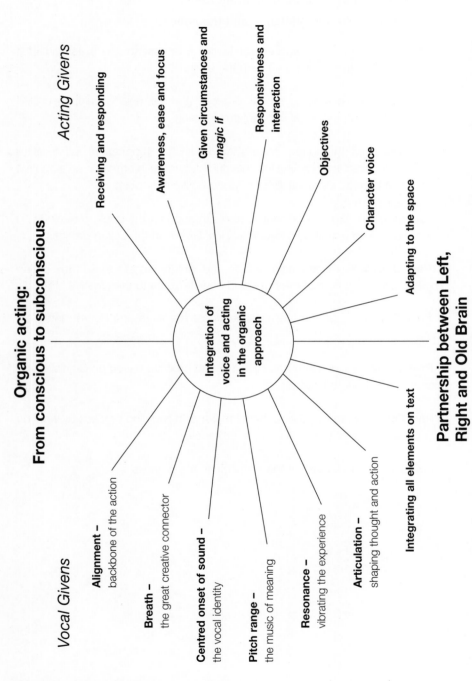

Figure 1 Map of the integrated organic approach

PART ONE

LAYING THE FOUNDATIONS

INTRODUCTION

In Part One, we lay the foundations for our approach by focusing on:

The organic acting approach and the voice – we give an overview of the organic and representational acting approaches and how they can affect voice.

Disconnection and integration – we look at the reasons and possible solutions for the gap that may appear between the actor and the text, action and circumstances, and between the voice tutor and the acting process of the actor.

The creative brain – we assert the need for a partnership between the different areas of the brain, between intellectual control and intuitive, imaginative release.

1
THE ORGANIC ACTING APPROACH AND THE VOICE

In this chapter we look at the obstacles to integrating voice into acting and possible solutions.

In the organic approach to performance we aim to integrate impulse, language, mind, body and voice so that we recreate a human experience in performance that is coming from the whole human being, not just the conscious brain. Modern scientific thinking places the brain, mind and consciousness firmly within the body: '… a mind, that which defines a person, requires a body, and (that) a body … naturally generates one mind. A mind is so closely shaped by the body and destined to serve it that only one mind could possibly arise in it. No body, never mind' (*The Feeling of What Happens – Body, Emotion and the Making of Consciousness*, Antonio Damasio: 143).

Because psychological impulse will affect the body, and physical impulse will affect our psychology, our approach is called *psycho-physical*. We aim for a receiving and absorption of experience through which the actor's intuition, subconscious, inspiration and independent creativity are released, and we create *the life of the human spirit of the role* within a full physical expression.

Making circumstances and character your own

To experience a role, rather than pretend and demonstrate it, actors have to act as if they are a real person, albeit within imaginary situations, and make the text their own, inhabiting it as a natural and full response to impulses created within material circumstances. We need to use *ourselves,* our human make-up, as the basis for this embodiment of the role – to find ourselves in the character and the character in ourselves. This means *going to* the character, and neither *bringing it to us* as we are in everyday life (as in some manifestations of American Method), nor offering an external imitation of a person lacking in full dimension and real life (as in some representational acting). We *experience* as ourselves as the character rather than *pretend*.

STANISLAVSKI'S BASIC PRINCIPLE IS THAT DRAMA IS ESSENTIALLY ABOUT *ACTION AND IMAGINATION.*

Ease and focus

In order to perform and communicate well to an audience in *any* art form, the practitioner needs to achieve ease and focus, a concentration of attention without tension. For the actor, their whole body and being is their instrument, which has to be filled with this quality if voice, physicality and action are to be responsive to thought, senses and feeling.

'If'

We examine and imagine the circumstances then place ourselves within them and ask '*if I am in these circumstances what do I, or what do I as the character, do*?' Stanislavski called this the *magic if* because of its far-reaching creative effect on inner and outer life and action. If actors don't use such a connection, which relates to their own human experience, observation and imagination, they will be locked into a purely cerebral processing of text and circumstances. The actor's imagination needs to be so free and fertile that it can create all the detail of the present and past circumstances of the character suggested by the text.

Communication

Once placed in the circumstances, we need to *interact* with other people, creating a genuine, dynamic and spontaneous responsiveness to create real communication in performance – as opposed to learning how to say lines in a particular pattern without really listening or reacting to others.

What do I want?

In addition, within the dynamics of the action, we have a whole chain of *objectives* – wants, aims, needs, intentions or tasks – that drive us through the imaginary life of the play.

Feeling and physicalizing

We enrich the action through our *sensory* awareness, engaging our *feelings,* and incorporating *images* of our imaginary world.

We discover the *full physical and vocal characterization* of the role through imaginative absorption of the world of the play.

We explore how to communicate the whole performance to different audiences in a variety of spaces.

We shall look at all these areas of acting process and how they relate to voice as we go through the book, and each element above is dealt with specifically in Part Three.

Integrating the voice

Actors need to believe that they are the character *vocally* and convince the audience of this. The individual voice of the actor has developed due to family, education, environment, class, etc. It needs to change into that of a different character by exploring such elements and finding where the new voice lives and resonates in the actor/character's body.

What voice do I have 'if' I am this character within these circumstances, with this accent, with this age, in this era, in this place, presented with this set of problems, with these objectives and actions? For example, the circumstances will affect the character's breathing and where in the body the resonance is; the objectives, the meaning of the language and responsiveness to others will affect the character's pitch range and intonation; the character's background, job and class will affect posture, accent and dialect.

Voicing and speaking are a learned ability that becomes automatic and habitual. The student actor has to develop awareness and control over the various elements within vocal expression so that they respond to any impulse happening in the moment like a finely tuned orchestra.

Representational or organic – how is voice affected?

The two opposing acting approaches make corresponding demands on voice work.

The representational approach *describes* the world of the script, and 'the language' may be seen as a sealed entity, reality itself, totally self-sufficient and revealing all we need to know. The form of how content is presented becomes the prime focus. Voice here is required to interpret the text – its structure, rhythm, sounds, figures of speech, images, literal meaning – and express it with the appropriate articulation, phrasing, intonation, accentuation and pitch range.

We decide *intellectually* what a script is about and *how* it should be delivered. We design a key to unlock the box, which, when opened, is expected to reveal the world of the play, but too often the box will be empty – all we have is the casing, the form.

This approach often prompts actors to develop early speech patterns, character states, vocal mannerisms and faked emotions, and fails to do what it sets out to do – to connect to the all-valued text. Actors get into a rut and produce external results. Any input from a voice specialist in this process will most likely focus on the purely technical role of how to make the actor more audible and clear or to improve an accent. In other words, it polishes the actor's mettle, or tinkers with some problems, but doesn't get through to the root causes of them. To attempt the latter may well incur the accusation of 'interfering with the acting'.

Stanislavski's approach sees the text as the only basis for the action, expressed in a form and genre that has to be respected, analyzed and explored. However, looking at the script in an *imaginative* way, it is the *result* of the world of the play, and all the given or imaginary actions, thoughts and feelings – the *subtext* – that give rise to it have to be accessed and explored. *Then the form of the language, which is of crucial importance because it expresses this content – both given by the writer and imagined by the actors and production team – can be fully brought to life.* The structure, rhythm, sounds and literal meaning of the text will be given imaginative colour, visualization and spontaneity by the actor inhabiting the world of the play and finding the impulses, the *need* to speak, behind the words in the given circumstances of the script. In this process we go from the conscious to the subconscious, imagination and intuition, and from the text to the subtext and back to the text. As Stanislavski says in Creating a Role (224):

> Therefore begin with the text and put your mind to work on reading its depths. Your feelings will not hesitate to join your mind and lead you deeper down into the subtext where the writer has concealed the motives which prompted him to create the play. The text thus gives birth to the subtext in order to have it recreate the text.

The actor will use rehearsal to probe and explore the text, subtext and circum-stances, absorbing information and other actors' responses, building up a sense of the action and inner life of the characters. Stanislavski argued against pushing for premature results, but he emphasized the importance of both a full physical life for a role and the mastering of the written form of the script: 'Without an external form neither your inner characterisation nor the spirit of your image will reach the public' (*Building a Character*: 1). In rich forms like Shakespeare's we are also given helpful indications in the metre, figures of speech, pauses and punctuation about the condition of the characters, and a detailed examination of form is needed at points in rehearsal when it helps, rather than hinders, the actor's organic involvement in the play's content and communication of its themes.

In this process, physicalization of the character through the body and voice will emerge as a *response* to the imaginative world developed, not as a cerebral decision. The voice and body must be sensitive and responsive to psychological creative impulses (as Michael Chekhov, one of Stanislavski's brilliant actors, says in Chapter 1 of his famous book, *To the Actor*). Then we can find freedom and spontaneity within the structure and discipline of the language and the production as a whole. The idea of speaking language like a jazz improvisation has been proposed by more than one prominent practitioner, but a representational approach works against that, instead encouraging something fixed and lacking in full reality and life.

Voice within the organic approach is an integral part of character development and voice specialists can have the role of harmonizing with actors' creative process and helping them to find full expression of their impulses through all the components of the language.

The table below gives a summary of elements that arise in representational and organic acting, and how they may be reflected in the actor's voice and speech. All of these elements may not be found in any one performance of either type, of course, but are representative:

Representational acting	Voice	Organic acting	Voice
* pretending * imitation and demonstration * cerebral choices * *how* to do things	adopting vocal manner; mimicry; illustration of ideas; conscious decisions how to speak	* experiencing * recreation * imaginative exploration of world of text * *what* we do and *why*, leading to *how*	expresses physical, psychological and emotional experience through imaginative exploration of circumstances, text and subtext
* manners, states and effects	vocal tricks for effect	* impulses and actions	intonation and pitch range arise from the need to communicate
* external form	language tackled formalistically with intellect, and set into a fixed score	* from inner life to outer form: creating 'the life of the human spirit of the role' within a fully physicalized form	responsive expression of inner impulses through the language: jazz

Representational acting	Voice	Organic acting	Voice
* premeditated control	programmed way of saying the lines	* spontaneous involvement	free, spontaneous expression of text in response to the action
* fashion	patterns of stress, phrasing and intonation associated with popular performers	* universal	drawing on a depth of human experience to create a unique delivery
* faked emotion	externally determined vocal imitation of emotion	* experienced emotion	vocal expression of emotion as a natural human response during the action
* individualism	separate, fragmented, individual choices	* ensemble	character vocal qualities developed as part of a collaborative whole

We favour the organic approach because we believe it best serves the writer, the actor, the production and the audience. A purely representational approach, which can include both the technically efficient and the low-key 'naturalistic' mode of delivery, can create a *gap* between the actor and the text, the action and the circumstances of the script. Equally, voice work that sets out to illustrate the text technically will limit vocal expression to the range of the intellect, which creatively will always be smaller than that of the imagination.

What other problems can arise?

Cicely Berry and Kristin Linklater have both identified a *gap* between the actor and the text for a number of other reasons.

In *The Actor and the Text* (9), Berry says

> ... there is so often a gap between the life that is going on imaginatively within the actor in order to create the reality of the character he is playing, and the life that he gives the text which he finally has to speak. It is as if the energy and excitement that an actor feels when working on a part is not released fully when he commits to words, when he is bound by the language set down.

Blocks and habit

Linklater presents the gap as coming from a world in which we've built up inhibitions and defence mechanisms, adversely affecting the voice and communication; both agree that a bound habitual voice can be created by culture, family, education, environment, class, physical make-up and personality.

Actors, says Berry, may not be able to respond to words which 'spring from many layers of consciousness' because we are 'trapped in our sound and sound pattern' (*The Actor and the Text*: 21, 15). This habitual voice may, for example, lead to a delivery too inward and underpowered for theatre performance.

Linklater says: '… spontaneity depends on reflex action, and most people have lost the ability and, perhaps, the desire to behave reflexively … The nervous system impulses are blocked, rerouted, or crossed with countermanding impulses' (*Freeing the Natural Voice*: 19, 20).

Over-control

Linklater maintains that socially conditioned behaviour causes us to respond '*only* to secondary impulses rather than primary ones' (*Freeing the Natural Voice*: 19). This can produce a more superficial, controlled response to language. This relates to Berry's idea 'of a lost primitive response' causing the actor to respond as though words 'spring from somewhere around the neck up' and not from 'our physical self' (*The Actor and the Text*: 19).

Intellectualization

Both see a disconnection happening through over-intellectualizing and over-controlling our response to language, exacerbated by reading rather than hearing print on the page. The actor presents the *reasons* for language but not 'the discovery of the thought' (*The Actor and the Text*: 19).

So, lack of connection to language and text is prompted through a variety of influences within our modern society, a loss of spontaneous responsiveness and an overly intellectual response to language on the page.

Fragmentation

This last point raises the whole issue of language and its function. The need to speak, to find the justification for words, is central to our approach. The language is an integral part of the script, the action, and dynamic between characters. If it is seen as a separate entity, something to be analyzed primarily from a literary or linguistic point of view; we have, on the one hand, the language to be formally dissected, and on the other hand, the business of acting and examining the character and situation. Both will be controlled somewhere in the conscious intellectual part of the brain and we won't see an integrated person centred fully in their body, experiencing from the solar plexus or 'gut'. There is a *fragmentation of performance*.

Whatever the origins of language – whether, for example, we think it derives from the gods, sounds found in nature, oral imitation of physical gesture, or specific human physiological development – it seems clear that humans developed it through gestures, signals, noises and possibly music in order to control their world better, to interact socially, communicate information and skills and perform tasks – like creating culture and civilization (see Chapter 1, *The Study of Language*, George Yule). The need to pass that knowledge on from generation to generation is likely to have been the main reason for *written* language. In a nutshell, language exists because of the need to communicate specific things between human beings to get things done in constantly changing circumstances.

From this we would say that any piece of language in a script is not the whole reality but a product of a wider, albeit imaginary, reality. It's about *communication* between people and has to be interpreted from our and our characters' experience of the world. It can only be brought to life if we explore the history and circumstances that have led to these words in this situation at this point in time, if we find the impulse behind them and the pulse running through them. This requires both research and imagination.

When we can identify with the text in this way, this is the time to uncover, reveal and execute all the – possibly numerous and complex – important elements of form. The form is the author's means for channelling the content, and the actor must embrace it in order to fully communicate the content in an artistic way; but if we begin rehearsal with a detailed dissection of, for example, a classical text, examining metre, stresses, figures of speech, sounds – whether sitting or physically moving – the danger is that the actor starts to set formal patterns that derive from the intellect and not from genuine creative impulse in imagined circumstances.

Linklater puts it clearly: 'The practice of form must be plugged into the electrical outlet of thought/feeling impulses or it will leave a mechanical imprint on the brain, and the actor will end up "speaking the verse" but not "acting Shakespeare"' (*Freeing Shakespeare's Voice*: 121). John Barton, in *Playing Shakespeare* (52), says that he avoids too much poetry at the outset of rehearsals because that 'blocks and inhibits' the actor.

A natural gap

There has always been a *natural* gap between the actor and a character's words because we are not the character at the start of rehearsals. The problem is that it isn't always closed through rehearsal. Here's Stanislavski's view:

> Our own words are the direct expression of our feelings, whereas the words of another are alien until we have made them our own, are nothing more than signs of future emotions which have not yet come to life inside us. Our own words are needed in the first phase of the physical embodiment of a part because they are best able to extract from within us live feelings which have not yet found their outward expression (*Creating a Role*: 84).

Here he refers to the role of imagination, improvisation and feeling to draw oneself close to the action and dialogue of the play. Connecting to the text isn't just about working on the words of the text.

He also refers to the temptation in the world of theatre to lose contact with nature and authenticity:

> All we ask is that an actor on the stage live in accordance with natural laws. Yet because of the circumstances amid which an actor has to do his work it is much easier for him to distort his nature than to live as a natural human being. So we have to find means to struggle against this tendency ... (*Building a Character*: 246).

So, these are not only contemporary problems, but ones that existed in the 1930s when Stanislavski wrote his books, and most likely way back during the first days of theatre. *How do we connect believably to the action, character, text and theme? How do we transform ourselves believably into someone else?*

Also, whereas the spoken word might have been valued more half a century ago, before emails, text messaging and Facebook, and actors' delivery of text might have been crisper and cleaner then, that doesn't mean they necessarily expressed the full meaning of the text, the world of the play, a sense of the inner life, and physical embodiment of a character: in other words, really connected to the text!

How we relate to the written word, and whether we stay within the calculating intellect or take flight into the imagination is also determined by how different parts of our brain work, and how we need to use them to achieve flexible creativity. We look at this in the next chapter.

Practical issues

When we go beyond these broad issues, there is also a range of practical issues that can create challenges for vocal integration and truthful acting:

- Voice training on some drama school courses may not include a sufficient number of classes, or sufficient integration within overall acting tuition, for voice learning to become so absorbed that the voice can simply respond to acting impulses.

- As many voice coaches will testify, their input on productions may be confined to making formal judgements on accenting, articulation, audibility, range, and so on.

- Some voice teachers may not have trained as actors and will not be versed in actor training or process. This may constrain their understanding of actors' problems and nature of their input.

- Rehearsal periods are usually short – four to five weeks or less – and actors can rush into presenting results too quickly.

- Some directors will have a production concept they want to fulfil in a short space of time and prompt actors into this sort of endgaming.

- There are very few genuine ensemble companies with both a collective vision and way of working. Actors with different training, attitudes and interpretations of a play are frequently thrown together for one production, which has already been worked out by the director and designer.

Many actors and other practitioners, though, would like to be part of a genuinely collaborative company in which they can develop their performances in a less constrained and more natural way, and in which voice and movement are fully integrated into their work and the production as a whole.

What are the solutions?

To deal with an actor's disconnection, Cicely Berry and Kristin Linklater both advocate removing blocks and tensions, as you would expect.

Berry emphasizes 'the physical connection between the making of the word and the emotional motive of the actor – in terms of Stanislavski, the want/need of the character in the scene'. She wants to 'release the language from its literal/academic meaning so that our responses can fly' ('That Secret Voice', in *Vocal Vision*, Marion Hampton and Barbara Acker (eds): 25, 27).

Her solution to this is often a form of physical struggling or other movement while speaking the text, a group 'displacement' activity not directly connected to the text. She believes this can 'free the speaker from over concentration and so release a subconscious response' (*The Vocal Vision*: 27).

Linklater aims to remove blocks in the body so that the voice and inner muscles can receive 'the sensitive impulses from the brain that create speech' and communicate with full emotion and subtlety of thought (*Freeing the Natural Voice*: 8). She uses imagery to connect the seen word, not to the intellect, but to imagination and physical and emotional experience, and then to the spoken word.

Her focus then is on the psycho-physical interrelationship between impulse, sensory response, emotion and physical and vocal action.

We hope to build on these discoveries. In this book, we'll maintain that the problems outlined here are best tackled by a comprehensive organic approach to acting and production because it focuses on breaking down blocks through the imagination; getting out of the head and into the whole body and being; on responsiveness, release and spontaneity; 'going to' the character from oneself; and on creating the impulse behind and through action and word.

Breakthroughs in voice understanding and training will not automatically carry over into the rehearsal space and performance. No one can accuse the modern voice practitioner of narrowness. Influences recorded in recent publications range from Elsie Fogerty to Tibetan Dynamic Meditation, from Bartenieff Fundamentals to Siberian Shamanism, from Dahnjeon breathing to holotropic breathing, from Reich, Feldenkrais and Alexander, to Sufi, Tao and Korean p'ansori, from Estill and Wolfsohn to Qi Gong, T'ai Chi, the South Indian martial art of Kalarippayattu and Apache storytelling. However, whatever the freeing and holistic effects of such practices may be, they don't add up to the proverbial hill full of beans unless we all bring the findings into the rehearsal and acting process; and if the acting process isn't organic we won't get consistently connected, responsive voices.

Essentially, acting process and voice work need to be unified: alignment needs to be linked to centre, identity and assertion; breathing needs to become responsive to impulses; vocal onset needs to identify the actor with the character; and vocal response needs to reflect the experiences of the actor/character in the present moment.

Achieving this connection and responsiveness is clearly often difficult. Student and professional actors have problems fitting the different jigsaw pieces together: acting creativity, good voice production, directors' demands. We hope to offer some solutions to these issues in the following chapters.

To sum up:

- A gap can appear between the actor's voice and the text, action and circumstances due to:
    - representational elements in acting approach;
    - blocks, habits and loss of spontaneity;
    - intellectualization and over-control;
    - treating language as a separate entity;
    - short and pressured rehearsals that put endgaming before process;
    - a lack of integration of voice work within acting process.
- An organic psycho-physical approach can integrate impulse, language, voice, mind and body: *voice and acting become one.*
- We 'go to' the character from our own natural resources, using 'if', interaction, objectives, feelings, and the vocal and physical embodiment of a role.

We *experience* the imaginary circumstances, character and vocal expression rather than *pretend*.

2

THE ORGANIC ACTING APPROACH AND THE BRAIN

To understand how voice production and other conscious work, and all our human resources – mind, body, imagination, will, senses and emotions – may be organically integrated into the acting process, we now need to look at how they relate to the brain and the nervous system. Although this may be specialist knowledge and it is not necessary for the voice coach, actor and student to understand it in entirety, it is useful to grasp a basic understanding of how information needs to be processed by the actor to access a creative, imaginative approach as opposed to a cerebral, mechanical one.

We believe like many, but by no means all, practitioners that once we have consciously understood and absorbed basic elements of text understanding, analysis and research, we then need to hand over to what we may call intuition, inspiration, the subconscious and the creative self. Holding on to conscious, intellectual control in rehearsal and performance will hamper the interplay of mind and body, imagination and emotion, will and action, and kill spontaneity, inventiveness and unpredictability. A gap opens up between the actor and the text, circumstances and action, as mentioned earlier. In looking at the processes of the brain and nervous system in this chapter we aim to offer extra insight into disconnection and integration, and representational and organic acting.

Impulses and psycho-physical connection

The brain and nervous system have an inbuilt communication system through which electrical impulses are sent and received via signals. The actor must respond to imaginative impulses created by circumstances, interaction and wants, from outer or inner stimuli, and draw on the responsiveness and sensitivity of the body and voice to express them. For example, 'For the actor who values truthful expression, breathing control must be diverted from muscle to impulse' (*Freeing the Natural Voice*: 44). The co-ordination of mind, body, feeling, wants and voice in performance needs to become second nature so that it can be accessed within the present moment of any experience; and we have a voice that in training may have been 'shaped by the intellect but not inhibited by it' (*Freeing the Natural Voice*: 8).

The brain

We develop from a helpless baby into an independent human being who has learned skills to survive. We *learn* everything: to walk, speak, eat, think. Riding a bicycle presents a difficult task of co-ordination and balance; but once it has been learned it becomes second nature, something we don't have to think consciously about. The skills an actor learns, like improving speech and posture or absorbing acting technique, also have to be consciously learned and then absorbed into a different part of the brain to become a new habit, automatic in a creative way. This learning involves a complicated co-ordination between the brain and the nervous system: the brain is part of our body and both *gives* orders and *receives* feedback, and some areas of the brain have more conscious control than others.

Old brain and new brain

The brain can be divided into the *Old or Primitive Brain* and the *New Brain*. The **Old Brain** consists of the *limbic system* (a sort of bridge between old and new brain)*, the mid and the hind brain.*

* The *limbic system* is concerned with basic emotions like anger, fear, pleasure, displeasure, fight and flight, and also controls motivation, memory and much of our behaviour (*Essentials of Neurology*, J. N. Walton: 89).

* The *mid brain* controls visual and hearing impulses.

* The *hind brain* controls the heart, breathing, digestion and movement.

The *Old Brain* is a subordinate centre and can be overruled by the higher developed *New Brain*. It is mainly concerned with reflex actions and is a control station for all stimuli before they go into the *New Brain*.

There is much less difference between our *Old Brain* and the brains of animals such as reptiles, from which we developed, since it is responsible for primitive feelings and vegetative and psychological influences on breathing and phonation.

The **New Brain** or *Forebrain* evolved later and makes us capable of higher activity such as consciousness, perception, reason, empathy, memory, understanding language and making speech. It has *motor areas*, nerve centres that control movement; and *sensory areas,* transmitting sensations from the sense organs.

The *New Brain/Forebrain* is divided into a *left* and a *right* hemisphere. This is of particular importance for our concerns in this book, and we shall shortly come back to an examination of this.

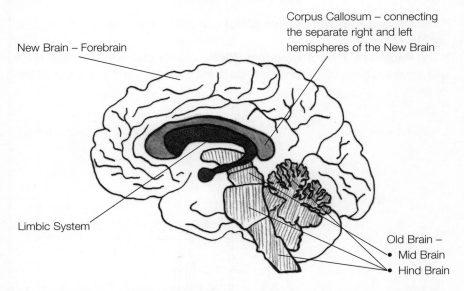

Figure 2 The Brain: The New Brain/Forebrain, Limbic System, and Old Brain/Midbrain and Hindbrain

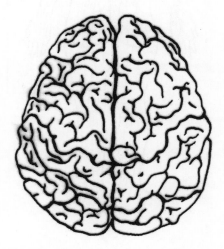

Figure 3 The Left and Right hemispheres of the New Brain

The nervous system

The centres of the brain are linked to the body by the *Nervous System.* This consists of a network of nerves that enable communication via impulses between the brain and the muscles, organs and glands of the body, and the outside world:

* The **Central Nervous System (CNS)** consists of the brain, the brain stem and the spinal cord.
* The **Peripheral Nervous System (PNS)** consists of nerve fibres that enter and leave the brain stem and spinal cord and connect them to the rest of the body.

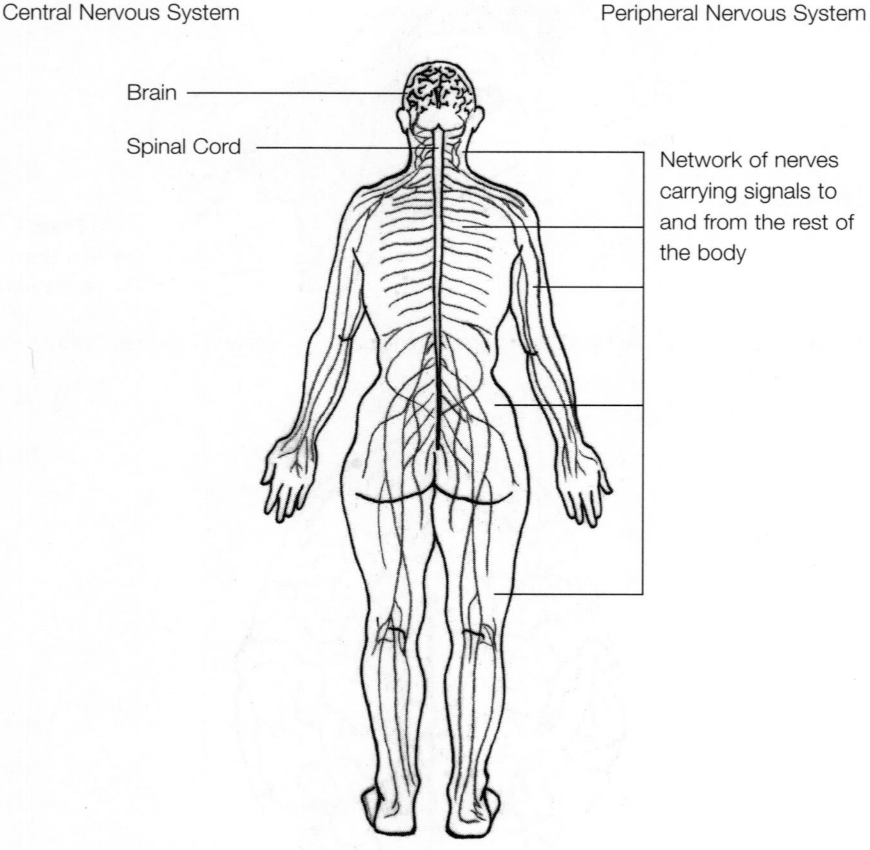

Central Nervous System   Peripheral Nervous System

Brain

Spinal Cord

Network of nerves carrying signals to and from the rest of the body

Figure 4 Central and Peripheral Nervous System

The **PNS** has two parts:

* The **Somatic Nervous System (SNS),** which has sensory and motor functions and conveys messages from the sense organs to the CNS and from the CNS to the striate (or striped) muscles of the body. These functions are mainly under *voluntary* control.

* The **Autonomic Nervous System (ANS),** which consists of those parts of the CNS and PNS that connect to glands, the heart, lungs and other organs. These functions are mainly *involuntary*.
    Within the ANS are the:

* **Parasympathetic Nervous System** (governing rest, e.g. digestion, heart rate)
* **Sympathetic Nervous System** (preparing us for immediate action, 'fight or flight')
* **Enteric Nervous System.** This resides in the gastrointestinal system, is made from the same tissue (the neural crest) as the CNS, and responds directly to CNS signals but can operate autonomously – earning it the name of 'the second brain'. It creates those well-known 'gut feelings' like butterflies, loose bowels and a tight throat, of which actors are well aware.

The activity of these different systems can be roughly divided into three categories: conscious activity, which relates to the *New Brain;* reflex activity, which relates to the *Old Brain;* and vegetative activity, which relates to the *ANS*.

An actor's work with the brain

An actor's work deals, on the one hand, with the *verbal* information of *what language is saying.* This is processed in the *left hemisphere of the new brain,* which decodes it to produce understanding and speech. Understanding is processed in the Wernicke area toward the back of the left hemisphere: a sensory centre holding the memory of what has previously been heard. Speech is associated with the Broca area, toward the front of the hemisphere: a motor centre holding kinaesthetic memory pictures that send signals to the muscles of the speech organs (*Sprecherziehung des Schauspielers* [*Vocal Education of the Actor*], Egon Aderhold: 64–5). The connection of the *left brain* with talking has given it the dominant reputation.

This isn't the whole story by any means, though. The actor, on the other hand, deals with the *non-verbal* aspects of *how language is said*, and this involves the *right hemisphere of the new brain* and the *old brain*.

Let's look now at the left and right brain differences in more detail. We are indebted here to Iain McGilchrist's wide-ranging and insightful analysis in *The Master and his Emissary – The Divided Brain and the Making of the Modern World.*

The two hemispheres, or brains as they are often called, look symmetrical but actually have differences, and also exist in animals and birds. The left brain controls the right side of the body, and the right brain controls the left side. Neuroscience and psychiatric analysis of brain disorders and the effects of strokes have revealed distinct differences in the type of attention and focus operating in each, leading to *a different approach to the world*. These differences have been observed as generally present, but of course there will be exceptions due to specific mental histories.

* The left brain has a narrow focus and sees the world in fragments. The right has a broader focus and sees the whole picture.
* The left produces unrelated events, decontextualized within a static focus, 'a Frankenstein's monster of body parts that never truly lives' (76). The right produces a sense of flow and narrative understanding, with the presence of change and opposite positions.
* The left needs quick closure and the certainty of being right. The right holds several positions together without premature closure.
* The left fixes experience and makes conclusions, plans, and asserts control. The right covers continuing experience in a changing world and perceives the new, the context and the circumstances.
* The left is closest to the world of consciousness, self-inspecting intellect, logic, linearity, systematic thought and rationalization, perseverance and stability: the controlling factor over our lives. The right is the world of creativity, athleticism and imagination, intuition and feeling, sensory awareness and the continuing experience of life.
* The left 're-presents' reality in a way that abstracts, distances, objectifies. The right connects to the subjective present of experience.
* The left is abstract and lacks realistic detail. The right presents a realistic, three-dimensional world and the opportunity for intensity and beauty.
* The left deals with the literal understanding and speaking of language, with form, syntax and vocabulary: a conscious processing that sees language as cut off from the world and as itself the reality. The right deals with the non-verbal, non-literal aspects of language like contextual understanding, metaphor, humour, associations, intonation and musicality: an expression of the world. *'Language … can never create experience of something we do not know – only release something in us that is already there'* (413).

* The left brain favours the Western sort of phonemic writing (based on units of sound) that goes from left to right. The right is more activated by the visual and tonal demands of, for example, Chinese.

* The left is unconcerned with others' feelings, identifies categories, remembers facts and focuses on mechanical things. The right brain is empathic and puts you in other people's shoes. It is more linked to the old brain, to the limbic system, the body and emotions, to the unconscious and the ANS; and also to the receptivity of the solar plexus, a key nerve, emotion and energy centre, to which we refer later. It remembers emotions and connects with nature.

* The left interprets the mouth and is 'involved in conscious representation of emotion' (62) (as you may have seen in what we call representational 'mouth-acting'!). The right interprets facial and eye expression, body language and gesture, vocal intonation and tone of voice. (In Tao, the eyes are thought to be the first to receive emotional signals and affect the organs and glands.)

* The left creates novelty, recombining what's already known. The right uses imagination to reveal something for the first time: a genuine originality.

* **'The left hemisphere is concerned with what it knows, where the right hemisphere is concerned with what it experiences' (78).**

Here is a table presenting these differences and revealing how use of left or right brain may affect the actor in the acting process:

Left brain	Actor	Right brain	Actor
Narrow, static focus. Sees fragments out of context.	Sees 'my character' in isolation.	Focus on whole picture. Flow and narrative understanding. Sense of change and opposites.	'My character' as part of whole script and action. Open to change. Sense of human contradictions in character. Sees voice and body as integral part of acting process.
Quick closure. Need for certainty.	'I'm right'. Early 'choices', fixed, inflexible.	Several positions together without premature closure.	Weighs up all information. Absorbs, discovers in rehearsal. Flexible, open. Allows voice to react.

Left brain	Actor	Right brain	Actor
Asserts control and plans: logical, rational, linear intellect, stability and perseverance.	Organizing work in rehearsal and performance: schedules, timescale, problem-solving, etc. Text understanding, analysis, research.	Creativity, imagination, intuition, feeling and sensory awareness, and the continuing experience of life and connection to context and circumstances.	Creative, intuitive development and release of character and vocal response through the rehearsal framework. Breathes in the given and previous circumstances.
'Re-presents' reality, distances, lacks realistic detail.	Representational acting, described performance. Conscious vocal decisions on *how* to speak and interpret. Focuses on the mouth, and demonstrating emotion and qualities.	The subjective present of experience, realistic and three-dimensional.	Experiences circumstances and role. Explores in the moment in rehearsal. Creates realistic human being. Voice as spontaneous expression of experience. Focuses on the eyes, and interactive spontaneous communication.
Understanding of form and content of language. Language as a reality in itself, cut off from world.	Cerebral focus on form and style and how to convey it. 'It's all in the language.' Gap between speaking text and circumstances, action, character.	Non-verbal, non-literal aspects of language: contextual understanding, metaphor, humour, associations, intonation and musicality: *an expression of the world.*	Imaginative discovery of how language can be expressed: *response to imagery, sensory and emotional elements; *vocal flexibility via breath, alignment, onset, pitch range and intonation, resonance and articulation; *voice as organic expression of actor/character in circumstances.

Left brain	Actor	Right brain	Actor
Relates to facts, categories and machines – not to feelings.	Calculated intellectual depiction of character, possibly according to type. Consciously cerebral working out of character actions, physicality, vocal characteristics.	Empathic identification with others, and connects to nature, body, emotions and the unconscious.	Acting follows natural human experience. 'If I am in the circumstances of this person what do I do, want, feel?' Emotion emerges organically through the action from memory, unconscious, empathy, observation, imagination. Voice responds to each experience while remaining artistically controlled.
Novelty: reshaping what's already been done.	Follows fashion in acting and vocal delivery, e.g. in phrasing, intonation, accent, gesture. General and non-specific.	Originality: imagination creates something for the first time.	Detailed, imaginative work that explores the uniqueness of a script in its specific and universal aspects.

Integrating left and right brains

What's crucial to understand here is that the left and right hemispheres do 'complementary but conflicting tasks' – but need to co-operate!

There is an actual physical barrier connecting the two hemispheres, the *corpus callosum* (see Figure 2). This inhibits interference from one to the other, keeping them independent. At the same time, paradoxically, it acts as a bridge so that information can be transferred from one to the other (see *The Master and his Emissary*: 210–13).

Without the right brain we would be intellectual and rational but cold, insular and narrow. Without the left brain we would be empathic, intuitive and creative but without focus, plan, control and will. We need an integration of the two. In both art and sport, we need to organize our lives, exert discipline, plan training and preparation, do research and understand things; but then we need to release into imagination, intuition, spontaneity and the free flow of living in the 'zone' or 'the moment' within the created structure.

As we see it, the left brain builds the rails and the right creates the journey.

Stanislavski's process embodies these two strands. There is a need here to combine conscious text understanding, analysis and research – largely left brain work – with imaginative, intuitive, sensory, emotional and spontaneous expression of text and character throughout rehearsal and performance – essentially right brain work. We need to organize and analyze, but then release. We have to build the runway, but then take flight. A predominantly left brain approach, which has more in common with representational acting, can resolutely hold onto the ground and avoid the unpredictability and risks of flying!

This raises some fundamental points for voice teaching within an organic acting approach, and we expand on these as we go through the book:

* The left brain helps us to understand the world of the play, but we then need to receive and absorb it and allow the right brain to respond through the body, mind and voice. This principle of receiving and responding is used throughout the book. The actor's voice requires technique, not as a mechanical skill but so that it can *react* to acting impulses.

* For example, when we use Stanislavski's 'given circumstances' and 'if' (see Chapter 1), we primarily use our experience, imagination and intuition to connect to circumstances and the world of the play. The theatre space becomes an imaginary space within which we also engage sensorily and emotionally. The voice should simply respond to these imaginative elements rather than attempt to describe them cerebrally.

* When using 'objectives', we relate to a series of character problems, needs, tasks, wants and actions, which involve us in the inner and outer life of the character. The actor will discover *how* thoughts and words are expressed by responding to these elements *as if* they are real.

This creates an imaginary but firm reality as a basis on which to draw out all the formal elements of language so that the script emerges in its full literal and imaginative shape.

So, the left brain deals with *what* is said, and the right brain, together with the old brain's feelings, memory and reflexes, deals with *how* things are said through the music of speech without intellectual domination – they simply play the tune that feels right.

We can see that the process of acting language contains a possible *struggle* within itself between the verbal and non-verbal parts of the brain. If the left brain dominates and intellectually determines *how* language will be delivered, it blocks the flow of intuitive processes sparked in the right and old brain, and musicality and spontaneity will be deadened. The left brain 'explains and rationalises the irrational, inexplicable energies of the right brain … It intellectualises the nonintellectual, and makes logically verbal that which is nonverbally logical' (*Performing Power*, H. Wesley Balk: 91). As McGilchrist puts it, we must not 'allow the right hemisphere's options to be too quickly foreclosed by the narrower focussing of the left hemisphere' (*The Master and his Emissary*: 164).

We may be faced with a highly sophisticated intellectual content in language but also a deeply experiential, emotional and physical content, as in Shakespeare. In order to achieve an organic way of acting language, there needs to be a left brain/right brain partnership. 'For example, the intellect may call the musicality of language into play, but it must then relinquish the control … It must allow the right brain system to do whatever needs to be done, trusting it while remaining in an observing, nonjudgmental role' (*Performing Power*: 90). It seems to be widely accepted among psychologists that at least 90 per cent of our mental life is subconscious. As Stanislavski said: 'Can, indeed, the conscious mind reach all the nuances of the human heart, for example, a complex mind like Hamlet's? Many … are accessible only to our unconscious, creative intuition' (*An Actors Work on a Role*: 165).

The left/right brain operations can be seen in two of the key vocal elements we examine in detail in Part Two. Articulation, as indicated earlier, is a later human achievement controlled primarily by the left brain. Breathing, on the other hand, is represented in the old brain and the new brain. It can work automatically, withdrawn from our consciousness and will; or, we can influence it consciously. The ability to breathe and to produce sound through crying happens after the first in-breath we take as a baby: an autonomic reflex action regulated by the old brain. The new brain takes over control much later. What is autonomic at first gains the possibility of voluntary steering and is therefore prone to *disruption* through control of the left brain (*Sprecherziehung des Schauspielers*: 54). As Linklater has pointed out, secondary impulses replace primary ones in the functioning of many adults; instead, we should aim to engage the autonomic and reflex functions of breathing and avoid the disruption from the left brain.

Learning a new skill

Actors may need to learn new techniques of vocal production affecting alignment, breathing, phonation and articulation. Initially this means that the new brain has to organize a conscious process to create a body memory. This can make us feel clumsy and unnatural until the skill has become automatic.

The brain connects to the muscles of the body via two conduction nerve paths that are extremely important for the processing of information for the actor. The conduction paths of the new brain are the *Pyramidal Paths*, and those of the old brain are the *Extra Pyramidal Paths*.

The *Pyramidal Paths* are responsible for the control of *voluntary* movements. Every conscious decision to move is controlled by the pyramidal system. It creates the initial model in the learning of a movement and new skill.

Once a skill is learnt via the *Pyramidal Paths*, control is taken over by the *Extra Pyramidal Paths*, which regulate an automatized way of processing and projecting information to ensure smooth integration of movement – if we were *consciously* to do every single movement, the effort would exhaust us. A new habit is created and the actor can then access this subconsciously while responding to impulses in performance.

If, however, conscious control keeps getting in the way, there will be no automatic smoothness in the exercise of the skill and no link to deeper emotions and responses: imagine the result if a dancer were to work out consciously every step in performance while actually doing it. **A partnership between new and old brain is needed.**

So, it's clear from the above that we need a smooth integration of the brain functions when working on voice, acting and text.

To sum up:

* Creativity in acting and vocal response requires harmonious teamwork between the left and right hemispheres of the new brain and between the new brain and the old brain to enable:

- **intellectual control, and intuitive, imaginative release, connecting to spontaneity, emotion and the subconscious;**

- **Verbal, formal reading of the text, and non-verbal interpretation of the full meaning and world of the text.**

* Stanislavski's approach embraces these different aspects of brain functioning, and emphasizes that in exploratory rehearsal and perfor-mance the actor needs to find ease, freedom and release and to respond to theatrical impulse with their whole being – including the voice.

*   *   *

In the next part, we examine the essential areas of vocal production governed by these different areas of the brain, and through which the impulses created in the acting process need to find pathways of expression.

These six essential vocal elements are:

- **Alignment**
- **Breath**
- **Centred onset of sound**
- **Pitch range**
- **Resonance**
- **Articulation**

PART TWO

THE ESSENTIAL VOCAL SIX – AND INTEGRATING ACTING INTO VOICE

INTRODUCTION

In Part Two, we'll examine each of the six essential vocal elements mentioned at the end of Part One:

1 **Alignment**
2 **Breath**
3 **Centred onset of sound**
4 **Pitch range**
5 **Resonance**
6 **Articulation**

We'll follow the same pattern of exploration for each of the six elements:
What is it? – a basic description of the element and what it does.
What is it for the actor? – what it means for the actor in the process of acting, not only physically, but psycho-physically.
How it works – a detailed account of everything that makes it function.
Exercises – these appear throughout the text to clarify how things work, to offer training advice, and to integrate acting process.
To sum up – the essential points made on theory and practice.
Symbols – we shall also introduce symbols in these sections to illustrate aspects of the vocal process. These will be used throughout the book to remind you of the need to keep the essential vocal elements constantly present in the acting process.

HOW TO WORK

At the beginning of the following parts of the book, we'll suggest how you can approach the work to get most benefit.

In Part Two:
1 Work with ease, openness and positivity.
2 Warm up before doing exercises.
3 Make sure you have time to do each exercise in an undisturbed, unpressured environment.
4 Do little and often – once exercises are learned, do maybe 15 minutes a day. Through this we can:
   • absorb new skills into our mind and body memory so that they become second nature
   • develop reflexive muscles so that we integrate our mind, body, and voice responses with each impulse
5 Take note of problem areas and tensions and work to overcome them.
6 Keep the link to acting ever present in your mind and practice – understand and experience it.
7 Memorize the symbols for the vocal elements to remind yourself of the vocal activity needed to meet the acting demands.

The Essential Vocal Six should become *Vocal Givens* for both your individual vocal practice and what's required by the acting process.

3
ALIGNMENT – BACKBONE OF THE ACTION

WHAT IS IT?

Alignment is the posture adopted by the body to work against the pull of gravity. The optimum alignment uses a minimum of muscular activity to sustain itself. All the components of bone and muscular structure align to achieve balance, stability and ease in the most efficient way.

Optimum, balanced alignment in a standing position is represented in the picture. A line runs through the ear, shoulder, hip, knee and arch of the foot:

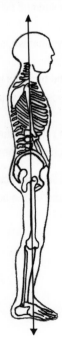

Figure 5 Optimum alignment

Various disciplines can help to achieve good alignment. Alexander technique aims to discover a new balance in the body by releasing unnecessary tension. Pilates works on strengthening the core muscles. Hatha Yoga seeks to balance mind and body through physical postures and controlled breathing, relaxation and meditation. All of these influence the approaches in this book.

Yoga and Tao emphasize, also, the flow of energy, a vital concern for actors. Good alignment means a co-operative relationship between the parts of the body, such as bones, joints and muscles, to create a smooth and co-ordinated action. The arrangement of a physical structure determines whether energy can or cannot flow, just as the riverbed determines the flow of water through it. For the body to be alert, responsive and animated we need to remove tensions that often block this energy. When the energy flows, it opens the spaces between joints, elongates muscles, strengthens the nervous system and heightens our perception.

Once the body is open and free, we can direct energy through the body and connect our movement to the environment: the earth below, the space around us, and the sky above. Donna Farhi calls this *engaged alignment*, and distinguishes it from the mere act of mechanical placement (*Yoga Mind, Body & Spirit*: 50).

What is it for the actor?

Alignment is the physical support system of the body, with the spine at its core.

It connects us to sense of identity, assertion of will and transmission of impulses

The spine is the backbone of the actor and the vertical sense of their identity within the imagined given circumstances and the character they are playing. The actor has to find their connection to the character and the circumstances imagi- natively, but at first may feel quite unsure physically and vocally. By lending the spinal strength of our own identity to the character, we build a bridge between imagination and our own flesh and blood. We assert ourselves through the spine, build ourselves up, stand our ground. We also live, interact and move in space through the spine. Spinal strength gives the actor belief and conviction. 'Being in the spine' means that we are in our identity and are giving our impulses and intentions a *backbone*.

It is the actor's support system for breath and voice

Because alignment determines our energy flow, ease and flexibility, balance and rootedness, it also affects the breath.

It determines whether energy can flow through the pathways of the body, whether there is space for breath and resonance to function without obstruction, and whether acting impulses can lead to free expression. So, it plays a crucial role in supporting the breath action as it carries the responses and experiences of the actor through the voice and text.

Also, breathing movements send cerebrospinal fluid from the brain through the spine down to the sacrum, affecting the nerves and the ability of the senses and brain to take in new impressions (*The Tao of Natural Breathing,* Dennis Lewis: 122) – pretty important for an actor.

It creates intrinsic equilibrium and balance

Good alignment means we are balanced through the head, spine, legs and feet. This *intrinsic equilibrium* within the spine enables us to return to an inbuilt place of ease and balance after we have thrown ourselves into physical and vocal activities. The spine will always return to this position, and frees up the actor's energy to be used for the dramatic task in hand.

If we are not balanced, extra muscular effort is needed to keep the spine upright, we lose openness and responsiveness, and our breathing is inhibited. Patsy Rodenburg, in *The Actor Speaks* (17), quotes an osteopath: 'When your spine goes, you age.'

In some recent training regimes, such as that of Wlodzimierz Staniewski of the Polish Gardzienice centre, the spine is seen as the foundation of the body, and the source of human energy and origin of movement for the whole body (see *Twentieth Century Actor Training*, Alison Hodge: Chapter 12).

Stanislavski became very interested in Yoga from 1906. It completely ties in with his own pursuit of integration between mind and body and inner and outer action. In the First Studio of the Moscow Art Theatre, established in 1912, he and his close colleague, Leopold Sulerzitski, introduced Hatha Yoga and Raja Yoga: within the first they focused on muscle release and relaxation (asana), and breath, breathing rhythms, and radiation of *prana*, life-force energy centred in the solar plexus (pranayama); Raja exercises focused on mental control through concentration, visualization, observation and meditation. Both influenced Stanislavski's techniques for communication and visualization of images, which we look at later.

How alignment works

To understand alignment and the spine fully we need to look at its anatomy and connection with muscles that control the body and breath. Breathing, as we'll see in detail later, involves the inhalation of air through the mouth and nose into the lungs, from where it spreads to fuel the whole body, and then is expelled back the way it came. The spine houses the spinal cord and is part of the Central Nervous System, has complex sensory and motor functions, and is the essential pathway for communicating impulses between the brain and the rest of the body (see Figure 4).

The human spine

The human spine is unique among all mammals in that it exhibits both *primary and secondary curves.* As a baby in the womb we had only a *primary* curve.

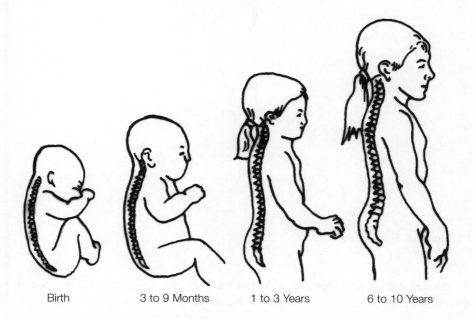

| Birth | 3 to 9 Months | 1 to 3 Years | 6 to 10 Years |

Figure 6 Development of the human spine

The *secondary* spinal curves emerge when the toddler learns to sit and stand. In order to sit, the baby (between three and nine months) needs to develop a cervical curve so that it can hold its head up. In order to stand, the child (between one and three years of age) must acquire a lumbar curve so that it can bring the weight of the head over the feet. This develops into its full adult shape by the age of ten.

The spine consists of four sections: *the sacral curve and coccyx, lumbar curve, thoracic curve,* and *cervical curve.*

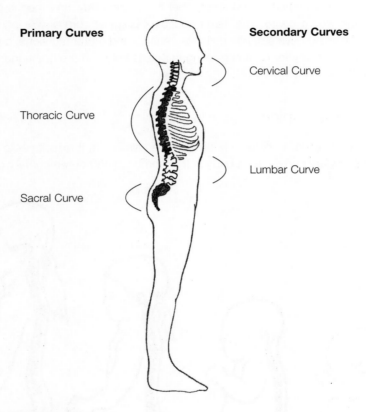

Primary Curves

Cervical Curve

Thoracic Curve

Lumbar Curve

Sacral Curve

Secondary Curves

Figure 7 Spinal curves

Sacral curve and coccyx – At the base of the spine are the five fused vertebrae of the *sacrum*, attached to the back of the pelvis. Connected to this is the *coccyx* (our vestigial tailbone) consisting of another four fused vertebrae.

The pelvis is the heaviest part of the body and therefore is our gravity centre, and arguably the core of vocal support. It forms a basin with a hole in the middle. The hole is filled out by the deepest breathing muscles, the *pelvic floor muscles*. These have deeper and more superficial layers. The more superficial the layer, the more it runs from side to side. The deeper the layer, the more it runs from front to back, from pubic joint to coccyx.

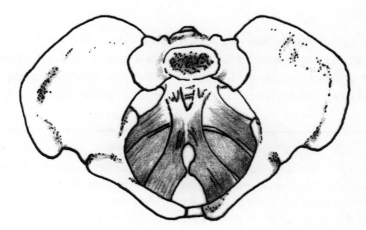

Figure 8 Pelvic floor muscles from above

The action of the more superficial perineal fibres of the pelvic floor muscles are associated with anal and uro-genital sphincters, which push downwards to eliminate solid and liquid waste. This muscular action, if used for the purposes of voice on the out-breath, can be harmful because it shortens the body and pulls the larynx down. On the other hand, the deeper muscles of the pelvic floor move back and up against the spine to help eliminate carbon dioxide through exhalation: they are the *floor* or *root* for the muscular breathing action that helps the diaphragm send the breath back up and out vertically.

Connecting this floor to the *onset of sound*, originating from the vibrating vocal folds within the larynx, creates the actor's vocal centre. Rooting the breath here also helps to unite the mind with the body: we become one with our life force, imagination, sense of identity, our intentions, feelings and action. This creates a stillness, focus and centredness vital for the actor, and enables ease, strength and responsiveness. This is why this area is of particular importance for the aims of this book. How we use this centre to connect our breathing process to our sense of identity and impulses will be explored in the breathing section.

This gravity centre also includes what in Eastern disciplines such as T'ai Chi, Tao and Hindu is called a *tan tien* or *chakra*, a source of *chi* or *prana*, that is, of *energy*. There are three main energy centres: here in the lower abdomen, the solar plexus, and the brain. This lower *tan tien* or *sacral chakra* is seen as the centre of the will, sexuality and life force from where actions flow. It is the 'basic storage battery of the body', and an abundance of energy in the lower *tan tien* 'makes it easier to assimilate all the other forms of energy available to us' (*The Tao of Natural Breathing*: 81–3). The actor needs a strong sense of this gravity and energy centre to feel connected with the present moment's experience.

Spanning from the thigh bones and pelvis to the vertebrae of the lumbar spine are the *psoas* muscles. These run either side of the sacrum and are important for the strength of the spine and alignment. They connect the upper and lower parts of the body, stabilizing their relationship. Located in our centre of gravity, they are essential muscles for big movement (e.g. flexion and rotation) and balance, and are important for voice because they connect with the diaphragm and help to push air out on exhalation. They can enhance power in the voice and tension in them inhibits breathing.

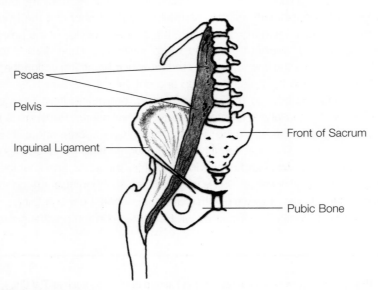

Figure 9 Psoas muscles

Lumbar curve – There are five lumbar vertebrae (the small of the back). From the age of 1 to 10, the lumbar vertebrae become a concave secondary curve. Attached to them are the main breathing muscle, the diaphragm, and the abdominal muscles, which enable rotation, flexion and stabilizing of alignment.

Thoracic curve – There are 12 thoracic vertebrae, and they form a primary curve to which the ribs attach. The diaphragm is attached to the lower ribs. Linking the ribs are the chest's respiratory muscles. Inside the ribcage are the lungs.

In the area of the diaphragm, between the navel and the sternum, is the *solar plexus,* a key nerve centre. It is often thought to be the centre of inner power and emotional drive, identifying us with the world around us. It is through here the actor responds to impulses from outside – more on this later.

Cervical curve – Seven cervical vertebrae make the neck, and this is a secondary curve. This is where the speech organs of the throat and larynx are.

The heavy weight of the head sits on top of the spine and needs to be balanced.

The muscles of the spine responsible for lengthening are the spinal raisers, the *Erector Spinae*: 'The most powerful muscles in the human body are those that run along the spine; they maintain posture and provide the strength for lifting and pushing' (*Human Body*: 84).

Spinal muscles

Figure 10 Erector Spinae muscles

Spinal and pelvic movement have a central role in supporting the voice in harmony with the breath. The movement of the spine and the inmost muscles linked to it make a psycho-physical link with the actor's need to communicate something with conviction and integrity.

In order to receive a full and easy in-breath and to control the release of the out-breath, stabilizing and strengthening the posture is essential. In voice work we can learn to enhance the secondary shapes of the spine during inhalation and the primary shapes during exhalation, resulting in an increase in the overall length of the spine. This counterbalances the common tendency to shorten the spine on the out-breath: when this happens, the spaces in the body close down and inhibit the free release of the voice through open channels.

EXERCISES

Prelude: relaxation and easy breathing

Deep natural breathing will only come through good alignment, but it will help us to work on alignment if we start with a sense of ease in our muscles and breath. So take ten minutes on this basic relaxation exercise.

* Stretch in all directions, up, down, to the sides, front and back using maximum space around your body. Yawn as you stretch. On an in-breath, reach up to the sky with both arms, on tiptoes, and then on an out-breath, sighing out, release and flop, hanging loosely from the hips with knees loose. Now roll up one vertebra at a time.

* Lie down on your back in semi-supine position with your knees to the ceiling. Sense your body, your contact with the floor through your feet, pelvis, back and the back of your head.

* On an in-breath, clench your fists and on the out-breath relax them. On an in-breath, tense up the fists, arms and shoulder blades and on the out-breath relax them. On the next in-breath, tense up fists, arms, shoulder blades, ribcage and pelvis, and on the out-breath relax them. Lastly, on an in-breath tense up fists, arms, shoulder blades, ribcage, pelvis, legs, feet and face, and on the out-breath let everything go and melt into the floor.

* Now listen to your body without applying any effort. Imagine that you are lying in a beautiful landscape. There is a perfect temperature around you. Sense how the pleasant surroundings influence your awareness of self. Allow yourself to quieten down and let your thoughts come and go. Don't try to change anything or to control anything.

* Tune into your natural breathing movements by simply allowing your body to breathe. Sense its movement but don't control it. If you feel self-conscious, wait for your body's impulse to breathe in. When you really feel it, follow it and allow your breath to come in. Place one hand on your navel and sense the warmth of your hand. Your breathing movements will be drawn to it.

On your impulse to breathe out, gently press your hand down on your abdominal area while making a sigh. Repeat. Your breathing will slow down and lengthen.

* Then, on your next out-breath movement, let yourself melt into the floor. Go deeply into the sensation of melting your body into the ground like ice melting into water: your face and jaw, your belly, back and chest, your pelvis and thighs, your calves and feet. Your breathing will slow down and become deeper. Allow your in-breath to happen automatically. The deeper your out-breath becomes with the melting sensation, the deeper your in-breath becomes in return. Your muscles will relax and the spaces in your body will widen and allow your natural breath to have more room to expand and contract.

Exploring spinal movements and balance

The first step is to picture your spine and its areas and to explore its flexibility through the vertebrae. Throughout the body, but especially in the spine, we can feel and organize how passive and active forces of release and support operate. The following exercises can only present a guideline. The important thing for you is to find your alignment physically (although aligning isn't just about creating an ideal structure), energetically (so that your energy and breath can flow) and psychologically (so that you find what it feels like to be in your spine, in your own identity).

Natural alignment is also often something that needs to be re-learned. Due to tensions and defence mechanisms alignment can lose its balance and equilibrium. Muscle groups that should be free to do other jobs become involved in keeping us upright. Tensions develop and muscles shorten. The key to personal growth is to re-educate our perceptions in order to experience ourselves in a new way – essential for the actor, who has to experience characters and situations without being stuck in a fixed self-image and personal habits.

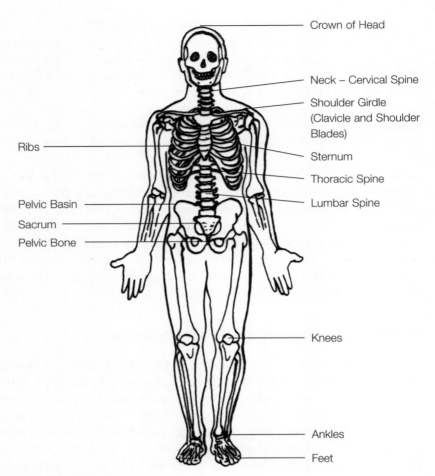

Figure 11 Visualizing your body

1. Visualize your body's alignment: preparing the channels for energy flow

Adopt this centred neutral stance, to which we shall constantly return, as your basic starting position for many exercises.

Stand easily with your feet parallel, hip-width apart and knees slightly bent. Allow your tailbone to release downwards. Imagine a string attached to the crown of your head gently lifting the spine. Imagine a balanced tray in your pelvis. This is the posture in the left picture. Now try the other two alignments, one with the coccyx tail tipped too far under and forward and one with it tipped too far back and up: see how uncentred and unbalanced they make you feel, as the tray tips its contents. Return to the first posture.

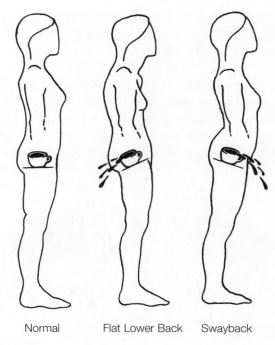

Normal   Flat Lower Back   Swayback

Figure 12 Neutral stance

Feet – Start by visualizing your feet and their three points of support and contact with the floor: one in the ball of the foot where the big toe connects; a second where the little toe connects; and a third in the heel of the foot. Sense this triangle of support. Feel how your weight is equally distributed between the three points. Feel how the feet carry the load of your whole body like the foundations of a house. Once they are balanced, we can concentrate on the rest of the body's structure. This is a neutral alignment (see Figure 13).

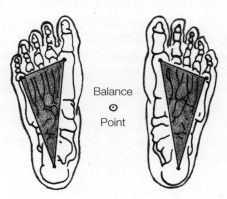

Balance
⊙
Point

Figure 13 Triangle of support – with balance point between the feet

Test your balance. First shift your weight from side to side and forward and back and sense what this shift of balance means for the rest of your body. For example, if you rock back onto your heels you will see how your back locks and inhibits action.

Now let's look at an *engaged alignment* that prepares for action. Rise onto the balls of the feet, feel the weight of your body resting on them through the balance line and sense a forward alertness. Roll back down through the soles of the feet and retain this sense of how the weight has shifted forward. This will free your back for supporting and engaging the breath in action (see Figure 14).

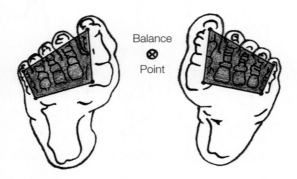

Figure 14 Forward engagement on the balls of the feet

Ankles and shins – Picture and feel your ankles. Then visualize your shins leading into your knee joints. Make sure that your knees are not locked. Feel how the breath and energy can move through them.

Pelvis – Visualize your pelvic basin and your coccyx tail. The sacral section of the spine forms a primary curve. Look at the picture of the sections of the spine above. Allow your coccyx tail to drop into gravity – don't push or hold it down. You can imagine your coccyx tail like an anchor rooting you down into the ground. This will tilt your pelvis up at the front slightly.

Adjust the balance between the balls of the feet, hip bones and shoulders so that they are in one line. Let your chin drop and sense the length at the back of the neck. Keep breathing. Don't just restructure your body's bones but sense the balance line through those shifts. You may find this uncomfortable because it goes against your habitual use of your body. This is normal but it is important to be open to this exploration so that we can find the organic way to align. Your breath will help you to find ease within these adjustments.

Lumbar curve – Now imagine how your spine grows out of the pelvis forming the lumbar vertebrae. Imagine the five vertebrae that form the lumbar curve in the small of your back. Picture your diaphragm and solar plexus in front. Sense the secondary curve this section forms.

Look at the picture of the lumbar section. You can stand sideways in front of the mirror to get an idea of the primary and secondary curves in your body. Or, you can use your hands to feel their shapes. Please note that if you are using a mirror, it is not a matter of outwardly readjusting things. Alignment is not like an army drill where you straighten parts. Muscle perception must be readjusted and the following exercises are guides to do this. Using a mirror can aid your understanding, though, because you can see what you might not be able to feel yet.

Thoracic curve – Next visualize the 12 thoracic vertebrae growing up between your shoulder blades. Here the ribs are attached, and enclosed by them are your lungs. Sense that this area is a primary curve. Look at the picture of the thoracic section.

Shoulders – Now visualize your shoulder girdle and how your arms hang from the shoulder sockets. Let this whole section drop into the weight of gravity. Feel your arms hanging heavily.

Cervical curve and head – The cervical area of your spine, the neck, is made of seven vertebrae forming a secondary curve. Visualize your heavy head on top. Sense the crown of the head and imagine the string pulling it up towards the sky. Let your chin drop slightly, creating a feeling of a fine dressage horse with a rounded neck 'on the bit', rather than a giraffe with a lifted chin.

Figure 15 Horse and giraffe

2. Spine roll

Do the following with the easy breath you have explored above. Don't hold your breath. Give yourself enough time to sense what is going on, but be aware that rolling down, when you are not used to it, can make you feel dizzy. This is nothing dangerous, but take a break before trying it again. If problems persist you can begin by doing the exercise sitting on a chair.

Stand in the centred position described above: feet parallel, hip-width apart, knees unlocked and your spine long. Allow your coccyx tail to drop into gravity and your chin to drop with a loose jaw.

Picture the areas of the spine.

Cervical curve and head – First picture the seven cervical vertebrae connecting head and neck, finishing with the big bull vertebra on top of the shoulder girdle leading into the thoracic area of your spine.

Now allow your head to drop forward and feel how it lengthens the back of your neck. Try to keep your coccyx tail dropped so that you feel a lengthening stretch occur through the whole of your spine. Keep breathing. Sense the weight of the head wanting to pull you into gravity. Keep the chin close to the chest so that the weight of the head can release you downwards rather than you leading with your chin.

Pause and breathe.

Thoracic curve – Picture the 12 vertebrae of your thoracic spine. Release them one by one following the weight of your head and the rest of your torso. Sense the movement of curling down through each vertebra between your shoulder blades.

Pause and breathe.

Lumbar curve – Now you have arrived in the lumbar area of your spine. Picture the five lumbar vertebrae. Move through these following the weight of the head and 'rolled down' part of your body.

Pause and breathe.

Sacral curve – Finally, picture your sacral spine with the coccyx tail attached to it. The vertebrae here are fused and are experienced as one portion. Release your pelvis and hang between your legs. Make sure your knees are bent and your head heavy and loose.

* Allow yourself to hang from your pelvis for a moment and breathe into your pelvis and lower back as well as the back of your lower ribs. Release a sigh.

Pause and breathe.

* Now roll up slowly from the coccyx tail, picturing the vertebrae and trying to build up one vertebra on top of the other by uncurling your spine. Do this fluently and on one out-breath if possible.

When you reach the top of the thoracic spine, while your head still hangs down, take a moment to pause and breathe. Make sure that your arms are released and heavy like monkey arms.

Keep relaxed for this and follow your body's need to breathe in and out as it wishes.

* On your out-breath, while keeping the chin towards your chest, gently lengthen the back of your neck with your jaw dropped, then on an in-breath induce a yawn to open your soft palate.

Imagine the string attached to the crown of the head pulling you up and let the head float up towards the zenith of the sky.

Imagine there are strings attached to your heels and big and small toes pulling you down towards the centre of the earth.

Check if your body is within its balance line so that your torso doesn't fall too far forward or too far back: see the balance line picture at the start of Alignment with ears above the shoulders, shoulders above the hips, hips above the middle of the feet. You will need this balance line for your energy to travel freely through the body on your breath.

* Do this several times more fluidly until you have a clear picture of your spine and its curling and uncurling movement, and of the two principles of gravity pulling you into the earth and anti-gravity pulling you towards the sky.

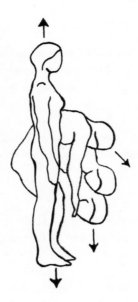

Figure 16 Spine roll

3. Grounding

'The earth is giving us more self knowledge than any book can because it gives us resistance.'
From *Wind, Sand and Stars,* ANTOINE DE SAINT-EXUPÉRY

Grounding – our rooted connection to the earth – gives us a sense of belonging, focus and direction. It helps us to experience things more deeply and strongly.

The symbol for grounding is the triangle, which we also use later for *centred onset of sound.*

The tip of the triangle is in the gravity point of the pelvis. The feet are the base of the triangle. The breath is centred and low and connects us with earth. The result is stability, strength, connectedness and stillness of mind.

T'ai Chi rotation exercise

This exercise is great for grounding and warming the whole body, especially the spine. It grounds the feet into the floor, makes the vertebrae flexible, opens the ribcage and centres and roots the breath into the pelvis. It asserts the presence of the actor – because without grounding there can be no strong experience of self.

* Stand with your feet more than hip-width apart and parallel. Allow your coccyx tail to drop. Become aware of the centre of your pelvis. Breathe as if through your feet and your pelvic floor.

* Start to swing to the left from the pelvis with the head and torso turning to the left and behind, and the right heel raising from the ground. Then swing to the right with the head and torso turning to the right and behind, and the left heel raising from the ground. The arms passively follow this movement, their weight swinging them round to hit the shoulder at the front and the kidney at the back, and with the shoulders dropped down. Feel the will in the pelvis while keeping it faced forward and your feet parallel. The balls of the feet should remain grounded into the floor as if they have roots anchoring you into the earth, from where they draw the breath like a plant drawing water. T'ai Chi practitioners do this for around 15 minutes.

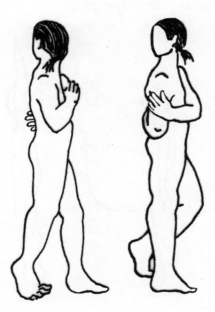

Figure 17 T'ai Chi rotation exercise

Connecting Sky and Earth

The following exercise is taken from *The Tao of Natural Breathing* (109). It's a good prelude to the next section where we explore gravity and anti-gravity.

* Stand well aligned with your knees bent, feet parallel and hip-width apart. Let your tailbone drop into gravity so that it points to the ground and gently lengthen your neck.

* As you inhale, slowly rise up on your toes and simultaneously raise your arms straight in front of you. Your arms should arrive over your head, palms facing forward, at the same time as you have reached your full extension, and fully breathed in.

* As you exhale, synchronize slowly lowering your arms straight in front of you and lowering the feet until you are in the original standing position by the time you have fully exhaled.

* Try this a number of times. Sense the upward and downward movement of energy. Sense your whole body breathing. Experience how your breath is putting you in touch with your own verticality, connecting sky and earth both inside and outside your body. Once you've felt this, walk around for a few minutes and see for how long you can maintain this sensation.

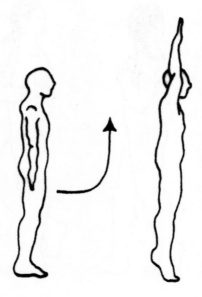

Figure 18 Connecting sky and earth

4. The Elastic Band

'What is happening within me?
My weight binds me to the earth whilst all the stars magnetically pull
me towards them.
Yet another weight throws me back onto myself whilst drawing me
towards so many distant things.'
From Wind, Sand and Stars, ANTOINE DE SAINT-EXUPÉRY

The opposing vertical forces can be imagined as an Elastic Band. This stretches through the whole length of the spine and can be imagined as a vertical balance line that runs through the crown of the head towards the zenith of the sky and through the centre of the pelvis toward the middle of the earth. Gravity pulls us down while anti-gravity pulls us up. Imagine a plant striving towards the light while pulling nutrition out of the earth. Sensing the movement of opposing forces from crown to feet will aid us in acquiring whole body breathing.

The symbol for the Elastic Band is two arrows pointing down into gravity and up to anti-gravity.

Now we shall do a spine roll exploring in *three positions* how the Elastic Band operates.

* We begin as before. Stand with feet parallel, hip-width apart. Keep your knees loose and your spine loose but long. Allow your coccyx tail to drop into gravity so that you will feel a lengthening stretch occur through the whole of your spine and let your chin drop. Let your jaw drop open.

* Start with the impulse to *roll down*. Allow yourself to breathe in this impulse through your solar plexus and down into your gravity centre, then when fully affected by it follow it through on an out-breath. Allow your head to drop forward and feel how it lengthens the back of your neck.

* Roll down your spine, one vertebra at a time, by following the weight of your head. Sense the pull of gravity all the way, allowing your out-breath movement to yield and melt into it.

POSITION 1: When you have rolled down, *release the body*. Let yourself hang from your pelvis between the legs and with your knees unlocked and breathe naturally.

On another out-breath continue to feel the pull of gravity towards the centre of the earth although your body might have come to the end of the movement. Imagine the string attached to the crown of your head that is pulled towards the centre of the earth. Keep your head released and your arms heavy. This will stretch you on your out-breath movement and will release your muscles.

Relax and breathe in. On an out-breath, as you hang from your pelvis between your legs, *sense the anti-gravity force by lifting the back of your pelvis and your coccyx tail up towards the sky while the crown of the head is pulled towards the gravity of the earth.*

Figure 19 Position 1

Now find the impulse to *uncurl back up.* Allow yourself to breathe this into your solar plexus and wait for your impulse to breathe out. On the out-breath, start with the lowest vertebra and raise one vertebra at a time while keeping your head hanging heavy and your arms dropped like monkey arms through the movement. Sense the anti-gravity force as you lift towards the sky. Follow it like the shoot of a plant follows the light of the sun.

POSITION 2: Come up as far as the top vertebra of your thoracic spine and leave your head hanging down, chin on chest, while feeling the gravity pull.

Sense the two forces operating on the Elastic Band and allow your breath to engage with their force and directions. *You will feel more and more how your out-breath engages with your intention to follow these two forces.*

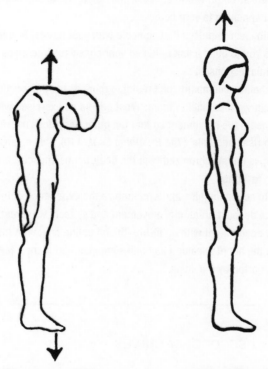

Figure 20 Position 2   **Figure 21** Position 3

POSITION 3: Find the impulse to align your cervical spine. Breathe it into your solar plexus and on your out-breath lift the head and lengthen the back of the neck.

Imagine the string attached to the crown pulling you towards the sky and another string on the triangle of the foot pulling you down towards the centre of the earth.

Sense that you are aligned between those forces and picture your spine as the centre of the balance line that goes through your body. Allow your pelvis to go with the pull downwards by dropping your coccyx tail. Lightly shift your balance forward towards the balls of the feet and come into your balance line.

The rolls should be done with ease. Balance means that alignment takes care of being upright while the muscles of the body are free to do other jobs if needed. The breathing movements will make the body's movements smooth. Gravity and anti-gravity work in a way that creates equilibrium within the body. They create strength within stillness and balance. Explore, observe and sense what is happening to your body.

Working with clear impulses that coincide with your natural breathing impulses helps you to build a link between your conscious intentions and the body's autonomic responses.

The spine should accompany the breathing movements that occur in the body, rather than work parallel to them: 'Most people do exercises where they breathe underneath the movement so that the outer body does not reflect the way the breath rises and falls' (*The Breathing Book*: 110). This means that when breathing is not synchronized with the body, bones, muscles and skin do not move in response.

Our aim is to act on impulse and synchronize the experience of the actor with the natural deepest breathing, movement and speech. We 'breathe the experience' by absorbing it with an in-breath and acting on it with the out-breath, so that the act of speaking embodies impulse, experience, feeling and physicality supported by the spine.

5. Primary and secondary curves

As we described earlier, we began as a baby in the womb with the primary curve. To connect to this shape, we will explore some positions from Yoga.

Our symbol for the shape of the spine where the primary curves are prominent on the out-breath is the C-shape.

Child pose

Sit on your knees, hip-width apart so that you can breathe easily. Allow your forehead to touch the floor. You can have your hands under your forehead or on either side of your knees. You can also lift your bottom off the ground if that is more comfortable. Breathe into the resulting primary shape of your spine. On your out-breath follow the breathing movement back towards your spine and sense how this further curls the spine into a C-shape.

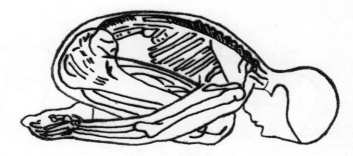

Figure 22 Child pose

Cat and cow

This is also a Yoga exercise. With this exercise we can explore primary and secondary shapes and connect them to the breathing movements of breathing in and breathing out.

* First, go onto hands and knees. Allow your coccyx to drop and your neck to lengthen to make a flat table.

* To make the cow position, emphasizing the secondary curves of the spine, on an in-breath let your abdominal area drop and the coccyx rise causing your back to arch downwards while your chin lifts up towards the sky, rather like a cow looking at the moon. Make the in-breath movement and spinal action one thing. If you have a partner, they can hold your abdominal area and sense the weight. This is useful if you have problems in releasing this area.

* Find the impulse to breathe out. Whilst breathing out, tuck your pelvis under and lower your coccyx as if it were a donkey tail dropping towards the floor. Let your abdominals move backwards towards the spine, and curl into a primary C-shape, rather like a cat stretching after waking up from a restful

sleep, emphasizing the primary curves of your spine. Make the curling flexing movement one with the out-breath.

* When you have the impulse to breathe in again, allow your abdominal muscles to relax and drop whilst your spine arches downwards.

* Repeat the movement from cow to cat to cow several times, fitting your breathing impulses to the action rather than doing it mechanically so that the breath and physical response feels organic.

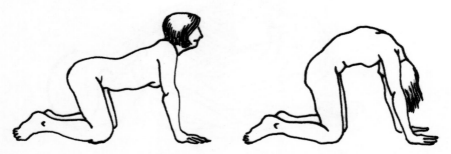

Figure 23 Cow and cat – emphasizing the secondary and primary curves

6. Exploring the movements of the spine that occur when breathing

Standing

* Stand well aligned, balanced and with your feet hip-width apart and parallel. Keep your hips parallel to your shoulders and let your tailbone hang into gravity. The pelvis should be in the neutral position shown in Figure 12. Find a forward balance in the balls of the feet. Note that when your balance is too far back on your heels it will lock your back, and if it is too far forward in your toes it will seize up the front of your body.

Here is a quote from Alexander Lowen, a well-known psychiatrist who studied with Wilhelm Reich:

Natural breathing – that is, the way a child or animal breathes – involves the whole body. Not every part is actively engaged, but every part is affected to greater or lesser degree by respiratory waves that traverse the body. When we breathe in, the wave starts deep in the abdominal cavity and flows up to the head. When we breathe out, the wave moves from head to feet. (*The Spirituality of the Body: Bioenergetics for Grace and Harmony*: 37–8)

* Place one hand below your navel and one in the parallel position on the back of the pelvis. Sense the rise and fall your breath creates in this area.

Feel how the tailbone and sacrum tip back, and how they draw slightly under on exhalation. This is the tiniest movement and might be hard to feel at first.

Feel how your lower back follows the movement of the rocking pelvis, arching up slightly on the in-breath.

Now sense how on the out-breath it lengthens and flattens, moving more towards the C-shape.

See how the entire spinal column responds to breathing.

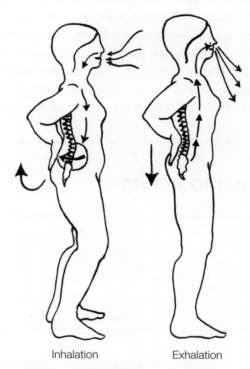

Inhalation   Exhalation

Figure 24 Spinal movement on inhalation and exhalation

Lying

* Now lie down with your knees up. Place one hand under your lumbar area where your back may create a gap with the floor, the other on your navel.

* *Allow yourself to be breathed by your deepest, involuntary breath.*

Sense how on your in-breath the pressure on your hand between your lumbar area and the floor gets lighter as the spine moves upwards towards the ceiling. When you breathe out, follow the journey of your out-breath: it will take you deeper into the floor and make your body press more heavily on your hand.

'CENTRED'

All the above exercises co-ordinate the movements of the spine and the pelvis, the gravity centre of the body, and create a sense of our connection to the sky and the earth and all the space around us. This creates a physical sensation we call *centred*: we feel integrated, easy, balanced, rooted and connected to our core. Walk around your space with this sense and you will also feel new psychological qualities as a result: confident, focused, relaxed, in the moment, in control. This is a basic feeling we need as actors at all times, and which Stanislavski referred to as self-possession and repose.

Integration into acting

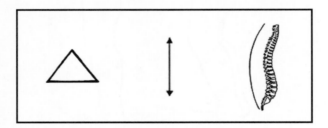

Take a look at the predicament of Dame Eleanor Cobham from Shakespeare's *Henry VI*, Part Two, Act 2, Scene 4. She is married to Humphrey, Duke of Gloucester, the younger brother of Henry V and next in line to the throne. Eleanor has been arrested for witchcraft and treason in pursuing her ambitions for Gloucester to succeed Henry VI. She is being paraded through the streets and publicly humiliated prior to being imprisoned in a castle on the Isle of Man. She is accompanied by the Sheriff of London and wears a white sheet with her alleged crimes pinned on her back and carries a wax candle. The people mock her when she hurts her feet on the rough flint and insult her as a witch. Humphrey has said to her: 'Be patient, gentle Nell: forget this grief', and she replies:

Ah, Gloucester, teach me to forget myself;
For whilst I think I am thy married wife.
And thou a prince, Protector of this land,
Methinks I should not thus be led along,
Mailed up* in shame, with papers on my back,   *enveloped*
And followed with a rabble that rejoice
To see my tears and hear my deep-fet groans.*   *fetched from deep inside*
The ruthless flint doth cut my tender feet,
And when I start, the envious people laugh,
And bid me be advised how I tread.
Ah, Humphrey, can I bear this shameful yoke?
Trowest thou* that e'er I'll look upon the world,   *Do you believe*
Or count them happy that enjoy the sun?
No, dark shall be my light, and night my day;
To think upon my pomp shall be my hell.
Sometime I'll say I am Duke Humphrey's wife,
And he a prince and ruler of the land;
Yet so he ruled, and such a prince he was,
As he stood by whilst I, his forlorn Duchess,
Was made a wonder and a pointing-stock
To every idle rascal follower.
But be thou mild and blush not at my shame,
Nor stir at nothing till the axe of death
Hang over thee, as sure it shortly will.

Imagine you are in the Duchess's circumstances as if they are real for you. Read the speech as an attempt to overcome your humiliation by standing your ground with dignity, head held high among the crowd. Feel this sense of 'standing your ground' through the whole of your spine. Lengthen your spine through the Elastic Band. Ground down and lift up and sense how this strengthens conviction in your objective, which is *to get Humphrey to stand up for me as a prince and husband should.* The spine will help you to get the sense of 'Me/I' – Stanislavski's 'I am' within the circumstances – to identify yourself with her situation imaginatively and physically.

To sum up:

- **Balanced alignment brings a vertical equilibrium between earth and sky, using gravity and anti-gravity forces.**
- **It economizes on muscular effort and is both easy and powerful.**

It is essential in order:

- to find the free flow of energy that enables creative communication between the brain and the body;
- to create spinal awareness that connects to our sense of identity, of Me/I in the moment;
- to find the spinal support system for the breathing movement;
- to bring conviction to our objectives when acting.

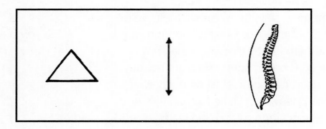

4

BREATH – THE GREAT CREATIVE CONNECTOR

'Where our breath goes, our attention can also go. By learning how to breathe naturally – that is, by learning how to breathe vitality into every corner of our being – we not only promote the expansion of our inner consciousness, but we also stimulate the healthful, harmonious movement of substances and energies throughout our bodies.'

The Tao of Natural Breathing (143)

WHAT IS IT?

When we breathe we take air through our nose and mouth and this enters the lungs and fills little sacs called alveoli. From here it enters surrounding tiny blood vessels and through these the bloodstream, which carries oxygen to all the cells of the body, giving us energy to think, feel and act. Conversely, carbon dioxide waste is carried by the bloodstream into the lungs and then exhaled.

However, the lungs are not muscles. They are moved into action only by the muscles around them.

The *primary* muscles stimulating the deepest breathing process are the diaphragm, the pelvic floor, the abdominal muscles and the intercostal muscles of the ribs.

The *secondary* breathing muscles in chest, neck, abdomen and back are smaller and thinner muscles, which tire much more easily than the more bulky primary muscles. Some of these are used in life-threatening situations or sport; some may create tension, for example, in shallow clavicular breathing, and are not useful to the actor. Others involved in posture, in the back and abdomen, have stabilizing and supporting functions and will be mentioned later.

The actor wants to avoid tension in the accessory muscles and allow the primary muscles to do the breathing movements. For this reason, we'll focus below on the primary muscles.

What is it for the actor?

We breathe because we have a physical need to inhale oxygen and expel carbon dioxide, and because we have a psychological inner impulse to express a thought, feeling or action.

Physiologically, breath is the fuel for the voice.

Psychologically, breath can connect us to inner experiences, reflexes and emotions.

How breath can enhance performance

* Breath can connect mind, body and voice.

* It can drive the will of the actor through sound and language.

* It can centre the body and calm the mind, helping us find stillness and focus by connecting with the gravity centre of the body.

* It can make us more aware.

* It can help actors to connect and interact within an unbroken line of communication that Stanislavski and Michael Chekhov called *radiation:* we constantly *receive* and *transmit* energy, breathing in responses from the other person and breathing out our own thoughts, feelings and actions.

* It can connect the actor to the theatre space and the audience.

* Breathing, or inspiration, can help us achieve *inspiration*, that sense of the subconscious creative forces taking over our performances and producing rich and unpredictable qualities.

* To be *on the breath* is the goal of any actor because it releases the actor's experience.

The actor's body needs to be unrestricted and free of tension to allow the breath to flow freely. The impulses and experiences that arise within an organic acting approach can be released by breath through the vibrations of sounds and words.

We say breath *can* do all these things. To actually *do* them we need to access *deep* breathing. It is important to realize that we have a facility to breathe both deeply and shallowly, for example, when we are in fight or flight mode.

Psyche, coming from ancient Greek, means breath, life, soul. Breath is essential for life and connects our impulses and experience to our bodies. It gives a rather wider meaning to the *psycho* in *psycho-physical* than the word *psychological*.

Breath connects us with the *gravity centre* below the navel in the lowest *tan tien*, where the intentions of the mind find responses in the body, and with the *solar plexus,* the middle *tan tien*. The solar plexus is a nerve centre, centre of energy and of the emotions – Stanislavski called it 'the seat of emotion' (*An Actor Prepares*: 172). It is also within the breathing centre of the diaphragm. Through taking in breath we can also *breathe in circumstances, action and language* and make them our own. We return to this idea throughout the book.

Breath training for the actor

The important thing for the acting student to realize is that we already have what we need in us. Nature has given it to us. Stanislavski saw Nature as the greatest artist: 'But the actor is not his own master. It is his nature which creates through him, he is only the instrument' (*Building a Character*: 255).

Jerzy Grotowski, the pioneering Polish director, saw actor training 'not as a collection of skills but an eradication of blocks', a *via negativa*, so that elements of 'natural' behaviour that obscure pure impulse are removed and inner impulse can immediately become outer action (*Towards a Poor Theatre:* 17).

The first step towards effective and connected breathing for an actor is to *liberate* the deep breathing rhythms that are given to us by the Autonomic Nervous System's (ANS) respiratory centre (this is in the *medulla oblongata,* part of the *old brain* near where the brain meets the spine).

The ANS causes breath at all times, by day and night, from the first breath we inhale until the last we exhale when we die. From here nerve impulses are transmitted to nerves within the spinal cord that cause the diaphragm and the intercostal muscles to start inhalation.

Also:

> The respiratory system is connected to most of the body's sensory nerves; hence any sudden or chronic stimulation coming through any of the senses can have an immediate impact on the force or speed of our breath, or can stop it altogether. Intense beauty, for example, can momentarily 'take our breath away' while pain, tension, or stress generally speeds up our breathing and reduces its depth. (*The Tao of Natural Breathing*: 35; also see 'The nervous system' in Chapter 2)

We receive constant nourishment from the oxygen provided by the incoming breath, which feeds every cell of the body and its organs. Also, the blood flows in harmony with the breath and all the inner organs are massaged and bathed by the free rhythm of the breathing movement.

Through breath we live and through breath we can breathe life into our performance.

* First we need to become aware of how the deep breath moves in our body.

* Then we need to centre and enhance the flow of breath for the actor's purpose of communicating.

Although breathing can be controlled by our conscious mind, it is the deep breathing rhythms implanted in us by the automatized action of the nervous system that can really guide us towards the most effective and connected way to breathe as the actor. However, we need to become conscious of how this process actually works in order that we can remove any obstacles that might have arisen to its free and natural movement and development. Then, in performance, the breath can connect with our deepest experiences, imagination and impulses, carry them through the sounds, words and thoughts of language and share them with our audience.

What it means for the actor and audience

Breathing patterns can be contagious. When an actor breathes deeply and freely and is connected to a real experience, the whole audience will adapt and copy the breathing rhythm of the actor, and enter the experience as if it were their own. If, on the other hand, an actor is tense and breathing is restricted, the audience will feel this tightness in sympathy. They will lose trust and even start to worry about the actor. Oxygen supply is lessened in the actor and the audience. Experiences no longer come out of the depth of the actor's experience but from more shallow places that are higher up in the body and have a strong link with stress responses. 'We've got to get in to get out', says one line of a song from Genesis. Shallow breathing will not get in touch with what we feel. In actual fact we might breathe shallowly in order to protect ourselves from experiencing what might cause us pain.

As we have seen earlier, it is essential to be still, balanced and focused in order to experience fully, and to keep a sense of centre and identity within the experiences of the part as if they were our own. Natural breathing rhythms will help us to achieve that, and to access our deepest layers of consciousness, which might have become buried under our defence mechanisms. To breathe out fully is to give back our version of what has been absorbed through the in-breath: to transmit our experience as the character within the imaginary world of the play.

We shall now look at how to promote deep and healthy breathing through harmonious team effort between the primary breathing muscles: the diaphragm, rib, abdominal and pelvic floor muscles.

How breath works

1. The diaphragm – the engine of the breath

The diaphragm is the principal breath creator: a large muscle looking like a mushroom but flexible like a parachute and divided into two domes connected by a central tendon. It extends from 'nipple to navel' and is attached to the bottom of the sternum, the base of the ribcage and the front of the lower lumbar spine.

The muscle fibres of the diaphragm run along the *vertical* axis of the body. The horizontal central tendon only moves in response to the muscle fibres connecting it. Although the diaphragm brings about a vertical and a horizontal movement within the breathing spaces of the body, the main movement of the diaphragm is up and down along the spine. This has relevance for the part the spinal movement plays in effective breathing action.

Inhalation – When the brain gives a signal to inhale, the diaphragm contracts and the domes are pulled down and fan outwards in the ribcage area, opening the ribs. The increased space in the torso means the pressure in the atmosphere exceeds the pressure in the chest and as a result air flows into the lungs. The lungs are pulled down, the abdomen is pushed down and our belly swells out and opens the pelvic floor.

Exhalation – When we exhale, the diaphragm relaxes back passively, and the lungs are pushed up, supported by the abdominal and pelvic muscles.

This mode of breathing is called *diaphragmatic* breathing, or *abdominal* breathing, and it is this form of natural, automatic breathing that enables acting impulse to synchronize with breath organically.

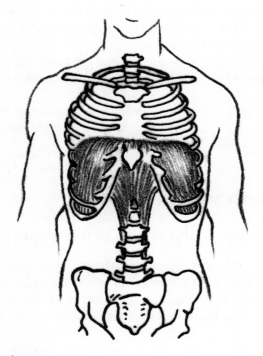

Figure 25 The diaphragm

Try getting a feel of the breathing movement. Place one hand on your navel and one on the lowest part of your ribs where they bulge out most. Sense the warmth of your hands and tune into your natural breathing movements (see *Prelude: easy natural centred breathing* in Chapter 1). Follow your *body's need* to breathe and don't interfere. Sense how your belly moves out and your ribcage expands when your body breathes in. Sense how your belly and your ribcage retract when you breathe out.

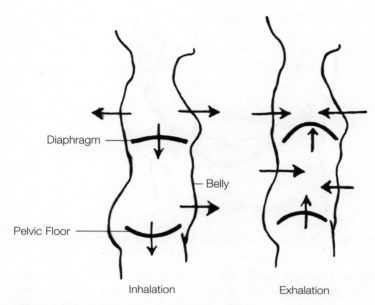

Diaphragm

Belly

Pelvic Floor

Inhalation Exhalation

Figure 26 Inhalation, exhalation from the side

2. Teamwork between the diaphragm, the pelvic floor muscles and the vocal folds

Breathing movements are enhanced by interactive teamwork between the diaphragm, the vocal folds and the pelvic floor and in Yoga they are actually referred to as the *three* diaphragms:

1 The respiratory diaphragm
2 The vocal diaphragm
3 The pelvic diaphragm.

The pelvic floor, which we met in the Alignment section, has been likened to 'an inverted parachute' (*The Breathing Book*: 56) or 'a hammock' (*Singing with Your Own Voice,* Orlanda Cook: 75). It is situated at the opening at the base of the pelvis and consists of the pelvic layer of muscles and the uro-genital layer. The pelvic muscles run from the pubic bone in the front to the coccyx tail in the back. This layer is the deeper of the two and has muscle fibres running around the anus and the genitals. Closer to the surface, the uro-genital muscles run from side to side and connect to the inside of the two sitting bones. When we inhale, the pelvic floor/diaphragm drops down and broadens, and when we exhale, it retracts upwards and narrows.

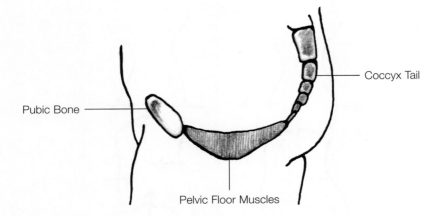

Figure 27 Pelvic floor muscles creating the vocal floor

The vocal folds are two folds made of five layers of fibrous tissue and muscle situated in the *larynx*, or voice box, at the base of the tongue in the upper passage of the air channel known as the *trachea* or windpipe. In the average woman they are only 18 millimetres long, and 23 millimetres in a man, and form a V-shape pointing towards the Adam's apple (*Your Voice: An Inside View*, Scott McCoy: 102). When we breathe in, the vocal folds open, and when we breathe out and create different degrees of air pressure on them, they come together and vibrate at different speeds and create the range of sounds – of varying pitch, length and volume – we know as speaking or singing.

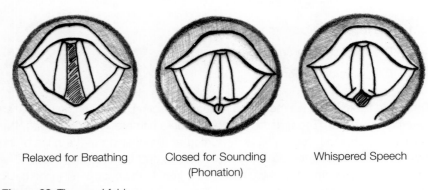

Relaxed for Breathing   Closed for Sounding   Whispered Speech
                               (Phonation)

Figure 28 The vocal folds

The three diaphragms perform a co-ordinated action aiding the flow of breath and energy through the whole body, and increasing awareness of this will facilitate an open, full-sounding voice.

When the diaphragm, which initiates the breathing process, moves down on the in-breath, the pelvic floor also drops down, but the ribs move out and upwards, and the larynx moves downwards and the vocal folds open. On the out-breath, the diaphragm relaxes back up and compresses the air in the chest while the pelvic floor narrows and rises up within the pelvis. Together with the abdominal muscles, it supports the action of the diaphragm and helps the lungs to expire, the larynx rises back as the air flows out through open vocal folds when we are silent, or presses through closed folds when we sound.

So, a *countermovement* is created in breathing and sounding: we experience the natural forces of the downward pull of *gravity* against the *uplifting* pull mentioned earlier in the alignment section. By enhancing these movements and by linking breathing to spinal movement in alignment, we can significantly improve breath support and the quality of sound. We need to work with this whole process of naturally occurring movements rather than mechanically contract isolated muscles.

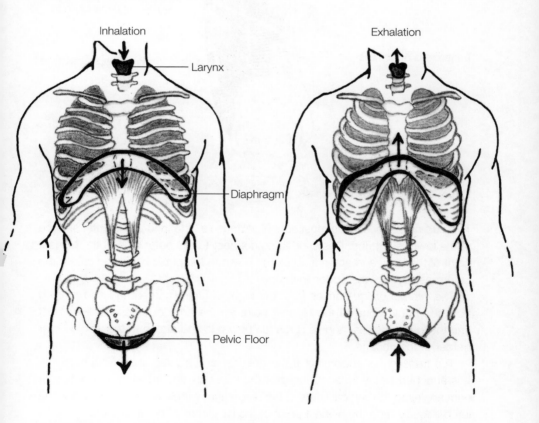

Figure 29 Movement of the diaphragm, pelvic floor and larynx on inhalation and exhalation

3. The abdominal muscles – core strength and support

The abdominal muscles involved in voice production and alignment are the *external and internal obliques* and, at the core of it all, the *transversus abdominis* muscles. The abdominals are the most powerful muscles of expiration.

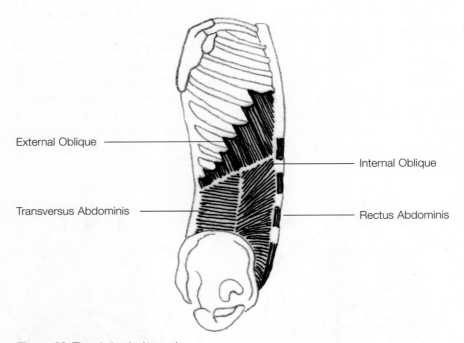

External Oblique

Internal Oblique

Transversus Abdominis

Rectus Abdominis

Figure 30 The abdominal muscles

The *external oblique* is the most superficial muscle, attached to the outer surface of the lower eight ribs. Posterior fibres connect to the outer side of the highest point of the hips, and anterior fibres run down to the pubic bone and create the outermost layer of the abdominal tube.

The *internal oblique* arises from the inguinal groin ligament (a band running from the pubic bone to the highest point on the anterior hips, the iliac crest) and the lumbar fascia, and its fibres fan upwards and attach to the whole lower border of the ribcage.

The *transversus abdominis* is the deepest of the three abdominal muscles. It is attached to the inner surfaces of the lower six ribs (running horizontally at right angles to the vertical fibres of the diaphragm with which it interweaves), the lumbar fascia, and the highest point of the hips from where it fans out.

The *rectus abdominis* is the powerful flexor muscle of the lumbar spine and balances the action of the powerful vertebral muscles behind the spine.

Another expiratory support muscle, which assists the abdominals, is the *Quadratus Lumborum*. This pair of muscles is rectangularly shaped and positioned in the lumbar area. It originates at the iliac crest and connects to the lowest ribs and the lumbar vertebrae. It forms a girdle around the back and helps to push up the diaphragm on the out-breath as the abdominals contract, and also stabilizes the lower back and ribcage (*Your Voice: An Inside View*: 88).

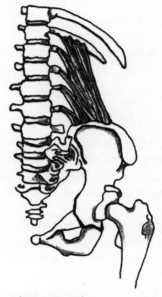

Figure 31 The Quadratus Lumborum muscles

Together, the abdominal muscles form a tube between the pelvis, the spine and the ribcage. This provides strength and support from the core of our body, creating an abdominal wall connecting with the ribcage. Support from the external obliques, internal obliques and *transversus abdominis* continues into support from the external intercostals, the internal intercostals and the innermost intercostals.

The *transversus abdominis* is the most internal of the abdominal muscles and responds best to impulses: its fibres interweave horizontally at a right angle to the vertical fibres of the diaphragm. It is also a muscle that releases energy over a long span of time and tires less easily than the more external abdominal muscles surrounding it. *Its engagement is the main contributor to support around the spine, pelvis and abdominal area.*

We believe that release of the *transversus abdominis* is preferable to mental control over it. When the diaphragm relaxes on the out-breath we observe that the abdominals engage automatically. This is preferable to actively tensing the abdominals to push the diaphragm back up. Again, it is a matter of working with what naturally occurs. As Christina Shewell maintains, the subtle engagement of the abdominal muscles on the out-breath and their release on the in-breath 'should become a natural part of the psycho-physical functioning of the body' (*Voice Work, Art and Science in Changing Voices*: 130).

The *rectus abdominis* is the powerful flexor muscle of the lumbar spine. We use it when doing sit-ups. If we use it too much, it can shorten the body by pulling the ribcage down, thereby restricting the neck and the larynx, and it can push too much breath against the vocal folds.

The general rule is that it is the inmost abdominals that will engage as a result of the impulse to speak.

4. The ribs

As we have seen above, the diaphragm is the engine and initiator of breathing movement that allows breath to enter the passive lungs. These are enclosed by the ribcage made of 12 pairs of ribs reaching from the collarbone right down into the lower back and its muscles. All the ribs are attached to the vertebrae of the spine at the back.

The topmost ribs (1 to 5) haven't got much movement. They are linked to the sternum and can only move in a 'pump-handle' fashion upwards and forwards and downwards and backwards. Put your hands on this area, breathe into it and get a sense of that movement.

It is clavicular breathing that primarily engages these topmost ribs, the shoulders and the clavicular bone – this superficial breath does not fill the lower lungs, only the top. Psychologically, it is connected to stressful situations, and physically it is very tiring because it engages muscles that are thin and small and situated around the neck and shoulders, and causes tension in the neck and larynx.

We aim to breathe with the lower ribs and to diminish tension in the upper body as much as possible. The lower ribs (6 to 10), called 'floating ribs', are not directly attached to the sternum and have more flexibility. They can move like a 'bucket handle', laterally (*Dynamics of the Singing Voice*: 34–5) – but also move forward and back. Put your hands on the sides of the lower ribs with the thumbs reaching to the back and feel how the ribs expand like wings in all these directions.

It is here in the more flexible part of the ribcage that true expansion can happen; and here is the bottom of the lungs, which can take in a large amount of air. So, breathing for voice work will engage the lower ribs surrounding the diaphragm and the solar plexus area of the body. Using the lower ribs in conjunction with grounded alignment and strong engagement of the core muscles of breathing will decrease tension in the upper body.

The rib muscles that help the diaphragm's action of enlarging the torso are the *external intercostal* muscles, also known as the *rib raisers*. These slope from the upper rib to the lower in the direction of the navel. They contract and cause the ribs to swing up, out and back during inhalation. The flexibility of the spine, the ribcage and the intercostal muscles will determine how much air we can take into the lungs. We need to open the entire body to allow free airflow to take place. The external intercostals are positioned more in the back of the ribcage, whereas at the front the internal intercostals are more dominant (*Your Voice: An Inside View*: 86). It is therefore beneficial to focus on breathing into the *back* of the ribcage.

The relaxation and recoil action of the external intercostal muscles releases the rib expansion so that the ribcage presses against air-filled lungs, helping them to expel air so that we breathe out. This out-breath movement can be enhanced by the action of the sheet of muscles that lie underneath, the *internal intercostal muscles.* These slope in the opposite direction, away from the navel (even deeper *innermost intercostals* cover the same area as the internal inter-costals and run in the same direction).

These are able to contract the ribcage beyond its rest position by drawing it down, and in creating greater pressure on the lungs can help sustain the airflow an actor may need to support long thoughts. However, this 'rib-squeeze' action can cause shoulder and neck tension, and to do it with ease spinal support is also needed. If a harmonious teamwork between diaphragm, pelvic floor, abdominals and ribs is achieved and becomes automatic, then we will find that the ribs will stay out longer anyway, and pushing the ribs beyond their natural resting position won't be necessary, which is preferable.

As we age, the ribcage tends to become more rigid, restricting deep breathing, so exercise to keep it flexible is very important.

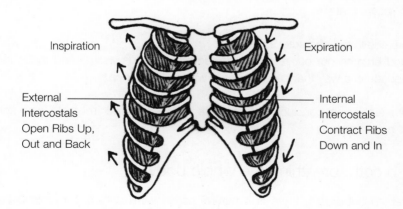

Figure 32 The ribs and intercostal muscles

Breath support and control

As actors we don't want to lose air quickly, because we need to sustain communication. We therefore have to support and control the airflow both under the vocal folds, known as *sub-glottic pressure*, and as it passes through the larynx in order to produce a rich and sustained sound (see the next chapter). This involves a balancing act between the inspiration and expiration muscles, responsible for the optimum functioning of both the diaphragm and the larynx and for creating the necessary air pressure. We need to avoid both shallow in-breaths, and collapsing the ribs and spine on the out-breath through a sudden movement of the abdominals and diaphragm.

We counterbalance the natural tendency for the diaphragm and abdominals to rise and ribs to contract on the out-breath, by dropping the pelvis, with the coccyx pointing to the floor, and at the same time lengthening the spine from the lumbar region up in the Elastic Band movement (see Chapter 3). The diaphragm is attached to the lower lumbar spine (see Figure 25), so this creates a sensation of leaning against the back (*Der Atem* [The Breath], Regine Herbig: 168). The back widens and opens and allows the ribs to close gradually. In this way the airflow is released up to the vocal folds in a controlled, but supported and easy, manner. This whole counterbalanced movement will feel strong if we keep the front of the pelvis stable using the psoas muscles, legs and feet to ground into the floor.

Breath support and control is the necessary artistic control over the natural breathing process, which will eventually become second nature (part of the skill learning we have discussed in Chapter 2 on the brain).

Training actors in muscular response to acting impulses and breath control will ensure that we:

* breathe in the character's impulses;
* and breathe out our response through the sounds, words and thoughts of language in a way that can be shared with our audience.

Here are some concluding comments on the passive in-breath and active out-breath phases.

In-breath: breathing the whole body

After an out-breath, there is a natural pause within which the brain delivers an impulse to the diaphragm for the next in-breath. As we have seen, the diaphragm is active as a muscle when it moves down to initiate air entering into our lungs. It presses against the body's abdominal content causing the belly to bulge whilst enlarging the ribcage in a three-dimensional way. When the belly-swelling predominates we call it *belly breathing*. When the action of the diaphragm, combined with that of the intercostal muscles of the ribs, predominantly opens the ribcage, we call it *rib breathing*. Indeed, both abdomen and ribs need to work together for the most harmonious effect, as well as for emotional and instinctive responses to take place. If we limit breathing to one action, we lose either connection to our very core and emotional responses in the case of using only rib breathing, or we lose the sustainability of the breath the ribs can provide when using only belly breathing.

Freeing the body from tensions within the muscles and ligaments will help the diaphragm to move down further. This has a beneficial influence on the volume of air that can be taken in at the bottom of the lungs, which in turn will give the organs vital oxygen. A freely moving diaphragm also gives internal massages to the organs thus enhancing their functioning. Restrictions on the diaphragm can arise from feelings of fear, stress and negativity.

The healthy movement of the diaphragm is also influenced by the mobility of the pelvis and the spine and their surrounding muscles. Natural alignment is therefore absolutely essential for deep creative breathing to work fully.

Although the diaphragm is *in action*, it is important that we allow the in-breath to flow in *passively*: only then can the body yield and make room for the breath to enter freely. If the abdominal, side or back muscles and pelvic floor are tense while breathing in, the muscles create a resistance which doesn't allow the torso to enlarge. As a result, the breath *cannot* enter freely. Tension starves the breath by closing its channels. With free breath, we are not aware of the diaphragm being active. We rather sense the effect of the action of the diaphragm: we feel the abdominal content yield and move down and the pelvic floor muscles open. This opening of the body's channels will allow the breath to connect with the solar plexus and release emotional responses. We need to become as absorbent as a sponge to breath and impulses so that they connect us to the experiences present in every cell and tissue of our body memory.

The breath should breathe us. In other words, we need to allow the automatic breathing rhythms given to us by nature to take place easily. Initially this means we have to undo tensions we've developed during life and rediscover the natural breathing rhythms of a baby, whose *whole body breathes*. If someone says to us, 'breathe in, breathe out', we can follow this order by *telling* our muscles to do so; but the deep breathing rhythms alone will connect us to the subconscious and all its experiences.

The opening of the vocal folds, the breath coursing through the open channel of the neck and imaginatively along our spine through to the pelvic floor, should make us feel as if we are actually *breathing in through the pelvic floor and into the expanding back and ribs*, which connects us to our gravity centre, core and sense of conviction. This will create rootedness, centredness and identity within the tones of our voice.

Out-breath: harmonious action

After the in-breath is complete there is another pause within which a new impulse is received for the next out-breath. On the out-breath the primary breathing muscles of exhalation become active and help the diaphragm, the initiator of breathing, to expel the air back up and out.

As we have seen when looking at the teamwork between the pelvic floor, the diaphragm and the vocal folds, the pelvic floor muscles narrow and rise up on the out-breath. They are connected to the inner abdominal muscles, which in turn are interwoven with the floor of the diaphragm, while the diaphragm and the abdominal muscles are connected to the spine by muscular fibres.

The abdominal muscles, in turn, have their counterparts in the rib muscles, which enhance the expulsion of the air. The spine, pelvis and back muscles also play their part in enhancing and controlling the out-breath (by using the primary curves and back lengthening through the spinal raiser and psoas muscles, mentioned earlier in Alignment).

From this it becomes very clear that all the muscles need to work *harmoniously as a team* in order to create the air flow and sub-glottic pressure needed to create intense sound, carrying the experiences of the actor to the listener's ear. This gives strength and direction to the actor's speech.

EXERCISES

Even if you have been trained how to breathe, it is essential that you come back to this kind of basic exercise, because it practises inner attention and awareness. According to Ilse Middendorf, a pioneer in breath therapy, perceiving our breath as it comes and goes, observing the physical, emotional and mental forces that act upon it, helps us to discover how the breath can access our subconscious and often unconscious life and will in time bring about an expansion of our whole self (see *Der Erfahrbare Atem, The Perceptible Breath: A Breathing Science*).

Exploring the breathing movements

1. Let the breath move you – sensing the movements of the breath within the body

Our symbol for free-flowing breath is the wave. The wave of the out-breath will carry the experienced thought or feeling to the audience.

The concept of the wave in breathing is a recurrent and international one. We have come across it as a major feature of Steiner training, and also in *Der Atem* (*The Breath*) by Regine Herbig, Barbara Houseman exercises, therapy and Yoga.

* Adopt your basic rooted stance described in the Alignment section. Stand quietly, with knees slightly bent, feet parallel and arms at your side. Let your pelvis hang without tension so that your coccyx tail is pointing towards the ground and your lower back is flat. As you do this, you will feel that both your perineum (the area between the anus and genitals) and your groin are open. Let your shoulders and sternum relax downwards and simultaneously feel that your head is being pulled upward from the crown, gently stretching the back of your neck.

* *Let your breath breathe you.* Respond to your body's impulses to breathe in and out. Follow your breath into the centre of your body. Sense how the flow of air enters through the nose and down the windpipe. Imagine the pipe continues all the way down to your pelvic floor. As you follow this journey of the breath, the abdomen and all your tissue will relax. This will help your diaphragm move lower into the abdomen. On your impulse to breathe out, notice how the pelvic floor muscles and abdominals engage, pushing the air back out. Sense the movements of your breath. Sense the skin around your body and how it expands and contracts with the breathing movements. Sense how they affect your pelvis, belly, chest, shoulders and neck.

Sensing your breathing movements will calm you and slow your breath down. Don't judge yourself. Sense any restriction that might not allow your breath to flow easily. Just allow yourself to get in tune with your breath that 'is'.

2. Exploring the breathing movements of the diaphragm

* You can do this standing well aligned, sitting or lying on your back. If you are sitting, place yourself on your sitting bones and keep your spine and back of the neck long and the jaw dropped. If you are slumped or tense, your breathing will be restricted and you will not fully feel the movements it creates.

* Place your hand on the soft solar plexus area between the breastbone and the navel and tune into your natural breathing rhythm. Let your breath breathe you rather than being controlled by you. Sense the warmth of your hand on your diaphragm. Let your breath *respond* rather than forcing it there. Sense the movement your natural breath creates in the diaphragm area.

* Think easy thoughts, for example: picture a peaceful environment, at the seashore, in a forest, on a meadow, for example. Peaceful images like this will slow your breath down and allow the automatic breathing movements to work better. What works well is if you imagine you are next to the sea, and waves come in and out of your body.

* The movement you feel under your hand is the *effect* the diaphragm has on the abdominal muscles, moving them downwards in the process of enlarging the torso to let the breath come in. The belly will therefore bulge outwards. On releasing the air upwards and outwards, the belly will retract inwards towards the spine.

You can breathe through the nose or the mouth for this exercise. Keep your jaw dropped a little even when you breathe through the nose. Breathing through the nose warms and cleans the air through the nose's filters. It also gives you direct access to and activates the ribs, and will increase the sense of the torso widening.

Breathing through the mouth will help you to find a stronger responding movement in the diaphragmatic and abdominal as well as pelvic area, accessing the lowest breath in your core. Once you master the recoil action of your breath, breathing through the mouth can create the instant dropping in of breath. Acting demands quick response to impulses through the text and a recoil breath action; this favours breathing through the mouth, which is a quicker process than breathing through the nose.

The rhythm and journey of your breath

Once you have become aware of the movement of the breath in your body, pay attention to how it is triggered by impulse and how a pause arises naturally after each phase:

In-breath impulse – air flows in;

Sense the pause;

Out-breath impulse – air flows out;

Sense the pause.

You will need to get to know your out-breath movement especially well because it is the transmitter of your vocal actions. When your body wants to breathe out, follow the journey of the breathing movement towards the spine: it will make your back lengthen, flatten and widen.

Once you are comfortable with being on your out-breath, your in-breath movement will happen passively whenever you need to refuel.

KEY FOR RELEASED BREATHING:

Do not tense or push the out-breath movement towards your spine. The aim is to tune into your breathing movements as they occur naturally, and to speak in the moment when your breath is ready to transmit your thought.

Observe the pause and sense of release that arises before your body is ready to go into the out-breath movement – like a gear change. If you don't, your out-breath movement will not be released or smooth.

Often, especially when endgaming for a result, the acting student tends to rush the process and starts to speak when still in the in-breath phase, which results in having to force the muscles.

The balloon

* Now lie semi-supine and picture a balloon around your navel, which expands on the in-breath and deflates on the out-breath. Sense if this movement can take place freely, unrestricted by tensions.

* If you feel that your belly does the opposite movement – if it pulls in when breathing in and bulges out when breathing out, you are most likely using your clavicular breath, where the rising of the shoulder girdle and sternum creates the in-breath. As we mentioned above, this is an emergency breath or one used in sports when you need a quick breath supply. It is not a deep breath and if you do it for a while you might start to feel panicky.

* If you feel you have connected to the clavicular breath, refocus and sense your body's need to breathe. Feel the warmth of your hands around your navel and let the breath rise into your hands to find the lower location of the deepest breathing rhythm. Feel the balloon expand in your belly on the in-breath, and contract on the out-breath.

Now, as you breathe, check if your sternum is relaxed by placing a hand on it. You should only feel a movement sympathetic to that happening in the diaphragm and abdominal area. The sternum and the shoulder girdle should not be the instigators.

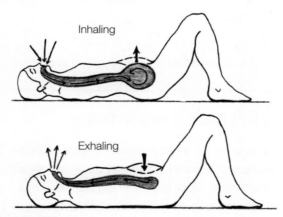

Figure 33 Balloon breathing

3. Exploring whole body breathing

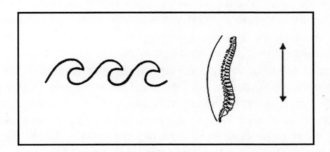

Now let's explore how the breathing movements triggered by the diaphragm create movements through the whole body.

Do this standing in your centred aligned position. Find your natural breathing rhythm. Imagine the breath is rising as you inhale and releasing through your feet like waves as you exhale. For the in-breath the knees should be bent, and on the out-breath straighten but don't lock them.

Diaphragm – Put one hand below the navel. Picture the balloon from Exercise 2 expanding behind your navel on the in-breath and deflating on the out-breath. As before, observe the pause that occurs between in-breath and out-breath and wait for the sense of release that triggers a smooth breathing movement.

Pelvis – Now place your other hand in the corresponding place at the back of your pelvis and sense if there is a movement happening there – up and back on the in-breath and dropping under on the out-breath.

Lumbar – Next place your hands on the small of your back and observe what happens here. You will probably feel how the area expands on your in-breath and retracts on your out-breath. This will only happen if the back muscles are released on the in-breath.

Ribs – Place your hands on the ribs towards the back of your lower ribcage. Sense how your ribs bulge out at the sides and up and back on your inhalation, and in and down on your exhalation.

Spine – Now get a sense of the whole spinal movement. Starting in the pelvis area, feel how your tailbone tips back and up on inhalation and draws under to point at the floor on exhalation. This sets up a rhythm. Feel how the whole lower back follows the movement of the rocking pelvis, arching slightly on the in-breath and lengthening and flattening on the out-breath.

Observe the effect on the entire spinal column and the neck. You might get a sense that the secondary shape in the lumbar area is accentuated on the in-breath, and that the lengthening movement of the spine and neck on the out-breath emphasizes the primary shape in the spine.

As we shall see later, vitality and intention must move through the spine on the out-breath when we act, so the spine must never collapse. We need to keep it long and strong so that the resonance spaces of the voice stay open. 'While the position of our spine is important, simply finding a balanced position is not enough … the spine lacks vitality until it is brought to life by the combined forces of gravity, the breath, and our directed intention' (*Yoga Mind, Body and Spirit*: 45). We'll look at the need for spinal support on an energized out-breath while acting later on.

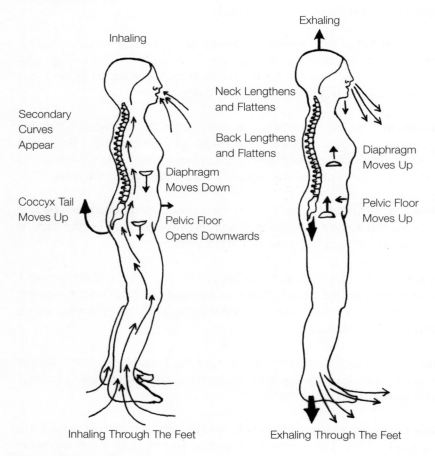

Figure 34 Lengthening the spine

DEEP AND SHALLOW BREATHING WHEN ACTING

Observe what happens when you:

1 *breathe deeply into your back*
- sense the expansion and strength in your back
- this will enable your vocal action, what you are doing to somebody through speaking, to drive forwards through your out-breath

2 *breathe shallowly into the front of the chest*
- this sends the out-breath backwards
- thoughts and words may be dropped and lack clarity and will to change a situation

Say 'Give me back my book!' with both types of breathing and see the difference in clarity and drive.

When playing a verbal action and filling a thought through the breath we need a forward energy, so breathing deeply into the back is essential.

4. The solar plexus – breathing in acting impulse

Our symbol for the *solar plexus* is:

This is about breathing an impulse, for example, from senses, emotions, images or objectives, into our centre and connecting to circumstances around us.

The information we get from our senses works on the nerves, emotions and energy of the solar plexus, which is linked to the diaphragm, the centre of breathing. If we *breathe in the circumstances* of the imaginary world of a play through our senses and free organic breathing movement, we get in direct touch with our sensitivity, feelings and core energy.

The sponge

This exercise will raise awareness of how imagination and sense memory affect your breathing, and how your breathing, if free and organic, will become the creative connector to your experience.

1   Lie on your back with knees towards the ceiling. Imagine you are on a beach and the sun is shining with a perfect temperature for you.* The floor is warm sand and the whole sole of the foot makes contact with it. Imagine there are sponges in your feet and start to breathe through them, absorbing the warmth of the sand. Feel the sand between your toes. Let the sponge feeling expand to your ankles, calves and knees so that you breathe through them; then to the thighs and the pelvis; and further, to your diaphragm and around your back, to your ribcage and between the shoulder blades; then to the shoulders, upper arms and lower arms and into the palms of the hands and the fingers. If you want to move at any point, do. Let it expand into your neck and face. Feel your whole body breathing, sensing and experiencing.

    *Of course, there are people who don't like beaches, sand or sunshine and for whom this exercise would not have the optimum effect. So, choose an alternative that will create the same warm, open, relaxed feeling for you.

2   Take in where your breath is present; how the channels of your body are opening and allowing the movements of the breath to happen. Also notice areas where the movement is blocked. You might have to give these areas some more attention. Feel how your breath responds to being on a beach in a holiday situation where there is nothing else to do but enjoy being where you are. Feel a breeze around the skin of your whole body. The breath response will become one associated with enjoyment and relaxation rather than one we may have when stressed out over work or travelling on the underground.

3   Now focus on the warmth of the sun on your solar plexus area. Sense this area in the middle of your torso as the space through which you can connect with the world around you – and with a character's circumstances and the world of a play. Don't control your breath in any way. The breathing response needs to come from your sensual experience.

4 Wait for the body's need to take in a breath – then allow the wave of the breath to come in. Wait for your body's need to breathe out – then allow the wave of the breath to move out. In between there will be the pause, a stillness. Adapt your breathing rhythm to the image of the waves of the sea coming in and out, as in an earlier exercise. Still feel the warmth of the sun on your body.

5 Respond to the sense of well-being with a voiced sigh. Allow the *huh* sound to respond to your circumstances without you listening to yourself. Let it travel on the weight of the wave of your out-breath, so that you find your supporting muscles yield to the movement rather than tense and hold. Do this again until you are letting your natural breathing rhythm breathe you. *The vocal expression will then feel as though it is jumping onto a surfboard that rides the wave of breath.*

6 Focus your mind on different sensory stimuli. What do you hear? What do you smell? Respond with the sound *huh* and let it release on the wave of your out-breath in direct response to your sensory impulse.

5. Pelvic rocking

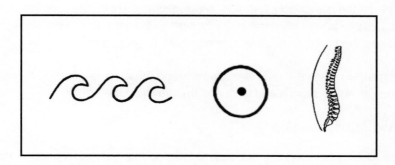

This exercise is about *teamwork* between body support (especially pelvic and spinal support) and the journey the free breath takes through the open channels of the body. As we have seen, the breath needs to *breathe us*, the body yielding to the movements of the breath rather than blocking them through tensions.

When dealing with the out-breath, we encounter the problem that the more we breathe out, the more the body contracts, which could potentially close the open spaces of the resonators down. Therefore the body needs to stay open by engaging a spinal counter-movement to anchor the body. This centres on the action of the pelvis and use of the primary curve or C-shape (see in particular Exercise 6 in Chapter 3, Alignment).

* Lie in semi-supine position. Tune into your deepest breathing rhythms. Imagine you are by the sea again and feel how the waves of your breath are flowing in and out.

Accompany the impulse to breathe in with the spinal movements that occur naturally. On the in-breath, allow your pelvis to rock forward slightly in an arch so that the lumbar area of the spine moves from the floor creating a gap as your pelvic floor muscles open. Your chin will most likely lift up slightly and the secondary shape in your neck will become more apparent.

Accompany the journey of the out-breath with the supporting movements of pelvis and spine. When the impulse to breathe out occurs, follow the journey of the out-breath movement and allow your pelvis to drop back into the floor so that the gap created by the in-breath disappears. The primary curves of the spine are now enhanced and the spine *lengthens* as the lower back flattens and widens against the floor. Lengthen your neck and point the chin down.

* Allow your breath to rock the pelvis slightly as if it floats up and down on water.

* Connect the pelvic rocking to your imagination. You're in your favourite nature spot. Breathe in your circumstances through your solar plexus. Find an impulse to voice a sigh on your out-breath in response to your sense of wellbeing.

So, again, we breathe in an imaginary world and the voice responds to thoughts, feelings, images, sounds and language that travel on the breath.

Pelvic floor muscles

When rocking back on the out-breath, imagine that your sitting bones come together gently and sense how your pelvic floor muscles come up and towards your spine. Do this on *fff, vvv, zzz, zoo, yaa,* using a separate breath for each.

Abdominal muscles

As a response to your sense of pleasure, get an impulse to voice a sigh to trigger the movement of the abdominals from navel to spine as the pelvis rocks back into the floor. Follow the journey of your out-breath movement. This will engage rather than force the muscles to act: they must yield, not hold.

Ribs

Sense how the ribs move outwards on the in-breath as you rock forwards. As you rock back into the floor on your out-breath, sense how your ribs remain open for longer, supported by your lengthening spine and back muscles. This will enable your breath to last longer.

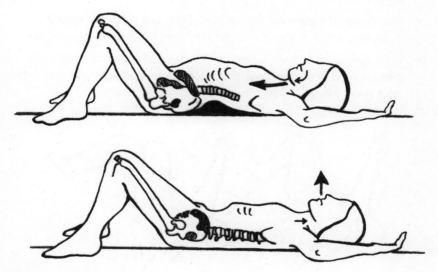

Figure 35 Pelvic rocking

6. The diagonal stretch

This exercise follows on from pelvic rocking. It opens the breathing spaces by stretching the torso diagonally.

- Start in a semi-supine position. Let both knees drop to the left side so that the thighs are at a 45-degree angle to the torso. Spread the arms to each side, keeping the shoulder blades on the floor. The head points to the right in the opposite direction to the knees.

- Sense the stretch between the neck, the ribs and the pelvis. Breathe into the highest point of the hips and on the out-breath pat the right side of the torso from pelvis to armpit. Now do this reversing the knee and head position.

- Go back to the starting position with the knees dropped to the left side. On an impulse to breathe out, do a voiced sigh on *huuh* and follow your breathing journey towards the diagonally stretched spine. This will increase the stretch further. Do this on both sides.

- Go back to the starting position with the knees dropped to the left side – but this time, raise your right leg over the left leg so that your right knee touches the floor. This might lift your opposing right shoulder blade and arm off the floor. Allow this to happen. Do a sigh on *huuh*. Do this on both sides.

- Go back to the semi-supine position. Sigh on a *huuh* and note the increased space in your torso and how the breath flows more easily.

- Now curl up into a foetal position on your side, and from there move into the child pose from Exercise 5 in Alignment. Rise to your feet and do a spine roll up.

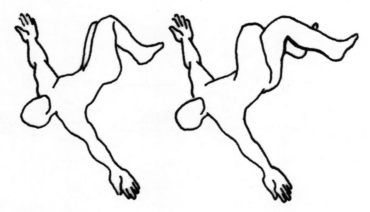

Figure 36 Diagonal stretch

7. The back roll

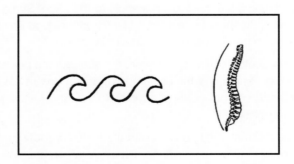

This stretches the whole back and creates more space for the in-breath, and on the out-breath, more support from the back (not to be done if you have back problems). Do this on a mat.

1 First sit on the floor with your knees held to your chest. Relax the head and sense a rounded back.

On an in-breath, roll backwards still holding the knees, and on an out-breath come back to sitting position. Synchronize movement and breath. Do this a few times. Now try it on a *fff* or *sss.*

2 On a new impulse to breathe in, roll back and let your feet and arms swing behind you to touch the floor.

On your impulse to breathe out, roll forwards and swing the legs back over the head until they rest on the floor. Reach forwards over the legs with the torso and arms, driving from the lumbar spine.

Now try this movement on a *fff* or *sss,* and a 'haah', and note how your out-breath has lengthened even further.

Now do the movement on the first line of Sonnet 18:
Shall I compare thee to a summer's day?

Start with breathing in what a summer's day means to you as you roll back.

As you roll forwards, say 'summer's day'. Feel the lumbar spine driving the breath forwards as you stretch your arms forwards.

Now try the whole line.

On the in-breath, rolling back, imagine someone so lovely that you propose comparing them to a summer day. On the out-breath, respond to this impulse through the line.

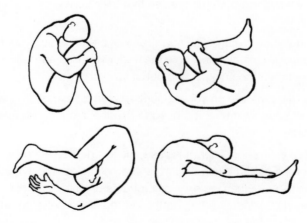

Figure 37 Back roll

3   Now stand and on an impulse to breathe in let the breath flow into your
    back, and on the impulse to breathe out sense how your whole back is
    involved in support.

8. Exploring the root of your voice

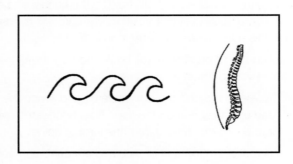

We shall now look at the vocal rooting muscles in the pelvic floor and the
innermost abdominal muscles that need to transfer the impulse into voice and
text in a reflexive manner.

As a preliminary, lie with your knees up towards the ceiling. Tune into your
breathing rhythm, letting yourself be breathed by your deepest breath. Imagine
waves coming in and out of your body with a pause between each phase.
Become aware of a sensation of release after the pause of your in-breath before
moving into the out-breath movement. Yield to the full journey of the out-breath
towards the spine and feel how your back flattens, lengthens and widens.

Now place a chair in front of you and lie on the floor on your back.

1   Place your calves onto the seat so that their full weight is resting on the
    chair.

2   Let yourself be breathed by your deepest breath. Place your hand on
    your navel so that you feel how the abdomen rises and falls. Imagine
    waves of breath coming in and out of your body.

3   Add a little pressure on your abdominal area towards the spine when
    breathing out. Wait until you need to breathe in again and release the
    pressure.

4   Visualize your pelvic floor muscles – the inverted parachute – at the
    base of the pelvis. When we inhale, the pelvic floor moves down and
    broadens, and when we exhale, it retracts upwards and narrows.
    Imagine the balloon inflating on the in-breath and deflating on the
    out-breath in the pelvis and abdominal area.

5   When you are tuned into your natural breathing pattern, place your awareness into your pelvic floor muscles. When you breathe in, and your diaphragm moves downwards whilst your abdominals bulge out, follow the movement of your in-breath as it travels towards the bottom of your pelvis and sense how the in-breath opens and widens the pelvic floor muscles.

6   On the impulse to breathe out, sense how the breath movement travels through the pelvic floor muscles, which narrow gradually inwards and up, and travels through the abdominal area, moving the abdominal muscles inwards, upwards and backwards towards the spine.

7   Now on an out-breath make the sound of a steam train: *ch–ch-ch-chooo*. Feel the sound bouncing up from the pelvic floor.

Yield to the full journey of the out-breath towards the spine. Gently press your lumbar spine into the floor, making a primary curve, so that the back flattens and widens and the spine lengthens. Make sure that you lengthen the back of your neck with the out-breath movement by gently bringing your chin towards the chest. Your breathing movement will then travel all the way up the spine.

Make three short *mmm* sounds on separate breaths, as though you are sucking them up like a hoover from the pelvic floor and along the spine: breathe into the pelvic floor and sense it opening, sound *mmm*, sense the contraction of the muscles and send it up and back against your spine. Make sure that on your in-breath you release the pelvic floor and the lumbar area so that the breath can flow in freely, and on the out-breath you flatten the lumbar area into the floor for strong support.

---

* As we saw earlier, the pelvic floor muscles connect to the cylinder of support of the abdominal muscles. All push up the diaphragm and are connected to the spine. If you follow the movement of the out-breath towards the spine all of the abdominals will engage – known in Pilates as 'navel to the spine'.

* To start with, lying on the floor is a good idea because the floor is an excellent teacher as far as alignment and release into gravity are concerned. Also, with your legs positioned on the chair, you can really open and broaden the pelvic muscles and relax while breathing in. By allowing your legs and pelvis to release into gravity you can feel the isolated activity of the muscles

much better. When standing upright, though, you may get a stronger sense of the support activity of these muscles.

* The pelvic floor accesses the qualities of what is known as the *root chakra* in Yoga. This is connected with basic survival, will to assert and fight, security and rootedness as the individual.

9. The beetle on its back

This exercise will strengthen and enhance the rooting of your voice and identity in the pelvic floor.

* Lie on your back in semi-supine position and bring your knees towards your chest. Sense the impulse to breathe in. Sense the widening of your pelvic floor muscles and enhance this feeling by letting your knees fall outwards. Follow their weight until they hang loosely and openly so you're like a beetle on its back.

* On the impulse to breathe out, move your knees back together. As you follow the out-breath, sense how the front of the pelvis raises and the lower back flattens into the floor. Lengthen the back of the neck gently by bringing your chin towards the chest. Sense how the pelvic floor muscles narrow inwards and rise and connect with the lower abdominals, which draw backwards towards the spine.

With this movement you will have to work against the sensation of heaviness in your legs. To do this safely so that your back doesn't suffer, you need to use pelvic, back and abdominal support.

* Now do the same sequence while sounding a *shhh* or *yeee* and sense that the support for it comes right from your pelvic core. Do this several times until you find the rhythm of it.

If you are doing this correctly you should feel that your neck and throat are relaxed and released. Dropping the pelvis and keeping the back of the neck lengthened, while engaging the pelvic floor muscles and the inner abdominals, will create a core support that enables the rest of your body to relax. The resulting breath support is powerful enough to rely on. Don't use your laryngeal or neck muscles to do the sound.

10. Shooting the arrow – playing 'I want …'

The bow and arrow is our symbol for the transfer of acting impulse into muscular response.

Just as the archer takes aim, draws on the string of the bow and then shoots towards the target, the actor has an aim or objective, breathes it in and responds through the text, supported by breath and spine.

* Following on from the sounding in Exercises 6 and 7, give yourself an objective: *'I want to make Mama come to me',* and call 'Mama!'.

Breathe this intention into the pelvic floor and respond through the word with the supporting pelvic, abdominal, back and spinal muscles.

* Do this with the imaginary bow and arrow above.

Draw the bowstring and take aim, breathing in the circumstances and objective and connecting them to the responding support muscles.

When you sense your muscles are ready to support, release the arrow pursuing the objective through the out-breath and summon 'Mama!'.

Now play the objective again without the action, but keeping a physical sense of it.

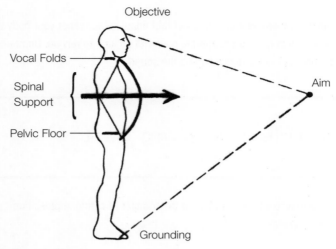

Figure 38 Bow and arrow

The co-ordination of this will take some practising. After all, this simple objective shows only an example of one thought. When performing, you can't waste effort to think about which muscles to use and how to do it. Your muscular activity must have become a reflex through repeatedly practising this link. When the skill is learned, the old brain and muscle memory take over and free the actor to stay in the present moment and respond freely.

11. Strengthening the objective by engaging the Elastic Band

* Imagine there's a fly buzzing around your head. Give yourself an objective: *'I want to chase this annoying fly away.'* Breathe it into your pelvic and abdominal muscles, readying them to respond. On the impulse to breathe out, use a *shhh* sound to get what you want.

Again, make sure that your will to change your circumstances by chasing the fly away comes from your core support and that the channels that release your sound are free. Sense how your pelvic floor is the place where your identity and will meet.

* Let's strengthen this intention now by involving the spine and the gravity and anti-gravity movements.

This exercise for continuous circular movement of the breath energy is adapted from one in *The Tao of Voice* by Stephen Chun-Tao Cheng:

> A smooth, continuous movement will assist the dynamic interplay of opposite forces and will help create the flowing vital energy required to produce a good strong sound or a soft lyrical one. It will also help you to control or coordinate your breath for singing and speaking without strain or rigidity, because your diaphragm will work effectively for you on its own. (17)

1 Sit on a chair on your sitting bones with your coccyx released downwards into gravity and your spine and neck lengthened into the uplifting anti-gravity force. This way your back is widened, flattened and lengthened yet released. Make sure that your feet are parallel and planted firmly into the floor for support. Feel your sitting bones and feet against the two surfaces grounding and stabilizing you.

Visualize the Elastic Band running through your body along your balance line, from the earth through the pelvic floor, the spine, the crown of the head into the zenith of the sky. Imagine the band as the channel through which energy, breath and sound are released.

Tune into your natural breathing rhythm.

2 Place one hand below the navel (at the position of the lowest *tan tien*). When you receive the impulse to breathe in, move your hand up to the point between your eyebrows in the first half of the circular motion. At the same time, allow the breath to drop into the bottom of the pelvic basin and your pelvic floor muscles to open – this should be a gentle movement rather than a forced action.

Complete the circle on the out-breath by moving your hand down to the navel, as the pelvic floor muscles engage inwards and up, the pelvis

drops under and the pelvic floor and abdominal muscles move back
and up towards the spine.

Do this a couple of times to get the hang of it.

3 Now do it on any voiced fricative like *zzz* or *vvv*.

Surf the wave movement of your out-breath on a *yeee* sound, then
yuuuh and *yaaah*.

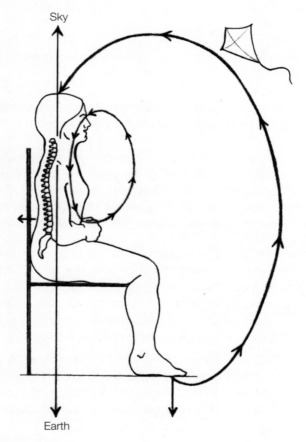

Figure 39 Circular breath

4 Now introduce the image of having a kite on a string.

As you breathe in and circle your hand upwards, imagine you hold a
kite string in your hand and you allow your kite to fly into the sky. Sense
how this image will deepen your in-breath and give it more space.

On the out-breath, pull the string of your kite back down to your lowest
tan tien. Sense how the 'pulling of the string' enhances your Elastic

Band energy, anchoring you down into the centre of the earth, which in turn enhances the muscular engagement of your core support muscles and your spinal stability.

To make this truly beneficial we need to enhance the other direction of the Elastic Band towards the sky, which aids the spinal lengthening: move close to the back of the chair so that your pelvis can press into it on the out-breath, while dropping your pelvis under and imagining a thread pulling your crown towards the sky. Gently tip your chin towards your chest and let your jaw drop open. You can sense how this opens the soft palate and releases the lower jaw. At the same time, press your feet gently against the floor for extra support. The vocal channels are now open and wide and powered by the core and spinal support.

Engaging the breath, spine and balance line through this co-ordinated movement will allow the core support of the muscles and spinal strength to work together in such an economical way that the rest of the body's muscles can release into gravity. This will free the larynx to move easily and unrestrictedly. The resonating cavities of pharynx, naso-pharynx and mouth will stay open and become widened and lengthened by the spinal stability resulting from this lengthened alignment. The spinal engagement will give you a feeling of conviction.

---

5 Go back to the objective to chase the fly away.

Get the impulse to chase it away, breathe it in as the kite pulls up your hand in the first half of the circular movement and then on the out-breath pull the kite string down and sound a *shhh* to make the fly go away.

Feel how the spinal lengthening and stabilizing enhances the assertion of your objective.

6 Now forget about the circular hand movement and the kite and focus completely on the fly.

See it and sense how it annoys you buzzing around. Let this give you the impulse of wanting to chase it away. Let it boil inside you until you find the connection between circumstance, impulse, breath and physical response:

- the experience of the annoying fly
- the need to chase it away
- the in-breath and the readiness of your core support
- the execution of the *shhh* sound while engaging core muscles and spinal support by going into the Elastic Band energy
    - and accompany this with a physical action, like flicking hand movements, to accompany the *shhh* sound to chase the fly away.

Now use a fully voiced line to pursue your objective: 'Get off. Get away!'

If you are doing this correctly you should feel how your vocal release is smooth and doesn't get trapped within the body, and is integrated with thought and physical action to chase off the fly.

7   Now chase the fly away standing, and imagine it's of huge proportions! The steps are the same as in the Kite exercise concerning the muscles used but the support now goes through the balance line of the entire body.

Reminders:

Get the impulse to chase the fly away on *shhh* and breathe it into your solar plexus contacting the muscles of vocal support.

On your out-breath, when your muscles are ready, root down and lift up into the Elastic Band sounding on *shhh* as you:

- let the breathing movement travel against your spine into the space behind you, the back space;
- point your coccyx to the floor and stabilize the front of the pelvis, anchoring you into the centre of the earth and enhancing the activity of your core muscles and the stability of your spine;
- lift towards the zenith of the sky following the thread attached to the crown of the head, while lengthening your neck and letting your chin drop and jaw open;
- make sure that your weight is on the balls of your feet so that the back is free to engage into this movement.

As a result you should feel at one with your spine supporting and asserting your objective. Add the hand movement once you feel your body support can release the breath and sound fully.

8   Try another strong objective.

Imagine you are Republicans during the Spanish Civil War stopping fascists from entering your village: *'You shall not pass!'*

Or – you're Gandalf in *The Lord of the Rings* trying to stop the ancient demon on the bridge.

Follow all the above steps to root this objective into your body.

If we feel the union between muscular movement and impulse then we can start to feel how mind, body, breath and voice connect within acting.

There is a vital difference between contracting muscles because I think about contracting them, and muscular activity occurring from an impulse. Head-controlled muscles can become held and tense and counteract release and ease and a psycho-physical approach.

Everything involves movement and change. Impulse is the electric energy that makes the muscles move. Breath and speech are movement. Objectives change the circumstances and create movement. As long as we move we are alive. As Stanislavski said: 'Acting is action – mental and physical' (*An Actor's Work*: 40).

Whilst moving through our in- and out-breath, breath by breath, we touch on being in the present moment. In the moment of in-breath we receive and prepare. In the moment of out-breath we respond and transmit our objective to change something within the circumstances.

Once we understand how breathing and being in the present moment of experience relate, we also understand what it feels like when we endgame and focus on the future, detaching from our whole experiencing system. Then we stand outside ourselves and our acting becomes studied, anticipated and wooden.

---

12. Exploring the ribs

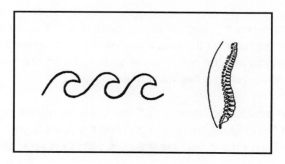

First, place your hands onto either side of your floating ribs – the ribs that bulge out most at the bottom of your ribcage – and with your thumbs at the back. Sense the warmth of your hands and add a little pressure.

Allow your deepest automatic breath to breathe you and follow its rhythm. Sense how, on the in-breath, your ribcage expands all the way round, pressing your hands outwards, in order to fetch air into the lungs. Following your body's impulse to breathe out, the ribcage contracts towards the spine in order to release the air.

Beach ball

This is one of the exercises David Carey taught on the MA Voice Studies Course at the Central School of Speech and Drama.

* First do a brief recap of what we have done before.

Stand aligned, centred and at ease with parallel feet hip-width apart and with your weight distributed between the big toe, the little toe and the heels of your feet. Centre your breath into the bottom of the basin of your pelvis and allow your coccyx to drop down and your neck to lengthen. Sense how the breath comes in and out like waves initiated by your deep automatic breath. Allow your sacrum to rise and fall with the waves. Find the balance on the balls of your feet. Let your arms hang either side of your body with shoulders dropped.

* Now imagine that where your diaphragm is situated you have a large beach ball that inflates when you breathe in and deflates when you breathe out.

Imagine that the palms of your hands are holding the beach ball, and on your body's impulse to breathe in, follow its inflation with your arms, which expand to the front and sides. To avoid tension, don't fully extend your arms. On your body's impulse to breathe out, follow the deflating beach ball, which becomes smaller and brings your hands back together.

* On your next in-breath, sense your ribs expand with the movement of your arms swinging outwards as the beach ball inflates, and contract back towards the spine when you breathe out. This will accentuate the ribs' movements. Do this several times to get into the swing of it.

*On your next impulse to breathe out, introduce resistance and *press* your hands against the deflating beach ball and ride the wave of your out-breath on a *yah* sound. Then on the next breaths, use *yuh*, then *yeee*, and sense how your natural breathing impulses and pressing the ball to deflate it engage more strongly the muscles of the ribs into support action.

Opening the wings

* Stand well aligned, arms at the side. Now put one foot behind the other.

* On an in-breath, open the arms as if they are butterfly wings and shift your weight onto the back foot and lean into the backspace. This will open the back of your ribs. Keep expanding the wings until you have the impulse to breathe out.

* On the out-breath, extend the arms fully forward, closing the wings until your hands touch in front of your body, while shifting your weight onto the front foot.

* Now do this movement again and on the out-breath sound on a *haaa,* then a *heey* and *huuh* on separate breaths.

Petrol pump

This is another David Carey exercise.

* Use a partner standing behind you and holding firmly your lower ribs, the area to focus on. Your partner is the petrol pump imaginatively filling you with fuel as you breathe in. Once you've filled up, sound on an *eee* and walk for as long as you can sustain the sound. Return to your petrol pump to refuel.

13. Automatic recovery of breath

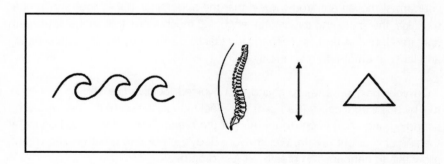

This is important for an actor who has to sustain lengthy units of thought and speech.

> Don't forget the principle of breathing: in-breath is passive, and out-breath is active. Muscles need to relax to let the in-breath movement, initiated by the diaphragm, happen unrestrictedly and move the whole body.

* Remind yourselves of Exercise 3, Exploring whole body breathing, and go through the steps.

* Imagine the beach ball again, but this time it's inside as well as in front of your body. It sits on your pelvic floor muscles, fills out the pelvis, lumbar area and diaphragm, as well as the ribcage. As you breathe in, feel the whole inner space opening and expanding in a three-dimensional way.

* On the out-breath, press against the inflated beach ball with your hands, while sensing how your pelvis drops under, the pelvic floor narrows and rises, your lumbar spine flattens (into primary shape), the abdominals rise up and back against the lengthening spine, and the ribs gradually contract.

* Observe the pause that will naturally occur once the breath is spent. When your body's impulse calls for the in-breath, let the breath drop in quite quickly yet passively.

* Allow your breath to come in fully. Observe the natural pause again. Then, on your body's need to breathe out, imagine the beach ball gives you some resistance when it deflates. This will slow down your out-breath as well as your arms' movement. You will feel that the abdominal, pelvic floor and lumbar muscles, the spine and the ribs are engaging much more. Follow the out-breath right through to its end, and engage the Elastic Band. Observe the natural pause and let your breath drop in quickly.

* On your next out-breath, sound an unvoiced fricative like *shh* or *fff*. Follow this by a voiced fricative like *zzz* or *vvv*. Feel the resistance of the beach ball on sounding and sound right to the end of the breath. Allow the natural pause at the end of your out-breath. Wait for your body's impulse to breathe in again and allow this to happen. The breath will just drop back.

14. Breath control

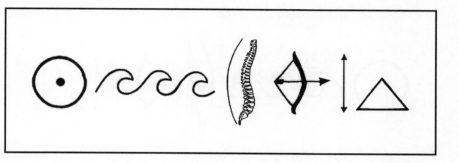

* Walk through the space imagining a golden ball of energy in your solar plexus, radiating energy into the space. It lifts you and propels you forward so that you have a sense of gliding over the floor. Stretch out an arm in the direction of your movement as if the walls are pulling you towards them as well.

* Take in an easy but full in-breath, and as you move, count to five on one breath. Then count to ten on a second breath. Then keep increasing the breath by multiples of five, keeping the breath and sound easy, controlled and supported.

* Let's look at this on text. Read *Sea Fever* by John Masefield below. Visualize the scene he creates, see the images and get the sense of yearning embodied in the poem. Let the images and words pull the breath out of you. Start by saying one line on one breath. Then say two, then three. Then try four.

I must go down to the seas again, to the lonely sea and the sky,
And all I ask is a tall ship and a star to steer her by,
And the wheel's kick and the wind's song and the white sail's shaking,
And a grey mist on the sea's face, and a grey dawn breaking.

I must go down to the seas again, for the call of the running tide
Is a wild call and a clear call that may not be denied;
And all I ask is a windy day with the white clouds flying,
And the flung spray and the blown spume, and the sea-gulls crying.

I must go down to the seas again, to the vagrant gypsy life,
To the gull's way and the whale's way, where the wind's like a whetted knife;
And all I ask is a merry yarn from a laughing fellow-rover,
And quiet sleep and a sweet dream when the long trick's over.

Integration into acting

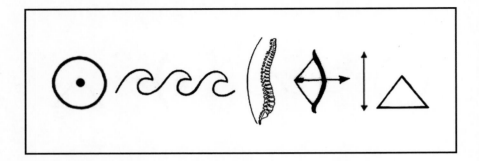

Let's now take the integration into acting further.

Imagine a stranger has just intruded into your living space and you suddenly discover them standing in your living room looking around. Your objective is to get rid of them quickly and you say:

'What do you think you're doing here? Get out! If you don't get out I'll call the police!'

Imagine the circumstances. Breathe them into your solar plexus so that you are affected as if this is a real situation.

Connect the objective to your breath and muscular engagement by breathing the objective into the pelvic, abdominal, back and spinal muscles.

When you sense your muscles are ready to support, release your objective through the lines like releasing an arrow. To strengthen your objective, engage the spine in the Elastic Band and sense what that does to your overall conviction.

Also, make sure that each of the three thoughts and actions within the objective are given full and different weight: for example, you challenge, command and threaten the intruder, finding the impulse for each within what you want to achieve, to get rid of them.

Make sure you go to the end of each breath for each thought and fill it with energy and conviction. Practise your automatic breath recovery combined with finding the impulse for each thought.

Blocked breath

We've emphasized in this chapter that the actor needs to be free, open and flexible so that a character's experience can be absorbed via a deep and automatic breathing impulse. We want to harmonize easily and effectively all the relevant breathing muscles and their relationship to the spine and alignment, and rediscover the child's open and responsive make-up. To this end, freeing the mind, body and breathing movement of tensions is an initial and essential step to be taken in any training (see Chapter 10 – Awareness, Ease and Focus).

Of course, certain breathing patterns hinder a natural, free and supported flow of breath and have physical and psychological causes and consequences. While the healthy baby breathes deeply and freely in an automatic way, life's experiences alter impulses from our nervous system, and patterns are programmed into us even if they are dysfunctional, as we pointed out at the beginning of the book.

Here are some patterns to avoid (with thanks to *The Breathing Book*):

Reverse breathing

Instead of allowing the belly to move *out* when the diaphragm moves down during the in-breath, the abdomen moves *in* during inhalation and out during exhalation. Likewise the pelvic floor contracts when breathing in and opens out when breathing out.

Actor problem: **Tension in neck, upper shoulders, back and jaw, reduces breath available to speak, tightens the voice, and inhibits spontaneity of expression.**

Clavicular breathing

This is the same as the survival breath in extreme situations (e.g., drowning, when we need a quick supply of air). It's quite common and may come from fear, stress or low self-esteem. Air is gasped high into the chest, pulling in the abdomen and pulling up the ribs. The diaphragm is prevented from descending fully because the abdomen tightens up, causing a lack of oxygen circulating through the organs. The secondary, weaker breathing muscles are engaged instead of the primary muscles. It can also lead to hyperventilation: quick, over-breathing.

Actor problem: **It's unhealthy, creating tension, breathlessness, poor concentration and rushed interaction. It weakens onset, limits range and resonance**.

Collapsed breathing

Here the chest collapses downwards, slumping the whole body posture, with the shoulders hunched forward and the belly stuck out. This might come from depression and dissociation from the body, which appears lifeless and burdened, with expression only happening from the neck up.

Actor problem: **Little breath or abdominal support, tension, breathy onset, no resonance or range.**

Throat holding

We close our throat and vocal folds, as a result of feeling overwhelmed by emotions, bottling them up.

Actor problem: **Constriction in the throat, neck, jaw and facial muscles impeding free intake of breath.**

Breath grabbing

The pause between in-breath and out-breath is a natural result of *relaxing* into the breath. Breath-grabbers snatch the next breath without a natural rest. They rush and finish other people's sentences for them because they feel insecure and uncomfortable with pauses and silences in a conversation.

Actor problem: **Tension, rushing, not listening, lack of organic receiving and giving.**

Frozen breathing

We tighten the whole body as if we're very cold, and contracting muscles block the movements of the diaphragm. This can result from endgaming – 'getting there' always supersedes 'being here' – or fear, stress or abuse. The body becomes rigid and frozen to cope with overwhelming feelings.

Actor problem: Very shallow breath, tension, weak onset, resonance and range, and experiencing is blocked.

So, from these patterns, we see clearly how vital free, deep breathing is both to our physical and psychological well-being, and to our ability as actors to speak easily and clearly and to creatively absorb and experience the circumstances of a script.

To sum up:

- Breath is *psyche,* a key source of inspiration.
- The creative breath is the automatic, involuntary breath that *breathes us.*
- This connects us, through the solar plexus, to acting impulse: to physical and emotional experience, energy, sensory awareness, our imagination, and to our deepest memories and subconscious life – so that when we breathe, our whole body and being is breathing.
- The breath carries the acting impulse on a wave through words and actions: with the in-breath we absorb circumstances; with the out-breath, we respond with our vocal expression, supported by the pelvic floor, the abdominal, lumbar and intercostal muscles, and the spine.
- To achieve the creative breath, we need to free the mind, body and breathing movement of tensions.

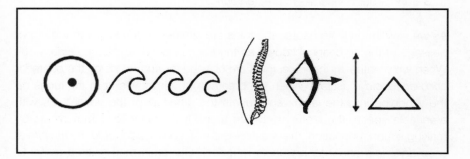

5

CENTRED ONSET OF SOUND – THE VOCAL IDENTITY OF THE ACTOR

WHAT IS IT?

Onset of sound is the initiation of vocal sound by breath flowing up to closed vocal folds, creating air pressure and making them vibrate.

Centred onset of sound is produced by teamwork between the onset of sound and the core support of the breath from the actor's pelvis, abdominals and spine.

The vocal folds actually have three functions:

1 to act as a valve to stop food entering the airways;
2 to block the airways to increase pressure in the abdomen and thorax, for example, when lifting, defecating, or in childbirth;
3 and – our concern – *to create sound.*

As we saw in the last chapter, the folds are situated in the larynx in the upper passage of the air channel known as the *trachea* or windpipe (see Figure 40). When we breathe in, the vocal folds are opened (or *abducted*, by the *posterior crico-arytenoid* muscles). When we breathe out, air moves from the lungs up the windpipe into the larynx and meets the gateway of the vocal folds with a variable space, the *glottis*, between them. If we want to communicate by making sound, phonation, the vocal folds are closed (or *adducted*, by the *lateral crico-arytenoid* and *inter-arytenoid* muscles). Our brain then gives a signal to create air pressure that sets the vocal folds vibrating at different frequencies, creating sounds of varying pitch, length and volume as they resonate in the resonators of the head.

The vibration or oscillation of the folds – a speedy opening and closing releasing bursts of air transformed into sound – happens at a rate no muscles could produce themselves. Blow air through your lips so that they vibrate in a similar manner, then try to open and close them as quickly through conscious muscular effort – not possible. The vibrations actually occur due to changes in air volume and pressure above and below the glottis, and the nature of vocal fold composition and elasticity (the myoelastic-aerodynamic theory).

Onset of sound becomes clear, focused, easy and centred when airflow is automatically controlled by the actor and is fully supported by the spine and abdominal and pelvic muscles we've already looked at.

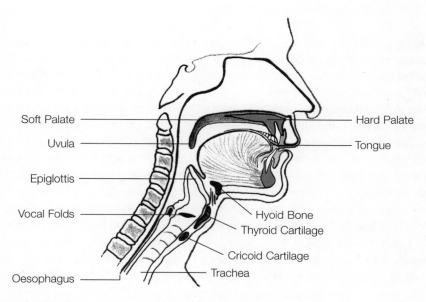

Figure 40 The vocal folds within the larynx and trachea

What is it for the actor?

* A place of focused and centred vocal identity and presence in the actor and character, helping to create the sense of 'Me/I' mentioned in Chapter 3.
* The centre of vocal will and drive – a centred onset enables the clear expression of the actor's objectives.
* The centre from where we radiate the voice into the space.
* The centre from which the voice has clarity, regardless of vocal quality, emotion, or volume.

So, it is in the centred onset of sound that the actor's identity, conviction, belief and intention meet within the voice and radiate outwards into the space.

How it works

A centred onset is achieved by:

1 Control – synchronizing the closure of the vocal folds, airflow and subglottic pressure to make a clear and easy sound in the vocal folds.
2 Support – connecting it to the innermost abdominals, the pelvic floor, the root of the voice, and the spine.

This co-ordinated gathering of muscles under the breath should create a feeling of vocal sound crystallizing to the *point of a needle.* For this sound to be expressed with focused and easy clarity, the vocal folds must be *closed* so that they create a clear point of vibrating sound. If they remain partially open, we produce a breathy sound (see Figure 28). On the other hand, if we do a hard attack, snapping the folds open, we produce a clucking or quacking sound.

The more we can create a precise point of sound in the column of air under the vocal folds, the more we will hear a centred identity and conviction through the voice of the actor. The more energy we need, the more we have to gather this centred support and the more we will need to keep the body open; and the actor needs a *lot* of energy to be present and centred and to carry the voice and intentions into the space. This does not mean we always have to be high-powered and loud in vocal delivery. The actor has to adapt to every set of circumstances, however adverse and difficult, and create a truthful but communicated response.

In addition, as made clear earlier, it's the *innermost* abdominal muscles, closest to the skeleton and organs and under control of the involuntary nervous system, that will offer most responsive and sensitive support. The external layers of muscle, on the other hand, are at the front of the body and do not connect to the spine at the centre of our body. They are cruder: to use them would be like using a whole football pitch of muscles under the breath, creating an onset of sound that is coarse, fuzzy and potentially harmful. It will be experienced as off-centre. Because this sound would not release through an opened, anchored body, we would only push and shout rather than resonate and release.

The spine is our means of staying balanced, open and upright. In the out-breath phase, the body, by contracting all those muscles responsible for the breath support of the actor, will have a tendency to fold inwards and will potentially close the resonance spaces and the neck around the larynx. This will create tension, prevent the larynx from tilting freely and result in a constricted sound and pitch range hampering expression (see the next chapter, Pitch

Range). As we've emphasized, the spine can counterbalance this by lengthening and anchoring the body into the Elastic Band. This keeps the alignment, the resonance spaces, the neck and larynx open.

We've already used the triangle to express grounding, but it is also a great image for the centred onset of sound.

It expresses the *rooting of the voice* in the pelvic floor and spine, and crystallization of sound in the point of a needle. The vocal centre that expresses 'me' within the voice needs this rock-like strength and sharp precision. We shall use this image to remind you of the importance of this idea as you go through the book.

EXERCISES

Exploring the centred onset of sound

Prelude

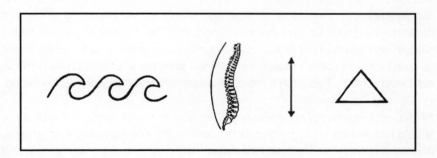

Stand in your centred aligned position.
Make sure that you:

• ground, by dropping the pelvis under and sending energy into the floor;

- put your weight into the balls of the feet so you have a clear balance line, rather like being ready to jump;
- lengthen the spine in both directions of the Elastic Band and press slightly away from the floor.

This will create a solid breath column right under the vocal folds and in the balance line, as we saw in the previous chapter.

As you breathe out, get a sense of the gathering point of support under the breath: it should feel as precise as the point of a needle, which will create identity and conviction in the voice. The more energy needed in performance the more we need to focus this support while keeping the body open.

1. Connecting to a centred onset

Lie in a semi-supine position on the floor. Tune yourself into your centred breath. Imagine the balloon that fills out your pelvis and up to the navel. Wait for your body's impulse to breathe in and allow the balloon to expand and open the pelvic floor muscles. If you have problems feeling these muscles expanding and contracting, go back to Exercises 8 and 9 in Chapter 4.

* Rock forward with your pelvis on the in-breath and backwards into the floor on the out-breath. You are now creating a flat lengthening back on the out-breath, which is the anchoring position.

* Allow your body to relax and to release on the in-breath. Here we'll look at the *timing* of our sound. Breathe an impulse to sound a *mmm* into the pelvic floor muscles. Wait for your out-breath impulse to kick in and for the pelvic floor and lowest abdominal muscles to respond. Let the *mmm* ride the wave of the out-breath like a surfboard, following the weight of the breathing movement back into the Elastic Band of the stretching spine. The resulting sound will have a smooth and released rather than a forced and tense glottal onset. It is important to wait for the breathing muscles to change from the in-breath phase into the out-breath phase. If you don't, there will be tension and the onset will be forced.

* Now, do it again and concentrate on *the definition and clarity* of the onset. It should feel and sound as precise as the point of the needle, rather than general, breathy and fuzzy. You should identify with the needlepoint as your centre and identity, your 'me'.

Do the same on a long *huuh*, like a voiced descending sigh, and connect impulse, breath, muscular and spinal support to the onset. Don't push the *huuh* – it should feel as precise as threading a needle. The sound should be definite and strong. You are now making sure that the surfboard is firm yet easy when you ride your wave along the channels of the spine.

Rather than being tempted to shorten the muscles and the body as you sound, you should see the out-breath and sound as a journey into the lengthening back wall of the body. Make sure you surf the whole wave of your breath. The sound should now really release and drop in. It will start to sound three-dimensional and resonate with the space – a centred onset.

* If, though, you find that your sound is breathy, it's because your vocal folds are not coming together fully. So try a 'puppy wants to go for a walk' or 'cat wants feeding' noise. This will thin the vocal folds and bring them together. Now sound a voiced short *huh* and then a long *haaah,* and you should feel a much more centred sound.

> It is not enough to open and free a voice technically, though. The physical apparatus needs to be integrated within the whole human being. Stanislavski identifies three *inner motive forces – mind, feeling and will –* at the core of our psycho-physical make-up, which work in conjunction with each other. The actor/character will need to change an imaginary situation by engaging the will and acting out objectives, and the will is seated in the lower body with the pelvic area and sacral nerve centre at its core. The will, then, connects with qualities associated with this area of intuition, creativity, sexuality and vital force, and the actor's voice needs to plug into this. If we cannot bring this focus into the voice, it will sound unrooted, uncommitted and unconvincing. Actors' voices that are connected to this and act on impulse with truth and sensitivity can be incredibly powerful.

2. 'Me'

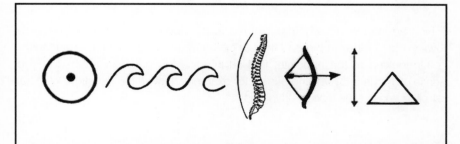

This exercise puts you in touch with the feeling of identity and conviction.

Using your centred onset of sound, say 'me' with full conviction and assertion from your pelvic centre and spine. You can play the action of 'introducing myself' and try to summarize what is you in the word 'me'.

* To gain this identity in your vocal onset is important, because you will need to have the same conviction of identity when you play a character. 'If I am this character in these circumstances what do I do?' Remember that if you convince yourself you will convince the audience that you are the character. You will discover that in order to define yourself in the word 'me' you will most likely use quite a lot of your pitch range within this little word.

* If the word 'me' sounds flat, then your breath isn't connecting deeply enough with the root of your voice, with that Elastic Band energy rooting you right into the earth and up into the zenith of the sky. Let the word 'me' ride the wave of the out-breath like a surfboard, following the journey of the breathing movement back into the Elastic Band of the stretching spine. You are bringing the word 'me', which sums up the sense of who you are, to a needlepoint and are grounding and strengthening it. 'Me' will stand on the ground, as *solid as a rock* – like in the song!

> By anchoring into the Elastic Band you will open all the resonance spaces and your spine will lengthen and create a back wall of support. This will create extra space at the back of the pharynx and release the larynx allowing it to tilt freely and expressively. Your breath and body support will melt together and your voice become one with the body, creating resonance that sounds rich and full. Because your larynx releases there is no strain on the vocal folds. You should feel that you are connecting with your spine and core, which will give you confidence and conviction. The anchoring and centred onset work will also greatly centre and widen the expression of your range.

* Find an impulse to say 'me', rooted in conviction, self-assertion, defiance, loyalty, etc. – for example, say the old classic movie line: 'Me! I'm Spartacus!'

Or, looking at the opposite, find an impulse for 'not me', earthed in your sense of integrity, loyalty and pride – for example, answer the question 'Who has rebelled against the king?' – 'Not me!'

Or, look at a *timid* response while keeping the onset clear: admit weakly to a scary head teacher that *you* were the culprit – 'Me'.

* Now imagine your whole body is a stage, with the pelvic floor as the boards. Rather than just playing downstage in the front of your body, you should move into centre and upstage, towards your spine, the back wall of the stage, and then over the soft and hard palate in your mouth, the arc of the ceiling above your stage. The voice will become full and three-dimensional rather than thin and one-dimensional.

* Once you really connect with 'me', play the action to 'impress someone', saying 'I can go high and I can go low', exploring the full potential of your range.

3. Optimum pitch – the centred note

> The optimum pitch is the pitch around the middle of your range, with the larynx in a released position, and from which you can go fully up and down; it produces the most easy, natural and supported tone. When trying to fill a theatre space, especially a big space, the optimum pitch is essential, because it has most carrying power. For spaces with poor acoustics an actor may need to pitch the voice higher.
>
> Our symbol for optimum pitch is:
>
>

Although the following little exercise has to do with pitch range, we've included it here because you might feel that your sound has deepened as a result of the above exercises. This is due to the releasing of the larynx, allowing it to tilt more freely – more on this in the next chapter.

Ask yourself a question that you can happily answer with 'Yes'! For example: 'Do you like holidays?' -'Yes!' You may find the note that comes from this positive answer is slightly higher now and more in your optimum pitch, easy and in the middle of your range.

4. On a chair

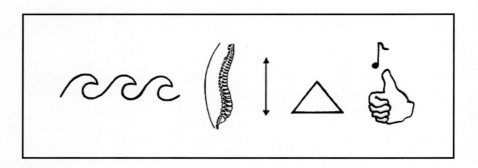

In this exercise we will explore how the feet can assist the support of the vocal rooting muscles and your spine. By pressing your feet against the floor, you will gain extra resonance because your spine and breath-support muscles will gain strength; and by making your spine lengthen, your resonance spaces will become open cavities with strong walls resonating the sound more strongly. When your resonance spaces don't have the elasticity created by an open lengthened body, your voice will sound weak and fuzzy rather than rich and full. Once your voice knows how to do this, the effort will become minimal.

- Sit on a firm chair with back support. Sit on your sitting bones and in balance. Make sure the balls of your feet can touch the floor.

- Give yourself an impulse to make the long descending sound *huuuh*. Breathe the impulse into your vocal rooting muscles, let them engage on the out-breath, then sound.

- Drop the back of the pelvis against the chair while pressing your feet (mainly balls of feet) into the floor.

- Feel the strength of your back support by lengthening your spine and neck. You should experience the Elastic Band where your spine lengthens and your breathing movement glides along the back wall of your body. Sit completely balanced and as tall in your spine/back wall as you can. Use all of the breath and melt the sound into the Elastic Band.

5. Against the wall

- Stand in balance against a wall with bent knees, as if you were sitting on a tall stool. Only your pelvis/bottom touches the wall, not the rest of the body. Your feet should be hip-width apart and your weight on the balls of the feet.

- Give yourself an impulse to make the *huuuh* sound. Breathe the impulse into your vocal rooting muscles, engage them on the out-breath, then sound.

- Connect the out-breath movement of these muscles to the Elastic Band by dropping your pelvis backwards into the wall and by pressing your feet gently against the floor. Don't allow your neck to fall backwards, lifting up your chin. Feel the support from the back of the pelvis all the way up the back wall of your body into the lengthening neck wall. Use your full breath.

- Now stand away from the wall, do the exercise again and maintain this heightened sense of back support

6. Standing with heightened balance

Here we add the importance of standing in balance between the counterforces of grounding down into the earth and lifting up towards the sky.

* Stand in balance, feet parallel, hip-width apart. Imagine you are standing on sun-warmed earth and you sink into it while growing into the blue sky above. Make sure your weight is slightly forward on the balls of your feet as if you are ready to jump. Aim for a heightened awareness of your balance line – this will take you into the present moment of action.

* Now press through the balls of the feet and raise your heels away from the floor. Lengthen your spine and back of neck, creating the back wall of your body, as you stand in balance on the balls of the feet.

* On an out-breath, release a *yeee* sound and connect to the Elastic Band and the vocal rooting muscles. Do the same with a *huh-haaah* sigh, descending through your range.

* Feel how the floor support and the spinal back wall of the Elastic Band give you strength to reach into the space above, below and around you with your voice.

* Now come down from the balls of the feet and stand in a normal aligned position, maintaining a heightened sense of balance line through the body and sound on *yeee* again.

The picture below represents the elements that create the centred onset of sound:

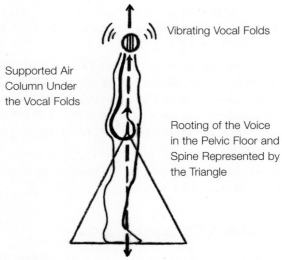

Vibrating Vocal Folds

Supported Air
Column Under
the Vocal Folds

Rooting of the Voice
in the Pelvic Floor and
Spine Represented by
the Triangle

Figure 41 Centred onset

Integration into acting

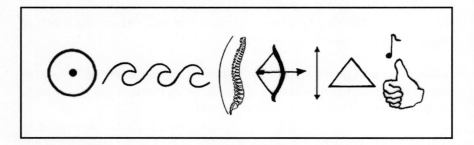

Start by connecting to your centred onset of sound by finding an impulse to say: 'Me, it's me!' Make your solid as a rock connection to sound, muscles and spine. Make sure your onset of sound is in optimum pitch.

Now make someone understand how to count to ten, or to learn the alphabet.

Take a focus point where the person might be. Connect the impulse to your reflexive muscular engagement: breathe the objective into your solar plexus, connect to your centred onset of sound and surf the wave of your out-breath, and change the other person by teaching them.

- Connect your sense of 'me' with the will drive of your objective engaging the Elastic Band.
- Put your object of attention, the person, further and further away from you. Breathe in the distance and find how much more you have to root your sound and engage the Elastic Band to reach the other side of the room.

To sum up:

- **It is essential for an actor to have a focused and centred onset of sound expressing the root of the voice.**
- **It is created by the vibration of the vocal folds and the core support of the breath in the actor's pelvis, spine and abdominals.**
- **It has the focus of a needlepoint and the solid base of a rock.**
- **It is the place where identity, belief, conviction and intention, as well as power and drive, meet, creating the sense of Me/I in the moment.**
- **It is the centre from which the voice has clarity, regardless of vocal quality, emotion or volume.**
- **It is the vocal centre that drives the voice into the space and its periphery.**

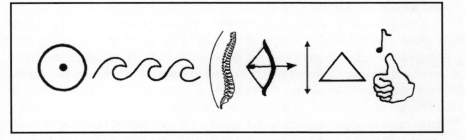

6
PITCH RANGE – THE MUSIC OF MEANING

WHAT IS IT?

Pitch range is the variation in notes from high to low, which gives speech musicality. It contributes to the wider pattern of *intonation*, the variation and accenting of the voice according to what we're saying, why and to whom. It also affects and is affected by other vocal characteristics like *tone* and *power*.

What is it for the actor?

Pitch range, in everyday life, naturally and automatically reflects our need to communicate, our expression of thoughts, desires, wants and emotions. This natural adaptability must be present for the actor playing a character.

So, rather than being determined in a skilled but mechanical way, pitch range and overall intonation needs to respond to what's happening in each moment in performance spontaneously – to all the elements of circumstances, previous history, images, thoughts and feelings that give rise to the words we're speaking and actions we're doing.

If the pitch range is dull, meaning and intention cannot be communicated. The result sounds lifeless and cerebral. Pitch range connects the actor to their creative musicality. In music we are given the melody. In acting, on the other hand, we have to improvise our own music to convey the language of the play most clearly and expressively. For example, a volatile and jerky range will create a different understanding of a character's situation from one that is constrained and monotonous, or easy, calm and flowing. It is the meeting between *what we say* and *how we say it*, between a *left* brain and *right* brain process. It helps to define who we are as the character through the sound, our *per sona*.

How it works

First of all we have a thought, feeling, or response, and this engages our brain to instruct the breathing apparatus and vocal folds to produce a particular note of particular length and power: for example, a low sustained groan of disappointment or a short high squeal of delight.

The high and low notes are created by the frequency at which the folds vibrate, i.e. the number of times per second. The high squeal will come from the folds stretching and thinning and vibrating at an amazing hundreds of times per second. The low groan will emerge from slacker, thicker folds and fewer vibrations. The thinner, lighter first 'E' string on a guitar, like a woman's vocal folds, produces a higher note than the thicker, heavier sixth 'E' string, like a man's folds.

Pitch range can be affected by other factors such as health and tension. To get maximum flexibility, the neck and vocal tract should be free, with adaptable length and diameter. The mouth and tongue must be relaxed, because tension will directly affect the larynx and vocal folds just below them. The whole larynx needs to be able to move freely and easily.

The larynx

As we can see in Figure 42, below, the vocal folds are positioned within the larynx, which is made of bone, cartilage, ligament and muscle.

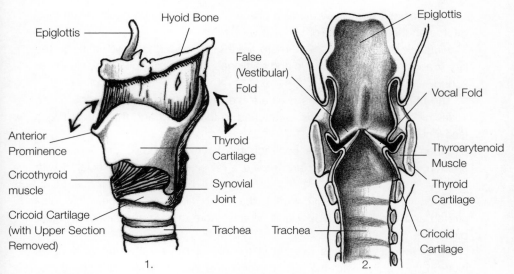

Figure 42 1. The larynx – side view showing the cricothyroid muscles and tilt direction
2. A cross-section of the larynx – rear view showing the thyroarytenoid muscles and vocal folds

It is suspended from the *hyoid bone,* located just below the jaw and attached to the base of the tongue and jaw muscles.

The *epiglottis* is a flap of cartilage that covers and protects the airways when we swallow.

The *thyroid cartilage*, looking like a helmet's visor, has a protruding V-shaped nick at the front – this is what we know as the Adam's apple.

The *vocal folds* attach at the front slightly below this point.

The *cricoid cartilage* is attached to the *thyroid cartilage* by *synovial joints* – these enable the larynx to tilt forward and back, changing the tension on the vocal folds and the notes they make.

The *trachea* consists of rings of cartilage allowing for flexible movement, rather like a vacuum cleaner tube.

The movement and the muscles

There are two main sets of muscles controlling the larynx and vocal folds:

The extrinsic laryngeal muscles: There are 15 of these and they raise and lower the larynx and affect the length and shape of the vocal tract (*Voice Work*: 158–9).

Put your finger and thumb on your Adam's apple, the thyroid cartilage, and swallow. The larynx moves up. It also rises with emotional stress, and with *higher* pitch.

Now yawn; it goes down. It also descends if we take in a deep breath (and returns on the out-breath), or use a *lower* pitch.

The intrinsic laryngeal muscles: There are 12 of these, and they live inside the larynx and move the vocal folds and cartilages, determining pitch and quality of sound.

The main relevant muscles here are the *thyroarytenoids* – the body of the vocal folds; and *crycothyroids* – attached to the cricoid and thyroid cartilages (see Figure 42 above).

When the *thyroarytenoids* contract, the larynx tilts back, the vocal folds shorten, vibrate more slowly and create a lower pitch (often associated with chest voice).

When the *crycothyroids* contract, the larynx tilts forward, the vocal folds stretch and thin like a rubber band, vibrate more quickly and create a higher pitch.

When louder volume is needed in the higher ranges, the *thyroarytenoids* work in partnership with the *crycothyroids* and create more resistance to the oncoming air by thickening the vocal folds as they also lengthen (*Your Voice: An Inside View*: 116).

Pitch range should flow freely through the whole vertical length of the body, so that it can create sound of amazing versatility and musicality arising from our need to communicate.

Each actor will have a different pitch range, of course. We will also have a range within that, with which we feel most comfortable. For example, soprano and contralto singers may have the same range but will have better tone, depth and ease in a particular area within it (*Dynamics of the Singing Voice*: 74). Equally, as we saw in the last section, we all have an optimum pitch, the notes on which we speak with natural ease and full resonance. There is no one optimum pitch. It varies from person to person.

The symbol for the freely responding pitch range is musical notes.

EXERCISES

Exploring pitch range

1. From relaxing into sirening

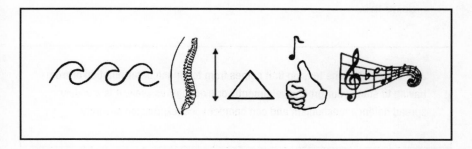

The centred onset of sound and the sense of the 'Me/I' in the voice should first be established, so repeat exercises from the previous section. Be aware that good alignment and breathing is essential for the success of the following exercises. Through working with the Elastic Band energy connecting creative breath and spinal movement into gravity and anti-gravity we will already have lengthened the neck and released the larynx, jaw and tongue as well as opened the soft palate.

Now we will focus on opening these areas further.

1   First give your jaw hinges a massage. Massage the area between your temples and the ears. Here are the muscles that keep the lower jaw closed. Release any teeth biting. Induce a yawn into the back of the soft palate. Sense how this releases the jaw and drops it open. Allow this to happen. Continue your massage all the way down the jaw line. Knead the base of your jaw line.

2   Try this Grotowski exercise (*Towards a Poor Theatre*: 120). Stand with the upper part of the body and head bent slightly forward. Rest the lower jaw, fully relaxed, on the thumb and index finger. Raise the upper jaw, and at the same time raise the eyebrows and wrinkle the forehead as if about to yawn, while slightly contracting the muscles on the top and back of the head and neck. Let the voice release on a vowel. Make sure the front part of the neck is relaxed.

3   This exercise is inspired by Kristin Linklater (*Freeing the Natural Voice*: 133). Hold the base of your jaw in place while you yawn with the upper jaw. Then close the lower jaw with your hands so that the lower jaw starts to become passive. Now let your lower jaw hang into gravity. Imagine there are little weights attached. Yawn again.

4   Check if the jaw is released by folding your hands together and shaking them while allowing your jaw to shake. Make a *huuuh* sound while doing this.

Jaw clenching is the tension that comes from too much determination or from having to stand your ground vehemently or even aggressively. It is a widely spread defence mechanism and can hamper vocal expression severely.

5 Once your jaw is released, do the following tongue rocking movement on your out-breath while connecting to the Elastic Band. Place your tongue tip behind the bottom teeth. With the jaw released, your body lengthening along the balance line, tailbone dropped down, rock the middle of your tongue forwards and in front of your lips, stretching it as far as it will go. You will enhance this stretch by connecting to the Elastic Band. On the in-breath, while relaxing your body and bending your knees, allow your tongue to come back naturally by itself and let it sit fatly in your mouth. Do this a few times until you feel your tongue releasing.

The base of the tongue is directly linked to the larynx. One can imagine the larynx hanging from the root of the tongue like a person from a parachute. Again, working with gravity will help us to get the most out of the larynx. If the tongue is tense the larynx will be tense, which will have an effect on its ability to tilt freely. The impact will go even lower into the diaphragm and hamper free breathing.

---

6 Now let's focus on the larynx. Put your index, middle finger and thumb on your larynx and feel its shape. Now massage the surrounding muscles gently. Hold your larynx and swallow. Sense the movement that is created as a result. You will first feel it rise up and then drop down. Swallowing will put the larynx into a neutral resting position. Try yawning. You will feel your larynx drop down.

Now make the whining sound of the puppy that wants to go for a walk. You will sense the larynx move up on the sound and down after the sound has finished.

7 Now give yourself an impulse to siren on an *ng* sound (as in sing*ing*) up and down your pitch range connecting to the Elastic Band. You will feel how your larynx now moves easily up when going higher and down when going lower. The Elastic Band will make your range more extensive through spinal support.

8 Now put yourself into your *optimum pitch* by asking yourself a question that you can happily answer with 'Yes!' as earlier. Go back to sirening on *ng* from this note as the centre, and get the whole body and breath involved.

2. The y-buzz

These symbols apply for the next two exercises.

This is a great exercise by Arthur Lessac that helps to develop what he calls 'tonal NRG' (energy): 'the control of a vibratory current of sound in a state of constant movement, radiation, and transmission propagating in the hard palate and teeth, nasal bone, cheekbones, sinuses, forehead and cranium. Like a beam of light or stream of water, the vocal sound current may be concentrated or diffused' (*The Use and Training of the Human* Voice: 139).

We shall extend this vocal current along the Elastic Band, rather than keeping it simply in the head resonators, so that it becomes a whole body sound.

We shall use the sound *yyy*. It sounds like the vowel 'e', but it is important not to make the sound a *yeeee* sound where the vowel takes over – we need to focus on rooting the 'y'. It is formed on the hard palate and is best for connecting sounds to the balance line because of its central position of formation. He calls this *yyy* sound the *y-buzz*.

* Get an impulse to sound a *yyy* in your optimum pitch from your vocal rooting muscles. Now explore a descending *yyy* in the lower half of your pitch range. Keep your neck long and the crown of your head lifted while staying rooted through the tailbone and your feet. Let your jaw drop. Sense how the *yyy* descends along the Elastic Band into the earth to give your sound feet.

* Now let's connect the *y-buzz* to the vocal root. Bounce the sound *yyy* on your pelvic floor as if on a trampoline. You will probably feel it bounce upwards because your pelvic floor/abdominal muscles send it up and back in a scooping movement.

* Finally, fold both hands together and start to shake them while keeping your body released within the Elastic Band movement. This shakes the vibrations

created by the sound *yyy* through the whole body. It will give you a sense of your gum-ridge vibrating initially; then the vibrations will spread through the bones of the facial resonators; and eventually through your whole vertical balance line. Through the shaking action you will find it easy to yield yourself to gravity, rooting down and lifting up. You will vibrate from head to toe through your spine.

3. The alarm clock

We'll now go further for more release. This exercise differentiates the muscles involved in support from those secondary and external muscles that should stay released.

* Make fast small steps with your feet while sounding on the *yyy*. Don't shake the hands for this. Instead, make the whole body, the tissues, bones and muscles, shake by stepping as quickly as you can against the floor while keeping your body relaxed and spine lengthened into the Elastic Band. The vibrations of the *yyy* will reach through the whole body.

* Now focus more on connecting to the Elastic Band. On *yyy,* engage the pelvic floor muscles, root down and lift up into it. Imagine your *yyy* sound is attached to the pelvic floor and is pulled in opposite directions, into the earth and up to the sky.

4. Connecting your pitch range to the balance line of your body

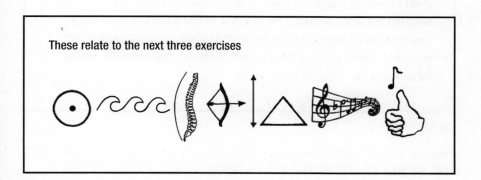

These relate to the next three exercises

* Next do this through your pitch range. While staying in the balanced support action of the Elastic Band, go up in pitch with your *yyy* sound, starting from

optimum pitch – remember to follow the sense of gravity of your out-breath taking you against the spine. Let your pitch rise from this centred note upwards towards the sky while keeping rooted into the earth. You will find release and more space in your pharynx as a result. Now, siren down again, making sure you lengthen towards the sky.

* Now explore your full pitch range from foot to head. Sense your feet, sound your *yyy* there – you will feel the vibrations in your feet eventually – and then siren up the legs, through the centre of the pelvis, along the back of the spine, to the crown of the head, along the imagined Elastic Band that connects you to the zenith of the sky. Experience how your body and balance line resonates with the vibrations created by the *yyy* with its various frequencies and pitch notes.

* Now siren from the floor to the ceiling, sensing how the Elastic Band energy expands through the space. Keeping this vertical sense while you siren up and down through your pitch range, try to draw diagonal lines from one corner of the room to another. Choose a corner and breathe it in, then let the out-breath and *yyy* sound take you to the next corner. This is an initial preparation for speaking in a space.

* Next, once the pitch range has been freed up, say 'Me/I' and note how your pitch range alters to convey this with conviction. If you have a partner to hand, say 'Me/I' to each other and take in how the pitch range changes intuitively as you assert this and respond to each other.

What sometimes happens is that people say 'Me/I' on a monotone unconnected to the centred onset of sound, so that there is no pitch range and therefore no expression. The other pitfall is to consciously explore pitch range in a mechanical way. Pitch range is a *natural* response to the need to be clear and give what we say meaning.

---

* Now say: 'I am here.' Feel the tonal energy buzzing through the Elastic Band from the floor through the spine to the ceiling.

Really go for the meaning of 'I am here.' Don't do a mechanical pitch range or attempt to be overly colourful. Just mean what you say.

* Do the following exchange with a partner:

   ' I am here.'
   'No, you're not!'
   'Yes, I am here.'
   'No, you are not here!'
   'I am here!'
   'I can't see you!'
   'But I am here', etc.

Engage with each other and experience how your pitch range gains more musicality and a wider range when you have to prove something against an obstacle.

Actors will only sound centred and assertive if they have their full pitch range at their disposal. Imagine your body as a building. Your range should find the lowest note in the basement and the highest on the roof. If you are not in optimum pitch where your larynx is in a released position, it will be much more difficult to use your whole pitch range because your larynx will be stuck either in a suppressed position or in too high a position. Always start from a relaxed position of the larynx – try swallowing first.

---

5. The responding voice through the vowel energy

Let your voice respond to colour. Allow your pitch range to communicate your experience. This exercise is inspired by Kristin Linklater.

* Explore the colour orange first. Breathe orange silently into your diaphragm/solar plexus. Allow the colour to affect you. Let associations of this colour come to you. Where have you seen it? Does it have a smell? A taste? A sound? A feel?

* Connect your experience to your vocal rooting muscles and whisper the word orange. Then start to give it a voice. Orange.

* Explore the vowel sounds of orange. Now the consonants.
   Go back to the vowel sounds. Just voice the vowel sounds of the word orange so that they carry the full meaning of your experience.

Do the same with the following colours. Don't move on unless you have a real experience of the colour and you sense that this experience is coming through your voice without you listening to yourself:

- blue
- red
- yellow
- black
- green

Take the experience of each colour into your solar plexus and express it through the vowel. Allow yourself to go with the out-breath movement and follow its journey against the spine. The out-breath becomes the river that picks up the experiences and associations you are expressing through the pitch range, vibrations of your voice and body resonance.

Engage fully in the experience of the colour and trust your creative and vocal responses to it. Every time you say 'green' it should sound different. If it sounds the same you have probably fixed how you say 'green', but this won't be connected to your experience within the present moment. Don't listen to yourself. Voice is response. The more you develop the response muscle, the more you can be in the experience of the present moment. The intuitive response will be richer and more colourful than anything you could think up.

Integration into acting

Objectives and pitch range

Let's now explore and respond to objectives.

Stanislavski talked about *the problem* that arises in the imaginary given circumstances of a scene. We need to take action to resolve it, we have a 'task' to do (*An Actor's Work*: 149–51). What he called our 'impulse to action' takes the form of 'I want ...', which is commonly called the 'objective'.

* Imagine a person you care about is standing turned away from you. You need

to talk to them and draw them closer. Imagine reasons why it is so important to you, e.g. you deeply love them and they've decided to break up with you. Give yourself the objective: *'I want to make them come to me to win them round.'* Let this desire and need for the person to respond boil in you like water in a pot with a lid on. Breathe the circumstances and objective through your solar plexus and into your back and vocal root support muscles, enhancing your sense of conviction and identity.

* Sense your pelvic floor muscles and lumbar spine in readiness and your impulse to breathe out. Follow the journey of the breath against the spine and into the Elastic Band energy through your balance line, and root into your centred onset of sound as you say: *'Come closer, come and talk with me.'* The spine will connect your whole body to the objective.

* **Now focus on allowing your objective and actions towards the other person shape the line musically.**

* Try working against an extra obstacle: the person is afraid of you, angry with you, torn between you and another person. Experience how this alters your pitch range.

* Try different actions, expressed by a verb: I coax you; I beg you; I order you. See how each gives you a different range.

Connect to these impulses in the same way as above: by breathing them into the solar plexus, letting them affect you, and readying the muscles before you respond vocally to the objective you are playing.

* Try the same with: *'I want you to go away.'* Create the imaginary circumstances, the problem to be overcome, the desire and need for this person to be made to go, and let your voice and pitch range respond as with the opposite objective above.

To sum up:

- **Pitch range is essential in creating the intonation pattern and music of meaning.**
- **It reveals the through-line of our experience, thoughts and wants and emphasizes what is important within them.**

- **It is the emotional reflection of what we are saying through the music of how we are saying it.**

- **Pitch range needs to respond to acting impulses freely and expressively.**

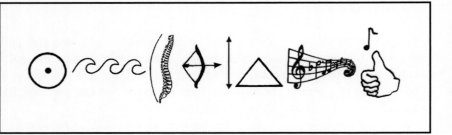

7
RESONANCE – VIBRATING THE EXPERIENCE

Resonance is the means through which the sound produced by vibrations of the vocal folds is given full tonal expression. Without this our voices would sound very thin, muffled and indistinct.

It takes place in the vocal tract, the flexible tube extending from the larynx through the pharynx or throat and naso-pharynx to the mouth – with its soft and hard palates – and nose (see Figure 43). The sound vibration in the vocal folds is amplified and prolonged in these spaces – they literally re-sound the vibrations in their hollow spaces, just like a guitar string vibration resounds in the hollow body of the guitar.

These resonating spaces can change shape and produce different sounds that enable our voices to 'carry' in a multitude of ways. It's as though we have unlimited vocal access to a range of wind instruments of different lengths and widths, such as recorder, flute, trumpet or oboe, which can play the same note but sound very different because of the nature of their resonating space.

Our quality of resonance will be affected by:

- our physical constitution – the shape of our vocal tract and vocal folds, and our health;
- our degree of ease and our alignment;
- our imagination, flexibility and technical control.

What is it for the actor?

Resonance colours the voice and enhances the actor's psycho-physical experience and communication with an audience.

Language and sound need to resonate through the actor's body to come

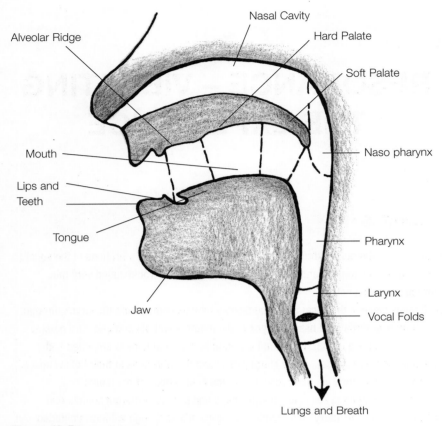

Figure 43 Resonance areas

alive. If they simply stay in the cerebral cortex they become separated from full human experience, merely an impression, an isolated fragment of life. The emotional life of the character is often released most strongly, but not exclusively, through the vowels in the text. To return to the river image, Stanislavski likened the vowels to a river full of emotional and spiritual content and consonants to the banks that keep them contained. This is not to say that consonants can't be filled with attitudes and emotion as well. He saw a piece of text like a symphony, and only *an unbroken line of sound* produced with imagination and skill will bring it to life. Sustained resonance is essential to achieve this.

Although the mouth, throat and nose are the only proper resonators, we can have the sensation of sounds resonating in a sympathetic way in other areas of the body. For example, brighter sounds like *eh, i* or *ee* are often released through the head, whereas darker sounds like *oo* and *oh* can connect with the pelvis and legs, and an open *ah* sound can find a chest resonance. Kristin Linklater has examined this, and it connects to the Yoga tradition where the body is divided into seven different *chakras,* or energy centres, each one possessing a specific function and experience and to which we can attribute a particular sound in the resonance scale. We will come back to this later.

From the point of view of our whole personality or that of a different character, we may experience ourselves as residing in particular parts of the body: the forehead, hands or eyes, stomach or pelvis, for example. Michael Chekhov calls these *imaginary centres*, and finding where we, or different characters, live in the body offers valuable psychological and physical insight. Chekhov also looks at whether a character is *predominantly* led by mind, will or feeling (Stanislavski's 'inner motive forces'), each of which has a corresponding centre in the head, pelvis or chest (see *To the Actor*, Chapter 6, and *On the Technique of Acting,* 'Afterword'). We can also focus on the areas of vocal resonance that relate to these centres in order to help develop what we call a *character voice* (see Chapter 13).

How it works

Resonance acts as an amplifier for the sound created by our breath in the vocal folds, and also by the *articulators* that form speech (see the next chapter), and without it our voices would sound fuzzy like the strings of an electric guitar before it's plugged into an amp.

Different sounds and frequencies/pitches will resonate in different ways according to where they are placed and how the resonance spaces are shaped, either by nature or by our design. Also, a particular resonance area will favour certain sounds and pitches.

If we round our lips into a Standard English *oo* sound, the vocal tract is lengthened and we hear a dark, full sound. If we say *ee*, the tract is shorter and results in a brighter sound. Generally, the wider and longer the space, the darker and more open the sound; and the narrower and shorter the space, the lighter and more constrained the sound. If we drop the soft palate and speak through the nose we have the distinct nasal sound of someone from Essex – very different from an RP speaker with a forward placement in the mouth towards the gum-ridge; or someone from Manchester, who will place their voice at the back of the mouth. A so-called *balanced resonance* mixes the resonance in the pharynx, mouth and nose. Our audibility and clarity often improves if we focus this resonance forward into a placement around the hard palate and gum-ridge in the mouth, and, to a lesser extent, in the nose, which allows us to speak with ease and at length (see *Vocal Arts Workbook*, David Carey and Rebecca Clark Carey: 115).

In *HOW TO DO ACCENTS,* Edda Sharpe and Jan Haydn Rowles call placement a *zone*. The different zones are the teeth and lips, the gum-ridge (or alveolar ridge), the hard palate, the soft palate and uvula, the pharynx the nasal pharynx, and the nasal cavity. Small changes in how we shape the throat, mouth, tongue, jaw and soft palate at the back of the mouth (which affects access of air in and out of the mouth and nose) determine which zone is used to resonate the voice. These changes are themselves determined by our intentions, feelings, images, responses and what they call our 'mimicry' muscles, which we've used to recreate sounds from an early age within our particular background and place of birth. The sound of the voice will change when focused in each of these different areas. In addition to the *zone,* as part of what creates our resonance, there is the *tone* of the sound we produce through different balances of tonal frequencies, creating a harsh or mellifluous sound, a rich or thin one, a bright or droning one (*HOW TO DO ACCENTS*: 29–32). All this helps to create what we know as the *quality* of the voice.

As introduced above, apart from the spaces scientifically identified as resonance areas, we can feel experientially that the *whole body* resonates in *sympathy* with the vibrations coming from the vocal tract. Vibrations travel through the body, particularly through our bones and spine. We talk of head resonance, chest resonance and pelvic resonance, and through these sensations we can get a better idea of how successful our primary resonance is. Just as sound resonates around hard brick, stone or wooden walls in a theatre or cathedral, so it vibrates in the bone of our heads and skeleton. Also, denser material like tissue and organs has its subtle vibrations. To achieve vocal brightness, a youthful or piercing quality, we might aim for head resonance. A rooted, earthy sound requires pelvic resonance. Warm and full sounds are associated with the chest area.

The vocal tract must be able to respond freely, without constriction, according to what is happening in each moment. Tensions of any kind are the killer of vibrations because they narrow the resonance chambers and muffle the sound. The more open the spaces the better the resonance and the balance of resonance from different areas. Any tension in the breathing muscles, especially the accessory muscles around the neck, chest and shoulders, needs to be released so that larynx, tongue, throat, lips and jaw can be agile. Getting into rigid patterns of behaviour and speech as a result of restrictive social conditioning and self-censorship will also have a constricting effect on these areas of expression.

Rooted and strong breath support, good spinal alignment and muscular ease will enable the column of air to produce a clear, focused sound in the vocal folds, and will make the jaw drop, raise the soft palate, release the larynx, tongue, neck and mouth, opening to the full all the resonance areas that amplify the sound and give it specific colour.

Our symbol for resonance, which vibrates our experience, is sound waves.

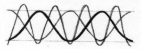

EXERCISES

Exploring resonance

1. Flow of breath, energy and vibrations through the whole body

These apply for the next three exercises

Exploring all the body areas

- Voice the sound *mmm* on your lips. Make sure the lips are loose and you feel a gentle vibration.

- Increase the vibration into the whole mouth and cheeks by chewing the sound *mmm* through the whole mouth like a toffee.

- Give your cheekbones and sinuses a massage and see if you can resonate into them.

- Now resonate into your forehead, maybe lifting the pitch a bit higher. Go under your scalp with your resonance and use your fingers to help you contact this area by massaging it or making raindrops with the fingertips. Go to the back of your head.

- Go to the chest: give it a pat to encourage the vibrations to go there. Also pat your shoulders, shoulder blades, upper arms and underarms and massage your hands and fingers encouraging the vibrations to connect to those areas.

- Rub and pat your lower back and the back of the pelvis. Experience which pitch range you want to use in those areas. You will most likely have gone lower in pitch to match the more gravity-oriented pelvic area.

- Rub your stomach.

- Now give your thighs a pat, then your calves and feet.

Partner assistance – If you have a partner, do the same again but let them do the massaging and patting on the different areas. This will help you to relax and become more aware of them.

- Now go through all the above while connecting the out-breath to the Elastic Band energy. Hum until you feel the vibration spread through the whole body. With further work on your body and breath awareness you can resonate out of specific body parts – from the toes to the tip of the nose – and this gives different imaginative stimuli to the voice in creating the physical life of a character.

Exploring back, middle and front for different resonance qualities

* Using the Elastic Band energy on the out-breath, sound a *ng* to get more sensations in the back of the body; *nnn* in the centre of the body; and *mmm* in the front of your body.

This exploration is useful because different theatre styles and characters require a different resonance from the actor. Just as instruments play different roles within an orchestra, the human body gives us different resonance through accessing areas of the nose, mouth, pharynx, chest and pelvis; the different zones within the mouth – used especially for accent work; and the back, middle and front of the body and their relationship to space.

* Rudolf Steiner, in his work on *Speechformation,* has used specific sound exercises to develop the various resonances appropriate for different theatrical qualities:

epic: resonance at the back. This quality relates to something behind us in the past, or with supernatural powers. It can be practised with back-of-the-tongue velar sounds like *g, k, ng,* which create a magical or mysterious tone for storytelling, or a cosmic resonance in plays where we connect to the gods determining human destiny.

Practise the velar placement with:
'The king knocked on the giant's door in the grey glow of the morning.'
Make the velar sounds resonate by leaning into your back support. Get a partner to pat your back while you say the line, and feel the back resonance and the quality that creates.

Try these lines from *The Odyssey* with the same sense of back resonance, even though the sounds are not all velar ones. Poseidon wants to destroy Odysseus with storms for blinding his son, the Cyclops:

> Thus as he spake he collected the clouds and stirred up the ocean,
> Both hands seizing the trident, and wakened to fury the tempests,
> Every wind of the heaven. All covered and darkened with storm-rack
> Earth was at once and the sea, while down from the sky fell midnight.
> Wildly together they rushed – East, South, and the furious West Wind,
> Air-born Boreas too, with a huge wave rolling before him.

dramatic: resonance in the middle. This quality relates to the present moment of everyday reality. It can be practised using alveolar sounds like *n, d, t, l,* which give a dynamic forward resonance. This creates a sense of readiness for response and action (with the weight of the body shifted towards the balls of the feet), fitting for sharp and fast duologues that are like tennis matches or fencing.

Practise the alveolar placement with:
'No, don't tell me lies, tell me the truth!'
Sense your balance line through the Elastic Band and the need to affect the other person in the here and now.

Try these lines from Act 1 of John Osborne's *Look Back in Anger*:

> Jimmy: I don't think I could take Webster tonight.
> Alison: I thought you said he was the only person who spoke your language.
> Jimmy: So he is. Different dialect but same language. I like him. He's got bite, edge, drive –
> Alison: Enthusiasm.
> Jimmy: You've got it.

lyrical: resonance in the front. This quality relates to the personal and heartfelt. It can be practised using sounds in the lips like *b, m, w,* which can give a delicacy of resonance we need for poetry and poetic drama like Lorca's, where musicality of pitch range, strong use of imagery and emotional release is called for.

Practise the front placement with:

'Warm waves move over foam-washed pebbles' (from Barbara Bridgmont).

Sense how your lips, face and chest vibrate – enhance this by stroking and pummelling around the heart area.

Try these lines from *Love Poem* by Christina Rossetti:

My heart is like a singing bird
Whose nest is in a watered shoot;
My heart is like an apple tree
Whose boughs are bent with thickset fruit;
My heart is like a rainbow shell
That paddles in a halcyon sea;
My heart is gladder than all these
Because my love is come to me.

To get a stronger sense of how particular resonances fit particular types of writing, try speaking the above pieces with *inappropriate* resonance qualities, e.g. speak the epic line with a lyrical resonance or the dramatic line with an epic resonance. See how ridiculous this sounds – it can of course be used for comic effect.

Rudolf Steiner, born in 1861 in what is now Croatia, developed artistic, educational and social ideas aimed at promoting a healthier human society. He created *Eurythmy*, a movement form aiming to embody speech and song in visible form: archetypical movements and gestures correspond to every aspect of speech and music. Steiner also developed an approach to speech he called *Speechformation*, where speech aims to embody expressive and archetypal movement, the gesture of experience, images and sensory content of sounds. Michael Chekhov extended Steiner's work on gesture in his own approach to acting, creating a bridge between him and Stanislavski.

---

2. Resonating in different body areas

The following exercises, inspired by Kristin Linklater, explore resonance throughout the body via response to the experience of specific consonants and vowels – we should respond to each sound with 'whatever energy, mood, feeling, or emotion it wants from you, activating the body into movement as it goes through you' (*Freeing Shakespeare's Voice*: 23).

When you focus your awareness into different parts of the body you will find they all possess different qualities and sensations. For example, you might connect your pelvis with feelings of a sexual nature; your heart area with love and courage; and you might find that your solar plexus area is the home of centring, sensitivity, emotion, unity with your surroundings, confidence, etc. The vibration of the sounds below will have their own unique experience for every person – but there are some archetypal qualities to them, which we shall explore. The whole purpose is that we connect the sounds to a body experience, making physical and vocal expression of an acting impulse one thing.

We are going to connect the sounds to the energies of the *y-buzz* and the Elastic Band (see Exercises 2 and 3, the Y-buzz and Alarm clock, in the last chapter). So, rather than *ZOO-OO, WO-Oe, SHAW-AW* etc. (as in Chapter 1, *Freeing Shakespeare's Voice*), we will use the sounds *YOO, YOE, YAW,* etc. in order to create the sound in the centre of the mouth and make it travel through the vertical line of the body on the Elastic Band. The sound will then become three-dimensional and have its very own unique vibrations through the whole body. Rather than projecting anything onto it, we shall allow the unique resonance of each sound to work on *us*. We are also using the sounds as they are formed with a Standard English accent.

Preparation

Stand well aligned. Connect to your vocal root centre and your deep and freely flowing breathing rhythms along the Elastic Band. Your deep breath must be able to respond to impulse. You might want to go over Exercise 8 – *Exploring the root of your voice* – in Chapter 4; then do Exercise 1 – *Connecting to a centred onset* – in Chapter 5; followed by Exercise 2 – *The y-buzz* – in Chapter 6.

YOO

1 Start by sounding a *yyy* from your vocal root centre in an optimum pitch. Now sustain a descending *yyy* by involving the Elastic Band. Do Exercise 3 – *The Alarm Clock* in Chapter 6, shaking your body as you make small and fast steps while sounding on the *yyy* to free the vibrations of your voice. Do the same again while sirening up and down your pitch range.

2 Next explore the first sound in the scale, *YOOO,* as in 'you'. Make a full round sound by rounding the lips, pushing them forward, and hollowing the cheeks. Sustain the sound using your centred onset of sound and the Elastic Band.

To make a real connection between impulse and sound:

- Breathe your intention to sound *YOOO* through your solar plexus and down into your vocal root muscles.

- Wait for your out-breath impulse to kick in and for the vocal root muscles to respond. Ride the surfboard of your rooted centred onset of sound on the wave of your breath.

- Allow the *YOOO* to be drawn back against the spine and into the Elastic Band on your out-breath movement, sustaining the sound *YOOO* until it travels along the full length of the balance line of your body.

- Allow your pitch to descend and follow gravity. The breath becomes a river that picks up the vibrations of the sound and its quality.

As the sound descends along the Elastic Band you will probably find that your legs are starting to vibrate. Sense what qualities and emotions it may trigger; for example, determination, confidence, conviction. Don't project anything onto the sound – simply allow it to affect you and tell you what it is.

3   Look at body resonance in words with the sound *OOO*.

A vowel sound can pick up almost any quality depending on the meaning of the word it is part of. Try for example, 'We are doomed', imagining you're trapped under an avalanche. Try 'Spooky', imagining you're in a haunted graveyard. Now try 'What a cool room!', imagining a sunlit room painted in your favourite colours. Let your sense of the word and your imagined connection to it enter your solar plexus on the in-breath, and then release the word.

The sound *OO,* often dark and low, can transform into something light and bright – but may retain depth underneath because of its timbre. The more you bring breath and sound back towards the spine, the more you will connect to your imaginative impulse expressed through the sound.

4   Go back to your optimum pitch question and answer with 'Yes'. Now do a shorter version of the sound *YOOO*. Imagine you recognize someone and say 'It's you!' quite shortly on your centred onset of sound, so that it is simply spoken rather than sounded in a sustained manner. Your pitch range will respond to this recognition by going up or down in an intonation pattern that fits the thought.

We should now have the full body resonance of the sound *YOOO* combined with the centred onset of the spoken word 'you' while allowing the pitch range to find its full potential up and down the body.

5   Let's now sound *OOO* within a longer sentence – do this, and the other sentences that follow below, in a Standard English (RP) accent:

Who moved to the blue room with the view to the tombs?

Give yourself an imaginative impulse to say this sentence; for example, challenge someone, and use the vowels to enhance and communicate your sense of your circumstances.

YOE

Now do the same process on the sound *YOE*, as in 'roe'. Sustain the sound on the Elastic Band and centred onset of sound, as in 2 above, and sense where your body vibrates. You will probably find that the sound vibrates in the pelvis. Allow the vibrations to bring about sensations of sexiness, flamboyance or power, or any other quality you find connected to this area.

Try words like 'stoat', 'road', 'crow'. Say to someone you imagine: 'You are so slow', or 'She's always moaning.' Say 'No' or 'Oh no!' in response to an imaginative impulse. Allow the vowel sound and body resonance to communicate your situation.

Now, in response to an impulse, for example, to tease someone, say:
You low rogue! You were slow but you floated my boat.

YAW

Let's look at *YAW* as in 'raw'. *YAW* will probably vibrate in your solar plexus, and you might experience warm, radiant or impressionable qualities. This is the centre through which we take in the world on a sensory level. While trying to win someone's sympathy say:
The daughter-in-law had a plausibly awful rawness.

YOH

Now try the shorter sound *Yoh*, as in 'rot'. You may find that it vibrates in the sternum area of the chest. Say 'I am hot.' Then using your body resonance to express your response through the sounds, warn someone that:
On the rock the moss is soft.

YAA

You will probably find that *YAA*, as in 'task', vibrates in the heart area of the chest, possibly with qualities of compassion, love and openness. While trying to console someone say:
The last part will calm your heart.

Try the above sounds, building one on the other:
YOO YOE YAW YOH YAA
and let your body vibrate through legs, pelvis, solar plexus, chest and heart.

Now we are going to explore the head resonators with the sounds *YUH, YU-UH-UH, YA, YEH, YEY, YI, YEEE.* Make sure you still connect your impulse to a centred onset of sound and surf the wave of the breath through the Elastic Band. The higher up we move in the body the greater distance we are from the root of the centred onset of sound, and the more the upper end of the Elastic Band will have to come into play. In order to let the sounds release higher up through the head resonators of mouth, cheeks, cheekbones, eye sockets, forehead and crown of head, as described below, you will need to make sure that you also keep the lower end of the Elastic Band well rooted – then the whole spine can keep the resonance spaces of the body open, through which the energy of the vibrations need to be released. Your sound needs enough fuel to vibrate through the body, so you will need to be on your full breathing wave: the surfer needs a strong wave to enjoy a great ride!

YUH

So, let's apply the above steps to *YUH,* as in 'bun'. You will probably find it sits in the lips area, with a quality of defiance, haughtiness or ridicule. Say 'I love fun.' Then find an impulse, for example, to defend your conduct with:
I had such a hunger I plundered the buns from the oven.

YU-UH-UH

Now explore the body resonance for the sound *YU-UH-UH,* as in a yawn: take in breath to find a real yawn and then sound the yawn on a *YU-UH-UH* and let it vibrate in your oral cavity, creating a sense of openness in the mouth and soft palate. The qualities might be ones of appreciation, affirmation or amazement:
Lovely, wonderful.

YA

You might find that the sound *YA,* as in 'sad', vibrates in your cheeks. Enhance this feeling by imagining that the sound comes sideways out of both of your cheeks. Make a gesture with your fingers and hands to bounce it through the cheeks. Find your associations with the word 'sad' and say it from an imaginative impulse: 'It is really sad.' Now try to correct someone's false impression and say:
He was sad, but bad and bit of a lad.

YEH

Again, apply the above steps 2 to 5 to *YEH,* as in 'ten'. Explore the vibrations in the cheekbones. Release the sound using a finger gesture. Say 'never' on an impulse: imagine someone has made you an indecent offer to which you reply emphatically. Now try to excite someone with the key to a great riddle while saying:
Ten men from the West will never rend the chest.

YEY

Explore the body resonance of the sound *YEY,* as in 'way'. Sense it vibrate in the eye sockets. Use your index fingers to spiral the sound forwards on its release. Qualities here might be excitement, surprise, joy. Say 'Wait', demanding someone wait for you. Or greet someone joyfully with 'Hey' at a party. Imagine someone is about to run away from you:
Stay and wait, it's not too late!

YI

Now try *YI*, as in 'kid'. You might discover that the sound resonates through the forehead. Imagine you are a unicorn with a horn through the middle of the forehead and make a hand gesture following the horn forwards when releasing the sound, but as with all these head resonance areas, keep it rooted. Now find an impulse to say 'Kids.' Find your association with them, e.g. they are annoying or delightful. Make people laugh by revealing that:
The kitten hissed as the kid hit the bin with the stick.

YEE

Explore the resonance for this sound, as in 'glee', around the crown of your head. Imagine your favourite team or athlete has won and express joy, exhila-ration and ebullience through the sound *YEEE*. Get everyone to celebrate with:
See. See. She's reached the peak!

So, in summary, we have explored sounds and their body resonance, and then expressed them through an acting impulse into words and sentences. Rather than skipping over the sounds, we need to fully vibrate them. The sounds will carry your experience, and will also build your vocal expression and the size and conviction of your voice. Impulse, words, sounds, voice and body need to feel as one.

It is essential to connect this exercise to impulse work and not just to indulge in the vowel sounds for their own sake. The vowels sounds, although they have a unique sound and quality to them, will carry what you want to express through them and transform accordingly. They are the notes of the music, but the music will only unfold if the whole piece is grasped and experienced. If you focus on projecting the qualities of the vowels, as you are making them, through the words, your mind will be fixed self-consciously on this and not engage with language, meaning, action and situation. We need to *respond* rather than *explain* through the make-up of the words, and let the sound pick up and vibrate our experiences within the present moment.

Integration into acting

The range of sounds and resonance areas explored above is a guideline and it makes you aware of links between them. We can develop this sense through practice so that vowels flow freely and spontaneously through the body.

We now want you to explore a piece of text and allow the sounds to take you where they will without consciously thinking about them, allowing your imagination to trigger what happens.

The following is from *Ballad of the Drop in the Ocean* by Bertolt Brecht:

> The summer has arrived, and the summer sky
> Shines on you too.
> The water is warm, and in the warm water
> You too lie.
> On the green meadows you have
> Pitched your tents. The roads
> Heard your singing. The forest
> Welcomes you. So
>> You're no longer poor? There's more in the pot?
>> You're being cared for? Content with your lot?
>> So things are looking up, then? They're not:
>> It's a drop in the ocean, that's what.

* Start by imagining what gives rise to the words. Bring summer and what it means to you in terms of sensory stimuli into the space around you: warm balmy air, blue sky, richness of colours in trees and flowers, the sensation of sun on your skin, the sounds and smells, the lightness of being. Although you might be poor you can experience this splendour. Breathe in the stimuli around you through your solar plexus until you feel prompted to speak the words:

> The summer has arrived, and the summer sky

Shines on you too.

Imagine you are swimming in a lake. The water is warm. You lie in a shallow bit and enjoy the pleasure of the water on your skin. Go with this sensation of touch.

The water is warm, and in the warm water
You too lie.

Now picture meadows with summer flowers and a place where you have pitched your tent. Imagine the noises of bees in the flowers; of birds singing; see butterflies. Enjoy the calm natural feeling and the sense of time spreading out in front of you. You don't have to go home, you can stay the night.

On the green meadows you have
Pitched your tents.

As you walk around you are in a carefree mood and sing a song. What is this song you would sing? What melody, rhythm and words are triggered by the surroundings?

The roads
Heard your singing.

You are drawn into a forest with its cool fresh air. What is the sensation of smelling oxygen created by the trees, the pines or leafy beech trees? How does your solar plexus and in-breath respond?

The forest
Welcomes you.

* Now you have set up these sensory stimuli, go through this part of the verse again and only speak the vowel sounds.

Start with the word 'summer' and explore what triggers it again but this time only respond on your out-breath wave through the two vowel sounds. This will create a space and vibrations that communicate your experience of this particular moment. Go through all the words like this, and communicate the thought in the lines through the vowels alone. Allow your vowels to be an immediate response to your impulses.

> To allow the vowel energy of a word to run through the body, always do this process:
> * Imagine the solar plexus is a funnel for the experience of the whole body.
> * Sense the vowel being absorbed through it and release it on your centred onset surfing the wave of your out-breath and backwards against the spine.
> * Solar plexus, breath and spine then really connect with the vowel and what it expresses and create a richly resonant tone.

* Now go through the full lines in this section with the same sense of the body resonance triggered by the vowels and imaginary stimuli.

* In the next section of the poem the carefree attitude is destroyed by a reality check, with provocative questions asked by Brecht. As soon as we have been enriched by nature at its best, we are now impoverished by the reality of inequality between people:

So
You're no longer poor? There's more in the pot?
You're being cared for? Content with your lot?
So things are looking up, then? They're not:
It's a drop in the ocean, that's what.

Explore the subtext behind this in the same way as before by creating images and sensory stimuli and then speaking the lines. Picture your bare house, your bare kitchen, your sparse meals. Look at the bicycle that carried you and your humble tent to the meadow. Watch a rich family drive by in their fancy car in complete comfort. How does this emotionally resonate with you? Sense the bitterness that creeps in and makes you forget your small blessings as nature becomes not so glamorous. Allow these feelings to resonate through the lines.

* Now respond through the vowel sounds alone, as above.
The *YOH* sound as in 'pot' and 'poverty' is frequent in this section of the poem and can enhance the sense of disenchantment that poverty brings. So, really connect to the resonance of this sound to help you vibrate the experience.

* Go through the whole lines again.

* Next, let's look at what Brecht intends to do to the audience with this poem. He addresses 'you' instead of 'I'. He wants to stir the audience into action rather than letting them make do with little moments of pleasure.

Place the audience in the idyllic scene you've imagined for yourself. Make the audience the reason for speaking the poem and play the objective: *I want to make you wake up from your dream in this idyll and get back to the fight for equality.*

Breathe in both the audience and their circumstances and connect with your pelvic floor and spine to speak the actions to sober, provoke, stir and galvanize the audience into waking up again to the fight at hand. So use your own explored experience but place the audience into it and connect your images to different places within the audience.

Now just focus on the vowel sounds to work on the audience, and then string all the lines together, keeping the sense of body resonance within your objective and actions.

You should find that you are now vibrating with your whole body resonance through the vowels without thinking about it: we receive with imagination, impulse, in-breath, and respond with out-breath, vocal support, and the objective filled with body resonance.

The idea that sounds resonate in different body parts is not new. Eastern disciplines such as Yoga and Tao have used sounds resonating in different chakras and organs since ancient times. Dennis Lewis relates that in ancient Tao breathing practice, six sounds are related to the major organ systems of the body and their associated energy channels (*The Tao of Breath*: 158).

In Steiner's *Speechformation*, vowels are connected to the energy of planets and harmonizing the organs' energies, and focus is placed on letting the sound tell you where it lives in the body. In his Eurythmy movement practice, vowels have specific gestures and spaces that are physically performed, e.g. *eee* is a vertical line that goes from the crown of the head down into the feet like a ray of light; *ah* is in the heart region and opens into the world by spreading the arms outwards; *oh* is a circular movement; *ooo* is a narrow searching gesture made with arms and hands.

Arthur Lessac's work on Vocal NRG states (vocal energies of consonantal NRG, structural vowel NRG and tonal Y-buzz NRG) connects sounds viscerally to experience. For example, his consonantal orchestra allocates different consonants to different instruments, e.g. N for violin, T for snare drum, L for saxophone.

'The human body is a musical apparatus capable of great precision and versatility: it can register, remember, implement, and play itself creatively. But humans, so used to masterly manipulating and controlling other instruments, seldom apply the same expertise to play their own inner *vocal life* instruments ... Any human voice can range from light, high, and bright to deep, rich, and dark. It can express sorrow, anger, melancholy, and joy in both speech and song and can adapt itself so well to each emotion that it seems the ideal instrument for each expression. Like any instrument, the body Stradivarius must be played with skill and artistry if most of the possibilities are to be realised' (see Chapter 5, *The Use and Training of the Human Voice*: 61).

Lessac considers his work as 'full-blown and ongoing actor training; actor training on "feeling" – instinctively, viscerally through the senses – and experiencing vocal, physical, and emotional characterisation and personality' (*The Use and Training of the Human Voice*: 244).

Various practitioners want to link sounds in speech with the actor's physical experience through the resonance. While this is an absolutely vital point, this work cannot be done truthfully if it is not connected to the impulse of the actor when acting. If done separately, the result may be a richly vibrating and physically committed sound but it will not communicate the experience of the actor as the character within the given circumstances – and again we hear a gap between the actor and the text.

To sum up:

- **Resonance is the means through which the sound produced by vibrations of the vocal folds is amplified and re-sounded and given full tonal expression.**
- **Resonance spaces need to be open and the actor must be free of tension for resonance to happen fully.**

- Breath creates a link to our experiences and emotions, which resonance helps to communicate. Vowels are particularly useful for resonance since they have different frequencies that will vibrate most in particular resonance areas of the body.

- Vibrating sound through our whole body resonance connects us with our creative mind and communicates a subtlety in text and experience that goes beyond the words and their literal meaning.

- Resonance of sounds carries the acting impulses of the actor.

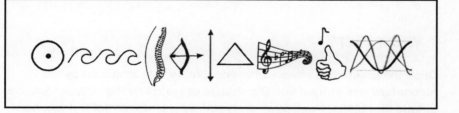

8

ARTICULATION – SHAPING THOUGHT AND ACTION

WHAT IS IT?

Once the breath has vibrated the vocal folds, it is amplified by the resonators and formed into the shapes of words by the articulators: the tongue (tip, blade, front, back and root), lips, teeth, alveolar ridge, hard palate, soft palate and pharynx. To communicate efficiently we alter these shapes fluidly and quickly in order to form sounds that become words; words that become sentences; and sentences that become whole units of thought.

What is it for the actor?

Without clear articulation the actor cannot communicate language. Learning it is very much a *left* brain function. Each letter, syllable, word, phrase and sentence is important for conveying meaning. If we miss sounds it's like dropping notes in a piece of music or cutting words in a book. We will fragment the flow of sense. Clear articulation must also carry each imaginative impulse of the actor, and express not only the meaning of sentences but the whole story of a text and its circumstances, relationships and emotional and sensory qualities. Poor articulation will break the attention and understanding of the audience and alienate them from the actor, their action and inner life. It is often an acting problem: the result of lack of clarity of thought, of the meaning of the language and the character's objectives and actions, or of lack of confidence. If clarity of meaning *is* there but speech is still not clear, then you have a speech problem, and work needs to be done on the articulators to produce ease, flow, clarity and full expression.

Articulation is also a key element in determining accents and dialects, which vocally define a character's particular background. Words of the same language are pronounced differently according to different geography, history, culture, climate, social class, occupation, age, gender, fashion and educational background. Unconvincing accent skills break the audience's belief in the authenticity of the character's origins (see Chapter 13, Character Voice).

How it works

The articulators

These consist of *fixed* and *mobile* structures.

- **Fixed** These are *the teeth, the alveolar ridge (upper gum-ridge)* and *the hard palate* and they support the movements of the mobile articulators.
- **Mobile** These are the *lower jaw, the lips (*and *cheeks), the tongue* and *the soft palate*. They are each controlled by different sets of muscles: for example, the lips have five sets of muscles (ten in all) controlling their shape and movement; the tongue has extrinsic muscles attaching it to the back of the mouth, including the soft palate and the pharynx, and four paired sets of intrinsic muscles within the tongue itself.

The lips and tongue are the main areas governing clear, defined sounds with maximum resonance. Any tensions in the lips will distort articulation, and tongue tension will affect the shape of the space in the mouth, the position of the soft palate and larynx and damage both articulation and resonance. The lips and tongue should work independently of the jaw, which can distort sound through clenching, protruding, opening too far or sliding to the side, and so needs to be used with ease and economy.

Speech sounds

These consist of *consonants* and *vowels*. Examples we give below relate to neutral standard speech (RP).

Vowels

'The most common view is that vowels are sounds in which there is no obstruction to the flow of air as it passes from the larynx to the lips' (*English Phonetics and Phonology,* Peter Roach: 10). They are formed in the vocal tract by the tongue and the lips, and consist of:

long vowels, such as *OO* as in room, *AH* as in rather, *EE* as in greet, *ER* as in bird and *AW* as in law;

short vowels, such as *u* as in hood, *uh* as in hut, *eh* as in pet, *i* as in sit, *a* as in cat, *o* as in hot, and a schwa as in broth-*er*;

diphthongs (a glide from one vowel to another), such as *ow* in loud or *ear* in pierce.

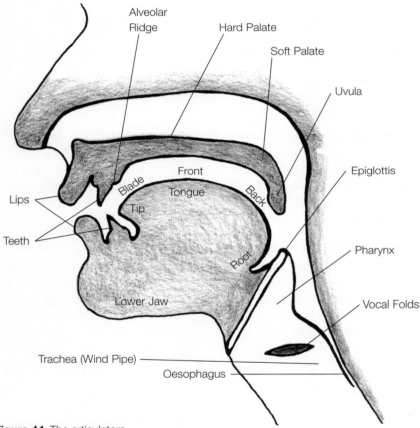

Figure 44 The articulators
        Fixed: teeth, alveolar ridge (upper gum-ridge), hard palate
        Mobile: lower jaw, lips (and cheeks), tongue, soft palate

Consonants

These frame the vowels so that full words are formed. Consonants are created in a variety of ways and with or without sound from the larynx, so they are voiced or voiceless – for example, *s* as in soup is voiceless and *z* as in zebra is voiced.

We distinguish between, for example, plosives, fricatives, affricates, approximants and nasal sounds. These describe in what way the articulators work with each other.

- Plosives are formed when two articulators are moved together to compress air and when released create a noise called *plosion,* as with *p, k, t, d, b, g* – e.g. **P**eter **t**ook the **d**og **b**ack **t**o the **g**arage.

- Fricatives are formed by air escaping through a small passage and making a hissing sound, as with *f, s, h, v, z, sh,* a voiced *th* as in feather*,* a devoiced *th* as in thing – e.g. The **fish**erman in **h**is lea**th**er apron **h**auled an ama**z**ing **th**ing onto **th**e **sh**ip.

- Affricates are sounds that begin as plosives and end as fricatives, as with *tsh* in chalk or *dg* as in congeal – e.g. The **judg**e and **j**ailer are like **ch**alk and **ch**eese.

- Approximants are consonants where the articulators approach each other but do not close completely, as with *y* in yellow, *w* in water, and *r* in rush – e.g. The **y**oung **r**unner **w**ent into the **w**ater.

- A lateral approximant, as with a light *l*, is unusual because the air flow is directed laterally over the sides of the tongue, instead of down the middle, as with laugh, lend or hilly – e.g. **L**ook at that **l**ovely c**l**oud above the hi**lly l**andscape. (A dark *l*, on the other hand*,* is used before a consonant, as in milk or sell, and is velar, formed by raising the back of the tongue towards the soft palate, e.g. Hold that eel! It's for our mea**l**.)

- Nasals are formed in the nasal cavity, as with *m, n, ng* – e.g. The so**ng**bird sa**ng** in the **m**or**n**ing.

Through *phonetics,* the general theory of speech sounds and how they are used in language, we can analyze sounds for their accuracy and also channel them into different accents, so this can be of considerable use in actor training.

Mastering articulation and accents, however, constitutes a whole area of training in itself. Actors must explore the formation of every vowel and consonant through regular exercise of the articulators and muscles involved, so that the process of communicating words and thoughts becomes reflexive – like a pianist doing scales or a ballet dancer exercising on the barre, enabling mental focus and muscles to become toned and responsive when in performance. The resonance of vowels and consonants in a word needs to be balanced. Clear speech is not limited to what is happening in the mouth, but should connect to body, breath and acting impulses. Changing accent and owning it convincingly is another challenge for the versatile actor. It also requires a lot of skill to fill a variety of theatre spaces with clear and resonant speech (see Chapter 14, The actor in the space).

However, a detailed examination of phonetics, accents and dialects, and articulation of every word sound is outside the scope of this book. We are concerned here with articulation as an easy, clear expression of acting impulses.

We shall give only a few examples of exercises in key areas, and recommend that you look at additional books for more exercises, for example: *Vocal Arts Workbook*, David and Rebecca Clark Carey, Chapter 5, pp. 162–89; *The Voice Book*, Michael McCallion, Speech, pp.125–90; *Voice & Speech in the Theatre*, Clifford Turner, Chapter 5: The Word, pp. 66–102; and *HOW TO DO ACCENTS* and *HOW TO DO Standard English ACCENTS,* Edda Sharpe and Jan Haydn Rowles. There are other relevant books in our bibliography.

Our symbol for clear articulation is a bell:

EXERCISES

Exercising the articulators

1. Preparing the articulators

Release jaw – First massage your jaw hinges, especially the area between your temples and the ears. Induce a yawn into the back of the soft palate, releasing and dropping the jaw. Continue the massage all the way down the jaw line.

Make sure the jaw is released: fold your hands together and shake them, prompting your jaw, lips and cheeks to shake, and make a *huuh* sound. Keep the lower jaw loose and take it between finger and thumb and gently move it from side to side and up and down

Wake up facial muscles – Give your whole face a massage. Start with the jaw, and extend it to the forehead, the top and back of the skull and down to the neck. Knead the eyebrows, and massage the sinuses and cheekbones. Rub your lips and cheeks. Rub your hands together, creating warmth and energy, then stroke them down over the whole face.

Stretch and release the tongue

- Place the tongue tip behind the bottom teeth. On an out-breath, rock the middle of the tongue forwards, stretching it as far as it will go in front of the lips. As you do this, release the jaw, lengthen your body along the balance line, and drop the tailbone, on an in-breath, allow your tongue to come back and naturally sit in the mouth, while bending the knees and letting your exhaling muscles relax.

Now do this again with the intention of scaring someone with your face as you extend your tongue. Raise your arms above your head as you lengthen your body (imagine you're a spitting cobra!).

- Drop the jaw and stick the tongue out straight and retract it several times.
  Flick the tongue up and down inside the mouth with the lips closed.
  Flick the tongue tip quickly side to side between open lips, like a lizard.
  Make a U-shape with the tongue between the lips.
  Stretch the tongue up to the nose, down to the chin, and to the sides of each cheek.

- Put your thumbs under your chin and gently massage the spongy tissue you will feel there – this is the actual root of your tongue.

Loosen and alert the lips – Put your little fingers into the corners of the lips and stretch them gently to the side and up and down. Take your lips in between your fingers and massage, pull them forwards and extend this into the cheeks, pinching them. Blow through open lips so they vibrate, like a horse blowing. Purse your lips tightly and make slow kissing movements.

Raise and lower the soft palate – Most sounds are resonated in the oral cavity only, with the soft palate raised to close the passage to the nose. However, the *n, m* and *ng* sounds are nasal sounds, and resonate in the open nasal passage, with the soft palate lowered.

To close the passage to the nose, put the back of your tongue against the soft palate and make a *k* sound. This will make your soft palate close your nasal passage. Now make a *g* sound and release through an *ah*, letting it resonate in the oral cavity only. The soft palate is raised here. Test the effect of this: squeeze the nose closed when sounding *ah* – it should not affect the sound of *ah* in the mouth.

To open the nasal passage, make a *mmm,* a *nnn* and a *ng sound* and feel the vibrations in the nose. Now say *Name a knight of Normandy. Name a Norman Knight*. This sentence is full of nasal sounds. If you squeeze your nose closed whilst saying this it will block your sound.

To create a swift change between a raised or lowered soft palate sound *ng* and open into an *ah* sound. Here your soft palate starts by hanging down, opening the nasal passage on the *ng* sound, and lifts up closing nasal passage on the ah sound. If the soft palate is lazy, nasality will occur on non-nasal sounds.

Contract and expand – Make your face and whole body tiny and scrunched up. Then expand everything to make yourself as big as possible. Open and widen your face and mouth as much as possible.

To sum up: your jaw should be loose, your lips and cheeks released, your tongue flexible and your soft palate responsive.

2. Playing with the articulators – 'articulatory agility is a desirable ability ...'

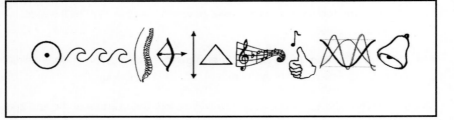

1. Create more space in the mouth

Drop the jaw and stick your tongue out. In this position and as clearly as possible, with your pelvic floor and spinal drive engaged, say 'Humpty Dumpty sat on a wall.'

2. Consonants to a rhythm

Choose any consonant described above, for example *b, m, d, l, z, k.* Now explore your agility forming the consonant in a rhythmical pattern such as:
bbb-bbb-bbb-ba
mmm-mmm-mmm-ma
ddd-ddd-ddd-da.

Use good support and engage into the Elastic Band so you feel your whole body is involved in making the sound. Articulation will benefit in clarity, tone and resonance if you imagine the spine as a magnet drawing the sounds to your core support.

3. Front, middle and back placements

Try the following sounds, making the transitions from front to middle to back swiftly and easily:
b-d-g, g-d-b or p-t-k, k-t-p and repeat several times

Now do this imagining you are playing the drums on a large drum set and involve your whole body in the sounds. Keep your arms released but your spine and pelvic floor rooted and strong. Put your back into it: imagine the consonants are glued to the lumbar spine as it drives them on the out-breath wave. This will give them more resonance.

4. Consonantal jazz

Use a mixture of any consonants, and create jazzy tunes to tone your articulators. Use different pitch range, resonance, rhythm and tempo as you find different combinations of consonants, whether fricatives or plosives, etc.

Once everything is warmed up and buzzing, try simple word constellations like *My baby is so blue today, my b-b-b-baby is so blue to-d-d-d-d-d-day.*

As above, engage your pelvic floor and lumbar spine when driving the sounds on your out-breath. Make sure that you are rooted physically by engaging into the Elastic Band.

5. Embodying vowel sounds

See the vowel exercises from Chapter 7, Resonance – we explored the resonance created in the body by every vowel, and gave each vowel a practice sentence.

6. Consonantal combinations

This exercise is from Clifford Turner's *Voice and Speech in the Theatre* (78), and is designed to create clarity of consonants through accurate movement of the tongue from position to position, and firm contact and sharp release of the articulators.

Stay rooted in the pelvic floor and engage your spinal support and Elastic Band. Imagine the consonants are glued to the spine.

OOP OHP AWP AHP AYP EEP
OOB OHB AWB AHB AYB EEB

OOPT OHPT AWPT AHPT AYPT EEPT
OOSPT OHSPT AWSPT AHSPT AYSPT EESPT

OOT OHT AWT AHT AYT EET
OOD OHD AWD AHD AYD EED

OOST OHST AWST AHST AYST EEST
OOZD OHZD AWZD AHZD AYZD EEZD

OOSTS OHSTS AWSTS AHSTS AYSTS EESTS

In well-articulated speech, the vowels and consonants are balanced and the tone is fully resonant.

Vowel energy: connect your out-breath wave only to the vowels until they flow easily and with full resonance. The lumbar spine should drive the out-breath wave through the vowel spaces and the pelvic floor root the breath and onset of sound. Make sure that you don't start with a glottal onset.

Consonantal energy: speak only the consonants and imagine them glued to your spine and pelvic floor as you drive them out on the out-breath.

Now go back to speaking the combinations. The vowels should flow on the breath and the consonants be rooted, crisp and precise.

Also, try starting with the consonants and flow into the vowels, e.g.

POO POH PAW PAY PEE etc.

Tonal Energy: tonal energy is achieved by activating the vibrations of a sound like *yyyyy*, Lessac's Y-buzz, which focuses sound into the hard palate and front of the mouth, creates a clear, supported onset, transmits sound along the Elastic Band balance line, and reaches with clarity into the space.

Do the above exercise again and imagine that each vowel travels along the Elastic Band. This will expand each vowel into a vertical line from the floor to the ceiling. Use your lumbar spine and pelvic floor as a driving force. The outcome will be an asserted and fully resonating sound.

7. Consonantal repetition

Here are two examples, using B and M:

B: Battered, broken and bound brothers! Beat back the bloody bands of blazing, bedevilled beasts, who besmirch our beautiful borders!

M: Many of you moaning mortal masters must mix meaningful moments in multifarious measures of music made for meandering past morbid musings.

Speak these sentences on your rooted, supported breathing wave with agility and clarity.

Play an objective – this will give your muscles and your breath a direction: needing to achieve something creates an urgency to be clear. Often when articulation is not clear, the necessary muscularity is missing because the speaker lacks intention.

Stand against a wall with your knees bent, your lumbar area pressing lightly into the wall and your weight rooted in the balls of the feet. Head and neck should be away from the wall, free and well aligned.

With the B sentence, play the objective *to stir people to resist the enemy* as if you were a political speaker. Visualize the audience that you want to stir up. Breathe the audience and your objective into your solar plexus, pelvic floor and lumbar spine. When you are ready to respond to the impulse, sense the pelvic floor muscles rooting your onset and the readiness of your lumbar spine to send the intention on the out-breath wave to the imagined audience. Your lumbar spine should press into the wall for support when driving your out-breath. Sense how your feet root against the floor and how your body engages into the Elastic Band for support. Feel the need to use the consonants to convey the clarity of your objective and message. Imagine the consonants are glued to your lumbar spine, which should be one with your strength of conviction, driving your message home to your audience. Your vowels should be freely flowing.

Do the same again but step away from the wall. Stay rooted, keep the lumbar drive going and engage the Elastic Band.

Try the M exercise against the wall. Play the softer objective *of soothing people away from dark thoughts*. Engage the pelvic floor and lumbar drive as above and communicate the soothing quality with strength.

Now, while playing the two objectives above, apply in turn the vowel, consonantal and tonal energy from the previous exercise and sense what quality each gives you.

8. Moulding

Mould words as if they are clay, offering resistance in the space.
For example, mould *A big brown bear* as you speak it. Use your arms and body to make the shape of the bear in the air, keeping your arms easy and your spine rooted and strong.
Try *A cruel cold king.*
Mould *A tall trembling tree shaking in the hurricane.*
Create not only the shape but the elements as well.

9. Vowel sounds

Practise the following word progression from Clifford Turner in front of a mirror in order to see how vowels are shaped (again, within a Standard English accent).

Through good tone all not part must serve and then shape fit speech.
    OO   u   oh aw o AH uh   ER   a   eh   ay   i   EE

See how your lips move from strongly pursed lips (*OO* in through) into increasingly open lips until you reach the most open position (*AH* in part). As you continue to say *must serve and then shape fit speech*, see how your tongue rises higher, decreasing the space in your mouth (*Voice and Speech in the Theatre*: 37).

Integration into acting

1. Action qualities

Try doing some tongue-twisters – but with a particular quality of speech and movement, for example:

Imagine an imaginary menagerie, so that the words and your whole body are **floating** through the air like feathers. Find a light, indirect and sustained drifting movement through the words.

Rubber baby buggy bumpers, **punching and thrusting** with each word through the space, in a strong, direct and sudden manner.

Are you copperbottoming 'em, my man? No, I'm aluminiuming 'em, mum, **slashing** with the words and your movements. Make the movement through the words strong, indirect, quick and sudden.

The swimming swans swam on the sea, **gliding** over still waters in a light, direct, smooth and flowing sustained way.

Gigwip, gigwip, **wringing** and twisting the sounds and your body in a strong, indirect and sustained movement.

Unique New York, New York unique, **dabbing** in a light, direct and quick manner.

The sixth sheik's sixth sheep's sick, **pressing** in a strong, direct and sustained way.

I'm a critical cricket critic, **flicking** through the space in a light, indirect and quick movement.

These various qualities were defined by Rudolf Laban in his analysis of movement as being based on weight, space and time, They are called *effort actions,* and we look at them in more detail in Chapter 13, Character Voice.

2. Physical actions in storytelling

Here we look at sharpening and embodying articulation by physicalizing the sounds, so that clarity of speech is not just stuck in the head. The sounds *are* movement and action and have a dynamic we need to express.

The following is from *The Birds* by Daphne du Maurier:

> He seized a blanket from the nearest bed, and using it as a weapon flung it to the right and left about him in the air … The blanket became a weapon of defence; he wound it about his head, and then in greater darkness beat at the birds with his bare hands.

In this story, people are being attacked by aggressive birds, as in Hitchcock's film – visualize this situation and the man's need to defend himself.

First, do the actions to seize, to fling, to wind, to beat that are there in the text.

Then do the actions as you say the words in order to embody them and conjure up the situation (go slowly if you need to, especially if you find your voice is tensing because of the drama).

Now, see the situation as if you're seeing a film, and describe what you see without the gestures. Make sure the physical dynamic is fully communicated through every vowel, consonant and syllable.

It's important to speak with the whole body: breathe the circumstances and actions into your solar plexus, pelvic floor and lumbar spine, and drive your response through your out-breath wave while engaging the Elastic Band.

3. Physical and verbal actions in dialogue

Here the focus is on giving articulation the weight of meaning, by meaning what you say.

Invite someone to sit down, making the appropriate welcoming gesture as you speak:
Please, sit down.

Repel someone who has offended you, sweeping them away with a gesture:
Get out of my sight!

Implore someone to come on a trip with you, and make the accompanying appealing gesture:
Come with me, please. You did promise.

Clarity of thought and action will maximize your chances of articulating clearly. The expression of the words and sounds must come from circumstances, meaning, intention and action.

Here are some lines from Shakespeare, with crackling consonants and elongated vowels, through which emotion and words are inextricably tied:
Leontes, in *The Winter's Tale*, Act 1, Sc 2, accuses himself of being a cuckold:
Inch-thick, knee-deep, o'er head and ears a forked one!

He is convinced that that his wife, Hermione, is having an affair with his friend, Polixenes. Imagine the two walking in the garden, arm in arm. Breathe in the circumstances and root into your pelvic floor and spinal support.

Explore the consonantal energy: with your consonants glued to the pelvic floor and spine, drive your self-accusing action through your out-breath, *tasting* the consonants. There are a number of plosives here that give a bitter taste and a sense of hitting against obstacles.

Explore the vowel energy: play your action on the out-breath wave through the vowels only, until they flow easily and with full resonance. Engage your lumbar spine to drive the out-breath wave through the vowel spaces and your pelvic floor to root breath and onset of sound. Make sure that you don't start with a glottal onset. Short vowels are followed by long, elongated ones: the repeated short *I* and long *EE* sounds are followed by the longer *AW* and *AA* sound, creating a disgusted quality. Let the vowels respond to the situation and sense the tale they tell.

Explore the tonal energy: imagine the vowels travelling along the Elastic Band. This will expand each vowel into a vertical line from the floor to the ceiling. Use your lumbar spine and pelvic floor as a driving force. The outcome will be an asserted and fully resonating sound.

Now try the same process on the lines below:

Macbeth curses his servant as the enemy approaches:

> The devil damn thee black, thou cream-faced loon!
> Where got'st thou that goose look?

Kate and Petruchio try to get the better of each other in *The Taming of the Shrew*:

> Kate: What is your crest, a coxcomb?
> Pet: A combless cock, so Kate will be my hen.
> Kate: No cock of mine, you crow too like a craven.

All such lines will only come to life if the intensity of the circumstances is absorbed and embodied and used to bite into the targets of attack. And for that to happen, the words need to ride on a strong out-breath supported by the pelvic floor and a rooted and lengthening spine. All the vocal elements we've looked at so far need to cohere in the process of articulation.

To sum up:

- Articulation is the formation of shapes of words by fixed and mobile articulators to produce meaning through units of thought.

- It allows full expression of emotional and sensory experience, the full 'life of the human spirit' of the character.

- Without clear articulation we fragment the flow of sense and break the link with the audience.

- Different types of articulation resulting from, for example, accent and dialect, class and culture, fashion and education, give insight into character.

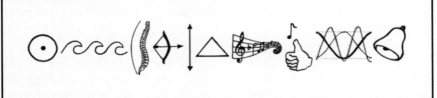

* * *

The *Vocal Givens* in symbols

In the table below we summarize the Essential Vocal Six, which we shall remind you about as we go through the acting process in the rest of the book. We'll refer to them as the *Vocal Givens*, because they should always be in place when speaking as an actor.

Vocal Given	Symbol	Where is it?	Exercises
Alignment Vocal strength and backbone rooted in the core muscles and Elastic Band of the Spine		Sacral curve and coccyx Lumbar curve Thoracic curve Cervical curve Erector spinae muscles Psoas muscles Elastic Band: gravity and anti-gravity force	Chapter 3 Prelude to 6

Breath
The voice rides the wave of the breath freely flowing through the body and creatively connecting us
		Diaphragm
		Abdominals:
		    external obliques
		    internal obliques
		    transversus
		    abdominis
		Quadratus Lumborum
		Pelvic floor
		Intercostals:
		    external
		    internal
		    innermost
		Lumbar area and Elastic Band in the spine
			Chapter 4
			1 to 14

Centred Onset of Sound A needlepoint clarity and focus supported by the rock of vocal muscles and spinal support, the vocal identity of 'Me/I'		Vocal folds Diaphragm Abdominals Pelvic floor Lumbar area and Elastic Band in the spine	Chapter 5 Prelude to 6

Pitch Range
The musicality of intuitive expression of impulse and meaning
 	
Optimum Pitch
The pitch around the middle of the range that gives the most easy, natural and supported tone
		Vocal folds
		Laryngeal muscles:
		Extrinsic
		Intrinsic:
		    thyroarytenoid
		    crycothyroid
			Chapter 6
			1 to 5

Resonance Vibrating the experience through sound and language in the resonance areas of the body		Open released spaces of the mouth, nose and pharynx Vibrations in the spine and whole body Vocal folds	Chapter 7 1 to 2

Vocal Given	Symbol	Where is it?	Exercises

Articulation
Clarity and muscularity
    in the shaping of
    consonants and vowels
    into thought and action
		The fixed and mobile
		    articulators
		Resonance spaces
		Vocal folds
			Chapter 8
			Articulators:
			    1 to 2
			Integration:
			    1 to 3

Symbols for Receiving and Responding are:

Receiving
Breathing an impulse
    into the solar plexus
    and connecting to
    circumstances
		Diaphragm
		Pelvic floor
		Intercostals

Responding Transfer of acting impulse into muscular response		Pelvic floor Abdominals Lumbar area and Elastic Band in the spine Intercostals Vocal folds Laryngeal muscles Resonance spaces Articulators

PART THREE

INTEGRATING VOICE INTO THE ORGANIC ACTING PROCESS

INTRODUCTION

In Part Three, we focus on integrating voice into key aspects of the Organic acting approach. As we summarized at the start of Chapter 1, these are:

Receiving and responding – the vocal and acting core of this approach that mirrors our natural process of living.

Awareness, ease and focus – we learn about the world through greater awareness, and we gain the ability to express our understanding through developing an easy focus through alignment, breath and centred onset.

The action – we explore 'the dynamics of action' created by breathing in the circumstances, responding with the voice during interactions, and supporting and driving objectives with the spine.

Seeing, sensing and feeling – in performance we see the past, present and future, and we'll focus on spontaneous vocal response to images and to sensory and emotional experience.

Character voice – we explore the elements in the text and imaginary world of the play that make up an individual voice.

The actor in the space – we look at different spaces and how to adapt, to prepare with others and focus for the audience.

HOW TO WORK

1 Work with ease, openness and positivity.
2 Warm up before doing exercises.
3 Work in an undisturbed and unpressured environment.
4 Keep all the Essential Vocal Six as *Vocal Givens* when doing acting exercises in each chapter – keep the link to voice.
5 Watch out for symbols – remind yourself of what should be in place vocally.
6 Revisit earlier chapters and exercises to work on elements that are not clear to you.

The acting elements we focus on here are essential for good performance and should become *Acting Givens*.

9
INTERVAL – RECEIVING AND RESPONDING

In Part One, we set out our aim of integrating the organic acting approach and the voice and looked at the brain's functioning in relation to this approach. In Part Two, we explained the essentials of vocal production in relation to acting.

Some of the basic principles from these Parts are summarized below before we move on to specific elements in the acting process.

Two travellers

Two travellers set out on a journey.

One is only interested in getting the journey planned, and is busy organizing train times, checking maps and guide books, finding the hotel's location, hiring a car. Time is tight and he wants to get as much out of the trip as he can. He books himself on sightseeing tours and will be able to tell you all there is to see and do and how to fill every moment of every day. He is ahead of the game. He uses his logical analytical brain as a guide.

The other takes in photos of the destination and local art, music, theatre and cuisine. Having arrived, he can't wait to leave the luggage and go for a walk to absorb the atmosphere. He breathes in the sea air, flowers and herbs, takes in the mountains, soaks in the sun and tastes the food. He forgets time and direction and gives himself to the new experience like a child. He is in the experience. He is in his senses, imagination and feelings.

We can be both these travellers.

The story shows the contrasting ways of processing information within our brain, through the *left* logical brain and the *right* creative brain, through endgaming and through receptivity. With one we give ourselves a direction and with the other we enter the present moment of experience. The endgaming brain can lead us towards shallow, rushed breath, taken high in the body. This can create tensions and cuts us off from full experience. The creative brain involves imagination, physical, sensory and emotional response. The breath associated with this is centred, calm and deep, the natural breath which is allowed to come in and out of the body freely and easily.

The following overview reiterates what each side of the brain deals with and how both are needed by the actor.

The Left Brain:

- has a narrow, specific focus;
- asserts control and plans work, using the intellect, logic and rationalization;
- analyzes the meaning of language;
- identifies facts and categories.

The Right Brain:

- has a broad focus and overview of a realistic, three-dimensional world;
- focuses on creativity, imagination, intuition, sensory and emotional experience of life;
- interprets non-literal aspects of language and expresses imaginary circumstances and character;
- is empathic and linked to the body, emotions, the Old Brain, the unconscious and the receptivity of the solar plexus.

From the first two parts of this book we can take the following as objectives for voice through organic acting:

- To integrate mind, feelings, will, imagination, body and voice into one whole psycho-physical process.
- To harmonize the processes of left and right brain functioning, so that the logical analyzing brain yields creative control to the right and old brain.
- To explore the role of the breath, its *receiving* and *responding* qualities, and how the impulses from this affect the other elements of the Essential Vocal Six; to explore how breath connects us to our deepest

emotional responses, sensual awareness, experiences and imagination, and then to our expression of these elements.

- To explore the voice as a natural and organic expression of the actor in the circumstances of the character, a voice that conveys the character's experience.

- To make language come to life as a need to speak in the imaginary circumstances.

Receiving and responding

The creation of something new is not accomplished by the intellect but by the play instinct acting from inner necessity. The creative mind plays with the objects it loves.

CARL JUNG (quoted in *Free Play, Improvisation in Life and Art*, STEPHEN NACHMANOVITCH: 42)

A principle running through this book, and introduced in Chapter 4 on Breath, is that of receiving and absorbing on the one hand, and responding or giving, acting, sending, radiating, transmitting, asserting, on the other. The two systems are constantly at work in life and in art, informing and adapting to each other, just like breathing in and breathing out.

In the process of *receiving*, we absorb imaginative influences that lead to *responding* and action. It is essential to work from impulse to engage both the voice and the acting process in the words and action with truth and conviction. The voice needs to be a natural and organic expression of the actor in the circumstances of the character. In the process of receiving impulses and responding to them within the present moment, we bypass the cerebral and endgaming focus on deciding how to say the text, and focus instead on exploring the world it expresses and discover imaginatively how to say it.

As we have seen in Chapter 1, to *experience* a role we need to use *ourselves*, our own natural human responses, to create a sense of 'I am' in the shoes of the character and act organically and truthfully. This is where our intuitive knowledge comes into play in combination with all the conscious research that has gone before. Stephen Nachmanovitch says:

Reasoned knowledge proceeds from information of which we're consciously aware – only a partial sampling of our total knowledge. Intuitive knowledge, on the other hand, proceeds from everything we know and everything we are. It converges on the moment from a rich plurality of directions and sources

– hence the feeling of absolute certainty that is traditionally associated with intuitive knowledge. (*Free Play*: 40)

We are searching for the character within ourselves and for ourselves in the character by entering into the imaginary circumstances of the character, allowing them to transform us; and we make the text our own by finding the impulses behind the words and actions.

Nachmanovitch again says: 'Impulse, like improvisation, is not "just anything"; it is not without structure but is the expression of organic, immanent, self-creating structure' (*Free Play*: 29).

Grotowski talks of 'creative passivity' and 'a passive readiness to realize an active role', in which the actor begins by doing nothing (*Towards a Poor Theatre*: 207, 17).

Michael Chekhov highlights three basic requirements for the actor: richness of the psychology, control of both body and psychology, and sensitivity of the body to inner creative impulse (Chapter 1 of *To the Actor*).

Receiving

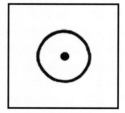

We receive information and stimuli through our five senses: seeing, hearing, smelling, touching, tasting. We process and assimilate this through our left, right and old brain on the basis of all our past understanding and experience stored in our mind/body. Our automatic breath will then serve as the creative connector between what we experience and its communication through the voice – breathing connects to our solar plexus, the nerve, emotion and energy centre that opens us up to receiving circumstances (see Chapter 4).

By placing ourselves into imaginary circumstances as if they are real, we can receive stimuli that will create an inner life and prompt believable action. Receiving is often neglected in rehearsal, and actors are pressed for results too early on because of lack of time, money or understanding. This usually takes the form of making cerebral and fixed decisions on how to play a character, using a generalized energy, and adopting external characteristics before any organic process can be engaged in.

In summary, here is the role of the breath in the receiving process:

- It can connect us to our deepest awareness, experiences, reflexes and emotions.

- It calms the mind and can centre and ground the body by connecting with the pelvic gravity centre and spine.

- Breathing and emotional response are integrated through the solar plexus.

- The centred breath connects to the actor's sense of self, the 'Me/I', Stanislavski's 'I am being', within imaginary circumstances.

- The breath can live within the present moment where everything is fresh and possible and a source for exploration and play, like when we were children.

Nachmanovitch describes play as something that is always a matter of context: 'It is not what we do but how we do it ... In play we manifest fresh, interactive ways of relating to people, animals, things, ideas, images, ourselves ... To play is to free ourselves from arbitrary restrictions and expand our field of action. Our play fosters richness of response and adaptive flexibility ... Play enables us to rearrange our capacities and our very own identity so that they can be used in unforeseen ways' (*Free Play*: 43).

When we receive we are like an absorbent sponge, or an aerial receiving signals. We are the second traveller, above, who takes everything in and experiences each moment as it happens.

Responding

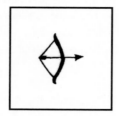

Responding involves all the elements that can express with clarity, ease, economy, form and conviction what you've received. We have looked at the the Essential Vocal Six elements in Part One. These require Michael Chekhov's sensitivity to psychological creative impulse and control of both body and psychology, so that stimuli received create spontaneous physical and vocal responses, rather than vocal muscles being consciously worked. Impulse – from circumstance, image, thought, will, feeling, action, language – needs to prompt reflexive muscle control, so that the actor experiences the acting process *through* alignment, breath, onset, pitch range, resonance and articulation. Look at the symbols below to remind you of the elements involved.

The essential thing here is that the outcome of what we communicate is entirely dependent on what and how information has been received and absorbed. Roughly speaking, you get out what you put in. If endgaming has been put in, demonstrated acting may well be the result. If imaginative experience has been put in, truly realized moments filled with life can be the outcome.

Likewise, if we train voice separately from acting process, the stimuli of the organic acting experience may always be missing from the voice. The danger is that we have a separate and mechanical vocal response rather than a seamless interplay between receiving and communicating.

The role of breath in responding is to:

- centre the body and connect the mind's intention to physical action;
- drive the will of the actor through the action;
- express emotional and sensory experience through sound and language.

We should also remind ourselves of the muscles, which make the voice respond with clarity, range and resonance so that it can fully communicate the experiences of the actor within the present moment:

- the muscles that anchor and lengthen the spine to support and assert the actor's will through the action;

- the vocal floor, inmost abdominals, diaphragmatic and rib muscles that enable centred onset, resonance and pitch range, and connect to our creative source in the sacrum and our emotions through the solar plexus;

- the muscles that articulate text and character.

Receiving and responding should work together like the breath going through its phases of inspiration and expiration. The one system stimulates the other. Too much receiving without responding and asserting could result in closing down, a mumbling introversion that fails to embody impulse. Too much assertive driving without received impulse results in empty reciting. The one is nothing without the other.

In the next part of the book we look at how this co-operation can be achieved in the different aspects of the Stanislavski approach.

10

AWARENESS, EASE AND FOCUS

In this chapter we look at the importance of the actor developing awareness as a human being, since inventive creativity depends on both imagination, and understanding and experience of life. Ease and focus are basic essentials for creativity to happen and for the body and vocal apparatus to be responsive to acting impulse.

Awareness and experience

Awareness, an informed state of consciousness, is a key element that an actor needs in order to enact action truthfully in the imaginary circumstances of drama. Our basic instrument when we act is ourselves. We *are* the characters in the sense that we are the raw material for them, the basis of transforming into someone else. The characters are created in the imagination of a writer, but we have to bring them off the page into living, breathing existence. Whether the characters become diminished or fully realized depends on our awareness and understanding of ourselves, and also of others and the world around us, which helps to create us. When we perform we need to play the action in the circumstances clearly, believably and economically in order to communicate it to an audience, and we do that as we are at our current state of development.

To understand a wide range of characters in different epochs and cultures, to grasp who they are and why they do what they do for psychological, social, political and economic reasons, and how they might express themselves vocally and physically, we need to expand our awareness and experience of life generally. To develop as actors we have to develop as human beings. We can develop our awareness and knowledge through some basic means:

- Observation – of people we know, strangers, nature, city life: examining the form and constituent parts of natural objects and how they change with time and the seasons; noting people's actions, appearance and mannerisms and how these relate to their job, living conditions, position in society, nationality, politics or religion; how their physicality and vocal quality have developed according to who and what they are.

- Understanding – ourselves and society. How did we become who we are through our backgrounds, environment, education and class? How did our vocal placement and tone, intonation pattern, pitch range and manner of articulation develop from this? We have so many variations in how we are with different people in different situations, all of which affects how we speak and move, that it's not a huge leap into transforming into different people with different vocal characteristics. How does a particular society form who I am? In a twelfth-century Muslim country I would not behave like I would in the royal court of seventeenth-century France or the streets of the Bronx in 2011. 'Where you are is what you are and how you are and what you can be', as Stanislavski told Stella Adler in 1934 (*The Art of Acting*: 139). It determines how you speak, eat, act, feel, dress and walk, so researching and understanding the differences between now and then, here and there, will enhance our ability to interpret characters in an informed and imaginative way and deal with different types of language and expression.

- Sensing – opening our senses of sight, smell, taste, touch and hearing so that we are always open and receptive to information and stimuli from the outside world, absorbing, assimilating and developing our perception.

- Experiencing – not just new events and people but our own physicality and sense of self. This involves exploring and developing our bodies and breathing and their sensitivity to inner creative impulse, connecting with our centres of energy, integrating our mind/bodies, so we develop the psycho-physical links between acting impulse and voice and physicality.

The vocal connection

EXERCISES

Connecting images to language

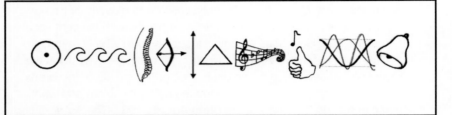

Let's look at a simple exercise that draws on past observation, sense of self and sensing to achieve a real experience of words and what gives rise to them.

For words to work on us we must explore the images behind them, and for the images to give full and free expression to the words we need an inner stillness. So begin by lying semi-supine, and find your natural deep breathing rhythm. Once you feel still and easy, let the following images form.

1   Imagine you are on a Mediterranean holiday, the weather is wonderful and you are looking at the turquoise waters of the sea. Focus on your solar plexus and allow yourself to receive this image here, soaking up the image until it fills you entirely. Then start to speak gently the word 'sea' as a response to your experience of the image, rather than listening to yourself speaking the word in a controlled manner.

Everybody experiences images differently, and you can experience them differently each time. If your voice is responsive the word will always sound fresh and alive and never exactly the same.

2   *Communicating the experience through vowel sounds.*

Connecting to the vowels through their vibrations and spatial size can create an immediate expression of the experience. It will feel as if the experience and the resulting words of the text are one.

See the image of the turquoise waters and respond with full voice through the word's vowel sound *ee*. If it sounds and feels as if the vowel is coming from an external place, allow yourself time to really let it into your solar plexus/diaphragm. Let the vowel vibrations travel on the wave of the breath, rooted in your pelvic, abdominal and spinal support action.

3 Now say 'sea' again and let the vowel *ee* vibrate your experience. If the drawing in of the vowel makes you under-pitch your voice, you can quickly get back on track by making a sound of agreement, 'Yes! Mmhmm!' to the question: 'Do you like holidays?'

4 Now link this experience to the following extract of text from *The Sea* by Barry Cornwall (1787–1874):

The Sea! the sea! the open sea!
The blue, the fresh, the ever free!

Connect to the language through imagined circumstances – where are you, when is it, and why are you there? Take the images into your solar plexus and start by sounding only the vowels of the text slowly, letting them convey your experience.

Then speak the whole words without rushing, letting your imagination trigger them until you feel one with them.

5 Add other sensations to your visual images: hear the sounds of seagulls, the waves lapping or the wind through leaves; smell the sand and seaweed; taste the salty sea-spray; feel sand beneath your feet. Say the lines out of this more complex picture, and allow their sound to change.

6 Now decide what the sea means to you. Imagine that your home is by the sea but you are far away and homesick. Use the text to connect to this experience.

Imagine that you haven't had a holiday for a year and have been working very hard. You long for the sea and the freedom and release it will bring you.

Or, you've travelled the seas for years and are only too glad to be away from them! See how this opposite impulse changes your relationship to the image and the expression of the words.

7 Now imagine any situation of your choice – a party, a wood, a railway station, a concert, a market, a restaurant – anywhere that is filled with sensory stimuli. Recreate something you've experienced by recalling all its sensory elements. Open all your senses, let the experience into your solar plexus. Take in how it makes you feel and how this affects your breathing, slowing and expanding or shortening and quickening it.

Now respond with a voiced sound in response to each of the sensory experiences of sight, smell, hearing, taste and touch. The sounds may be expressions of delight or revulsion, caution or enthusiasm, they may be guttural and sexual or yearning and ethereal. Feel free to use a sigh, vowels, consonants, speech or song to match your expression to your experience. Don't listen to yourself but stay in the centre and moment of the experience and avoid emoting. Stick with the sensory experience and when you've sounded each sensory element, explore the sound which sums up the whole experience. (Also see Exercise 5 from Chapter 6, Pitch Range.)

Sensing and breathing are closely linked, connect to our creative mind, and immediately evoke responses within us in the circumstances of a character. These exercises are a simple way to prepare ourselves for a more detailed exploration of the given circumstances of a play. These will be more complex and to a large extent will determine the character you are playing, and require a greater subtlety of vocal expression.

Ease and focus

To act, to perform action creatively, imaginatively and effectively, we need to find our centres. When we are centred we feel connected to ourselves, integrated, in control, undistracted and in the moment, energized, easy and confident. Stanislavski believed this self-possession enabled the actor to 'forget all about himself as an individual and yield his place to the character in the play' (*Stanislavski on the Art of the Stage*: 117). It is what Michael Chekhov meant by control of the actor over psychology and body. To achieve this, the actor needs ease and focus, both in the mind and body, and because of their mutual interdependence we refer to them as *focused ease*; an alternative could be *relaxed concentration*, or, as Dennis Lewis uses in *The Tao of Natural Breathing* (62), *effortless effort.* We neither want to be so relaxed as to be energy-less and floppy, nor so concentrated that we're like a wound-up clockwork spring. The balance needed is like that of a tennis player who is open, easy and responsive but has alert, engaged muscles that can snap into action in reflexive reaction to what the other player is doing.

If we are tense inside we will create physical tension. Equally, physical tension causes mental tension. Anything which detracts from an easy focus on the action as it happens moment by moment will be a source of tension, and that will break the actor's belief in the situation, cause self-consciousness, break contact with other actors and create more tension. Performing in front of an audience or technical crews in radio, TV or film studios can make us nervous.

The audience, for Stanislavski, constitute 'the spiritual acoustics for us', so the actor 'must act as the character and listen as the actor' (*An Actor Prepares*: 189). So, while we are aware of the audience, in order not to be unsettled by them and to communicate the imaginary action of the play to them, we need to focus on the action onstage.

A fundamental way of doing this is always to have *an object of attention,* whether an inanimate object, like a scarf you've been given as a present, or another person. The scarf might have been given to you by an estranged lover and it might prompt you to agree to a meeting. The person might be a friend relating a desperate story that requires you to help them. In these and all cases, the object of attention will engage us and prompt the basis of drama, *action*. It may help to create the feeling Stanislavski called *public solitude,* the sense of being alone onstage or in front of camera while being in the presence of many people. A focused and easy attention on an object also helps create *belief*, and the more we believe in the imaginary circumstances *as if* they are real the more *truthful* we will be. All of this helps us to enter the inner creative state Stanislavski called 'I am being', where we start to act in the moment intuitively, imaginatively and spontaneously.

In this state, we receive and create more *impulses to action* that need organic physical and vocal expression. Our physical instruments need to be very responsive and sensitive to impulse. For Stanislavski, 'freeing our muscles' is vital because of the limitations on the actor created by muscular spasm and physical tightness, which block energy. Voices become hoarse and inexpressive. Legs and faces tighten. Breathing becomes clavicular and short. Lesser tensions can produce unconscious mannerisms and twitches in the hands and face. What may go unnoticed in everyday life is highlighted in performance, particularly on camera. If an actor looks tense and wooden, then their whole inner life looks wooden.

Stanislavski's physical training regime involved gymnastics to improve the flexibility, muscle tone and expressiveness of the body; acrobatics for developing 'the quality of decisiveness' so that an actor can release and act on impulse more; and dance, for alignment and clarity of form. These disciplines, to varying degrees, will be evident in many acting schools.

More relevant types of discipline for vocal training are Alexander technique, for release of muscle tension and improving alignment; and Yoga, T'ai Chi and Pilates for posture, co-ordination and equilibrium, muscle toning, and integration of mind, breathing and body. Also, Michael Chekhov's exercises, specifically designed for actors, are very useful: his basic archetypal movements, and exercises on radiation, moulding, flying and floating all involve physical expression of an imaginative impulse. (See Chapter 1, 'To the Actor', and Chapter 2 of John's book, *Acting Stanislavski – A Practical Guide to Stanislavski's Approach and Legacy.*)

Stanislavski introduced Yoga into training. Eastern disciplines like Yoga, T'ai Chi and Qi-Gong relate to his concern for the interconnection between inner life and the physical, and integrating mind and body at all stages of the acting process. This psycho-physical connection may not come easily to us, given the stresses and emphasis on new technology in modern life, and the way our intellectual, physical and imaginative experience may be split during our working or studying lives. We can become dualistic, head cut off from body, thoughts from emotions, desires from action, alienated from others and from ourselves, rather than wholly integrated. As actors, we need to remove blocks and disconnections so that we operate much more as we did as a child, when thoughts, wants, emotions and physical and vocal expression were unthinkingly integrated.

Our acting process and acting and vocal training should focus on regaining this state, which opens us to sensitivity and creativity – and physical exercises to achieve a focused ease are central to this.

The vocal connection – Alignment and breath

The skilled actor does everything with ease. As we have seen in Chapter 3, in order to bring about ease, the actor needs to find a neutral alignment that is based on a balanced connection between gravity and anti-gravity forces as well as to free the muscles of tension. In a state of balance, muscular action is at its most economical and responsive. If the muscles work too hard to achieve an upright posture, the result is tension. Ease is necessary within the body for the breath to flow easily. Any tension impedes the breathing muscles and the breathing spaces. Tension is the enemy of resonance because it restricts the acoustic spaces of the voice. It limits pitch range and obscures articulation. Tension blocks impulses and our responses to them.

Any vocal training starts with releasing tension and finding an easy and neutral posture through which the breath can flow freely. To achieve this, we need to repeat exercises until the mind/body has learned and absorbed a new skill, and control passes to the old brain via the extra pyramidal paths so that we don't have to consciously think about it to perform it (see Chapter 2, Learning a new skill). The aim is for the actor to breathe and receive and to send out energy, thoughts, feelings and will in response and without tension.

EXERCISES

Opening the channels of the body

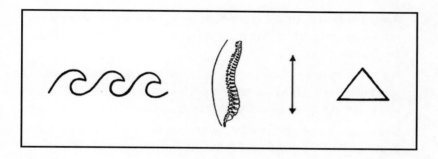

1   Stretch in your own way in every direction so that you tune into your body. Swing the arms in different directions. Skip and jog through the room, do sidesteps and constantly change direction. This generally loosens and wakes up the body and gets the blood flowing and oxygenated. Or try the T'ai Chi rotation exercise from Chapter 3.

2   Body isolation exercises are good to get the joints warmed up, for example, the *Snake Dance*.

You start by rotating your fingers, then the hands and wrists, followed by the lower arms and elbows and then the shoulders. All of these limbs should rotate separately and in different directions. This then expands into the ribcage, then the pelvis, the thighs and knees, then the calves and ankles and the feet and toes. Lastly let the head participate in the rotation. You are now doing a rather ecstatic snake dance that will be even better with some music.

After you've had your fun with this, start to reverse the process by taking the rotation of the feet and toes away but keep going with the rest of the body. Then take away the ankles and calves, then the thighs, etc., working your way up to the hands and fingers. Keep the areas where you stopped rotating as still as possible. In the end you will have come to a point of stillness and should feel the blood and energy flowing through your body.

3   Here's a stretch exercise along the Elastic Band to make you aware of the whole back wall of support from the coccyx to the crown of the head.

Stand well aligned with knees bent. Place your lower arm against the back of your head. Breathe in to your pelvic floor. On the out-breath, sound a fricative like *sshhh*. Press your arm against the back of the head and feel the stretch of the Elastic Band along your balance line, as the legs straighten but not lock, and ensuring that the back of the neck lengthens.

Repeat several times using alternate arms, making sure your coccyx moves up and back on the in-breath and down and under on the out-breath.

4   Now, with the left arm behind the head and the lower triangle well rooted, lean the upper body to the left and pat your ribs with the right hand as you sound out on an *aaahh*. Change the arm and pat the other side.

5   Stand well aligned, knees bent, and hands clasped behind the back. Breathe into the pelvic floor. On the out-breath, sound a *sshhh* as you lift the arms, engage the Elastic Band, straighten the legs and lengthen the neck. Do this several times, relaxing your body on the in-breath.

On the next out-breath, bend the upper body forward and lift the hands and arms towards the ceiling as you sound out. On the next in-breath, relax the arms and hang from the pelvis. Take several deep breaths, then on an out-breath, raise the body on a spine roll as you sound on a *sshhh*.

Now remind yourself of these exercises from Chapter 3, Alignment:

- Prelude: relaxation and easy breathing
- Visualizing and balancing the body's alignment and easy natural centred breathing, listening to your body – Exercise 1
- The Spine Roll, exploring each section of the spine – Exercise 2
- Grounding, connecting to the pelvis – Exercise 3
- Elastic Band, exploring gravity and anti-gravity – Exercise 4
- Primary curves, connecting to the primary curves of the spine – Exercise 5
- Exploring spinal movements when breathing – Exercise 6

And from Chapter 4, Breath:

- Exploring whole body breathing – Exercise 3
- The sponge – Exercise 4
- Pelvic rocking – Exercise 5

Letting your deep breath respond to imagination

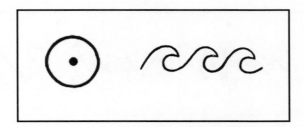

Imagine you're on the beach and you're jogging along the water's edge. Feel the resistance of the wet sand as if it's real, making jogging harder.

Then run into the imaginary sea and feel the water resistance work against you the deeper you enter. Run back out onto the beach and feel how it gets easier when the resistance of the water disappears. This gives you a sense of weight, time and space that will affect your breathing in different ways.

– Centred onset of sound

In order to communicate the response to what the actor receives from circumstances we need to create a vocal focus point of muscular readiness. This is achieved by a centred onset of sound (see Chapter 5), where identity, belief, conviction and intention meet within the voice, and the actor's impulses are expressed with energy. From here you should be able to radiate outwards into the space like sunrays.

Breath, muscles and spine must work in harmony to respond to impulses received and connect to the will of the actor, so that objectives are communicated organically, physically and vocally, not intellectually and mechanically.

EXERCISES

Remind yourself of the exercises in Chapter 5, Centred onset of sound, especially Exercise 2, the 'Me' exercise on the feeling of identity, conviction and creative centre.

Chekhov movements

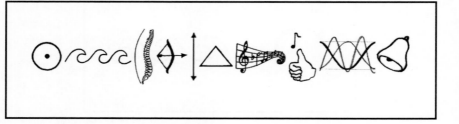

We'll now look at Michael Chekhov's basic movements, sometimes called archetypal gestures – gestures typical and representative of particular actions – recorded in Chapter 1 of *To the Actor* and in Chapter 2 of *Acting Stanislavski*. These are simple psycho-physical exercises that aim to increase the sensitivity of the body to inner impulse and the command of the actor over body and psychology. For Chekhov, only this will give the actor 'the necessary self-confidence, freedom and harmony for his creative activity' (*To the Actor:* 6).

As with all Chekhov's work, he emphasizes that the exercises should be done with *ease, form, entirety and beauty.* Ease makes a performance look natural and believable, and enables a free flow of breath and communication through an expressive body. Form gives shape, style and outer appearance to content. Entirety gives a sense and purpose to each action within the whole performance. Beauty, the intuitive inner quality comprising many qualities, brings out the real artistic meaning of a piece.

We shall introduce breath and vocal expression into these exercises.

Growing bigger/opening out

* Stand with the legs far enough apart to feel a pull on the leg muscles, feet rooted to the earth. Give yourself the impulse, 'I want to wake my muscles by growing bigger, using maximum space around me'. Then spread the fingers and raise wide the arms and hands until they reach up to the sky, palms facing up, and head and eyes lifted. Stay in this expanded and energized position for a few seconds, experiencing and radiating the sensation of having grown, then end the action cleanly.

This movement, and the others below, should have a clear beginning, execution and end, a clearly defined form and sense of ease and beauty. This, and the interpretations of Chekhov's exercises below, are based on John's own training and there may be equally valid variations on the actual form of each movement, but the aim and principles of them will remain the same.

Figure 45 Growing bigger

* Try the movement again. Give yourself another strong inner impulse to wake and revive your muscles by growing bigger and opening out. Now breathe in the impulse and on the out-breath execute the action.

* Now do the sequence again and this time on the out-breath find a rooted voiced sound from your centred onset that expresses the expanding, opening out movement – the sound needs to run through the whole sustained gesture on the movement of the out-breath, like surfing the wave mentioned earlier: a *haaaaahhhhh* perhaps.

Keep trying the action until you have created as perfectly formed and vocally expressed a movement as you can.

Growing smaller/closing down

* Stand feet together with the arms crossed over the chest. Breathe in the impulse, 'I want to wake my muscles by growing smaller, using *minimum* space around me', bend to the knees smoothly, dropping the head and curling down to the floor, closing and disappearing into a shrinking space. Hold the position again to really experience the sense of having grown small.

* Now do it again and find the voiced sound which expresses closing down into the smallest possible space: maybe a *mmmm* sirening down. Observe all the other instructions as above.

* Try starting from this closed down position and move on an impulse to grow bigger and with sound into the fully expanded opened out position;

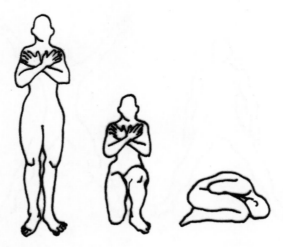

Figure 46 Growing smaller

and then from here, on an impulse to grow smaller, move back down to the closed position with a different sound. So we integrate in sustained, opposing movements, impulse, breath, physical action and sound.

Reaching out

* Stand with feet slightly apart and arms thrust back, fingers spread, in opposition to the movement to be enacted. Breathe in the objective, 'I want to wake my muscles by reaching out, using maximum space around me', then on the out-breath thrust the body forward on one knee as far as possible and swing straight arms through, reaching as far forward as possible, with the other leg fully extended. Hold the position a few seconds, then try on the other leg.

Figure 47 Reaching out

* Now do the gesture with the sound that you feel fits it, as above.

Dragging

* This has the same start position as *reaching out*. Breathe in the impulse to wake the muscles by dragging, then on the out-breath reach far out and down towards the floor with the front leg bending and back leg stretching straight, then pull back an imaginary object between spread fingers, and drag it to the back foot as the front leg straightens and back leg bends, with both feet flat on the floor. Hold the position, and then try the action on the other leg.

Figure 48 Dragging

* Now try it again with an appropriate voiced sound, as above.

Figure 49 Lifting

Lifting

* *Stand* with feet apart, legs straight and arms held out parallel to the floor with fingers spread. Breathe in the inner command, on the out-breath lower the body from the pelvis, swinging the arms down until the fingers touch the floor, then lift an imaginary object and hold it above the head.

* Now do it with a sound, as above.

Throwing

* Stand legs apart at a right angle, and arms outstretched forward and behind, parallel to the floor and along the line of the front leg, and the eyes looking forward along the front arm. Breathe in the impulse to throw using maximum space around you, and on the out-breath, with ease and control (not stiffness or floppiness), swing the front arm bending across the chest and the back arm as far behind and straight as it will go, while the front leg bends forward. Then swing the back arm over in an arc in a straight arm bowling action finishing parallel to the floor with the hand facing down; the forward arm simultaneously swings horizontally round in front of the body to behind it; as the arms move, the front leg straightens, and back leg bends. Try with the other leg facing forward, and other arm throwing.

Figure 50 Throwing

* Now do it with a sound, as above.

Beating

* Start in the same position as above, but with the palms facing up. Imagine you're a blacksmith wanting to beat a hammer on an anvil. Breathe in that impulse and on the out-breath, with the most expansive gesture, swing your rear hand over to slap the front one firmly.

Figure 51 Beating

* And do it with a sound, as above.

* Subsequent practitioners have suggested additional movements such as pushing, pulling, embracing, tearing, wringing, penetrating, slashing. Try these with your own sense of their archetypal quality and an accompanying sound.

* Try executing all these gestures with different tempos – this will elicit a new range of responsive sounds, altering in quality, pitch and resonance according to speed and energy used.

* While exploring the sounds that fit the gestures, try starting them with consonants, because it will help you to root your voice and release the vowel sounds on the breath, surfing it rather than forcing it. The more you throw a sound out, the more you need to root it. For example, try the *yyy* sound and release into a vowel sound like *yyyy-aaaaaaah.*

> Make sure that in all the above exercises you root the sound into your pelvic floor and release the sound through the whole breath movement. Even when your spine is bent you must still work with the principles of breathing out towards the spine and of gravity/anti-gravity pull, otherwise you may create tension in the larynx.

– Integrating mental and physical ease and focus

EXERCISES

Here are two group exercises that require mental and physical ease, focus, alertness, responsiveness and vocal connection.

Alphabet

This is suggested by a Stanislavski exercise recorded by Jean Benedetti in *Stanislavski and the Actor*.

Stand in a circle. Distribute the letters of the alphabet. Some will have more than one. Choose a well-known quote, e.g. *If music be the food of love play on*, or *To be or not to be, that is the question.*

You then spell out the line. Each person with a relevant letter steps forward into the circle and claps as they speak their letter, then steps back. Try to do it rhythmically and at a good tempo. At the end of each word, the whole group jumps together.

Once the line is complete, you can try spelling out the whole line together. Everyone speaks every letter together, moving rhythmically into the circle, clapping, then stepping back. Everyone jumps up at the end of each word.

Equally, if you don't have access to a group, you can do the whole thing on your own.

Zip Zap Boing

Stand in a circle, alert and easy. One person starts by sending an impulse of a clap with a voiced 'Zip' to the person to the left or right. They receive it and send another clap and a 'Zip' in the same direction, and so on. You can alter this by clapping and saying 'Zap' *across* the circle to a specific person, or sending a 'Boing' with opened arms *back* to the person who has just sent you a 'Zip' or a 'Zap'. All claps and arm movements should be done with great energy with the body fully alert, engaged and energized, and the voice easy and on centred onset. Whoever fluffs or goes in the wrong direction with their sound has to drop out. The game goes on until only one person is left standing!

Improvisation and text

Find two friends for this improvisation, and just focus on the elements we've raised in this chapter.

You own a bag. Another keeps taking it from you. The third tries to assist you and to restrain the other person.

Use the whole space with the action and improvise lines like: 'Give me my bag!', 'This isn't your bag', 'Leave it alone.'

The challenge here is to have high energy while sustaining ease, strong centredness and rooting, and sharp focus within your will. This demands easy breath flow, clear onset of sound and articulation.

Once you feel you're achieving these aims, have a go at them on text. Let's look at the scene from Act Two of Pinter's *The Caretaker* in which Davies wants to get his bag from Mick. This is full of initial verbal agitation followed by a very focused set of physical actions.

MICK. This your bag?
DAVIES. Give me it!
ASTON. Give it to him.
MICK. What? Give him what?
DAVIES. That bloody bag!
MICK (*slipping it behind the gas stove*). What bag? (*To* DAVIES.) What bag?
DAVIES (*moving*). Look here!
MICK (*facing him*). Where you going?
DAVIES. I'm going to get ... my old ...
MICK. Watch your step, sonny! You're knocking at the door when no-one's at home. Don't push it too hard. You come busting into a private house, laying your hands on anything you can lay your hands on. Don't overstep the mark, son.

ASTON picks up the bag.

DAVIES. You thieving bastard ... you thieving skate ... let me get my –
ASTON. Here you are. (ASTON *offers the bag to* DAVIES.)
MICK *grabs it.* ASTON *takes it.*
MICK *grabs it.* DAVIES *reaches for it.*
ASTON *takes it.* MICK *reaches for it.*
ASTON *gives it to* DAVIES. MICK *grabs it.*
Pause.
ASTON *takes it.* DAVIES *takes it.* MICK *takes it.* DAVIES *reaches for it.* ASTON *takes it.*

Pause
ASTON *gives it to* MICK. MICK *gives it to* DAVIES. DAVIES *grasps it to him.*
Pause.
MICK *looks at* ASTON. DAVIES *moves away with the bag. He drops it.*
Pause.
They watch him. He picks it up. Goes to his bed, and sits.

To sum up:

- **Awareness of self, others and the world comes from observing, understanding, sensing and experiencing, and enables us to create truth in the imaginary circumstances of drama.**
- **Ease and focus is essential for free, open and centred creativity and a flexible responsive voice.**
- **Breathe images into the solar plexus and let the voice respond to them spontaneously.**
- **Exercise regularly to develop an effortlessly balanced alignment and automatic full breathing.**
- **Expression of an easy voice must be focused through a centred onset of sound expressing the identity, conviction and actions of the actor.**

11

THE ACTION – GIVEN CIRCUMSTANCES, INTERACTION AND OBJECTIVES

We now focus on the key elements that create the essential sense of 'I am the character in imaginary circumstances', both psychologically and vocally/physically. We start with 'I in the circumstances of the character', then look at interaction with others and what I want to achieve in the situation: elements that create the basis for creation of character, narrative line and vocal response, supported by the breath, spine and support muscles.

The given circumstances

When we come to work on a text or improvisation, it's only once we have considered the events and circumstances surrounding us or our characters that we can know what we actually do: the circumstances are not only where we are but what we are, how we are, who we are and who we can become. Who you are and how you are with parents on a weekend out is different from who you are and how you are when in conflict with the landlord over the rent. The circumstances draw out different facets of personality, different ways of interacting, different objectives, and different ways of holding oneself physically and of speaking.

For Stanislavski the given circumstances mean the story of the play, its facts, events, time and place of action, epoch, the social, economic, political and cultural conditions of life, the actors' and director's interpretation, the production, sets, costumes, properties, lighting and sound effects, and so on – all the elements that are given to actors to take into account as they create a role.

So, as in real life I enter a set of circumstances; these set the framework for what I do, and my actions and those of others set off a dynamic that triggers organic responses and emotions, a process that is spontaneous within a created structure, intuitive and subconscious as a result of conscious preparation.

Knowing the circumstances in the head is one thing; believing in them with the imagination, senses and whole body and being so that we can be responsive is another. To prevent the process of entering and engaging with the circumstances from being an intellectual description, we need an imaginative springboard to launch us into them. This is provided by honing the circumstances down into four succinct questions, the Ws:

- **Who am I?** As myself the actor, or as the character in the script. My name, sense of identity, what has formed me in terms of background, family, environment, class, education, key events.

- **Where am I?** Where have I come from, where am I now, where am I going? What is the specific place, the district, town, country and what is in the space around me (objects, animals, plants, furniture, colours, textures)?

- **Why am I here?** What events, people, relationships and reasons bring me to this place?

- **What time is it?** Time of day, day and date, season, year, epoch.

The Ws provide the focus points to which the actor can respond intuitively, breathing in the circumstances through the imagination and the solar plexus.

The *magic if*

A further and essential question we should ask ourselves is, '*If* I am in these circumstances, here and now, imagined as if they are true, as a real possibility, what do I do intuitively, spontaneously, unpremeditatedly, in response to them?' A wrong interpretation of Stanislavski's 'if' would be to say, 'If I *were* in these circumstances, what *would* I do?', in the sense of 'What do I *think* I would do?', followed by an illustration of a rationalized idea. The 'if' is called the *magic if* because, if used in a non-intellectual way, it has such a substantial and far-reaching effect, prompting the actor's inner and outer life, the imagination and action, connecting the actor to different possibilities of themselves, the character and circumstances.

'If' doesn't demand that the actor believes something is *actually* happening, only that we imagine ourselves, or ourselves as a character, in circumstances *as if* they are real. We 'make believe' and respond truthfully like children. The actor draws automatically on past experience, knowledge and observation, and what is created will be organic as opposed to cerebral. We stop 'acting' and begin to focus on the situation, problems to be solved, and what to do. This will lead to actions that are coherent, real and justified by the situation.

So when entering given circumstances,

we should: respond truthfully to the imaginary situation, live moment by moment, allowing actions to unfold, find the impulse behind the actions, let each action be justified by the circumstances, allow any emotion to arise from the action, use economy, only doing what we need to do on any particular action: that is, *respond to the circumstances.*

we should not: play an emotional state (like anger, anxiety, frustration), demonstrate what is happening (e.g. indicating impatience by looking constantly at a watch), anticipate or premeditate what should happen, deliberately create 'dramatic' moments and imaginary conversations, do a lot of superfluous 'business', present a theatrical 'me' in trying to entertain: that is, *push through the circumstances.*

The vocal connection

Placing ourselves in circumstances as if they are real will trigger impulses that we receive through the breath and solar plexus and express through an immediate, unmediated vocal response.

To connect fully vocally to the sense of 'I am' in the circumstances, we need to find the place of identification in a centred vocal onset: the 'Me/I' rooted in the gravity centre of the pelvic floor. This keeps us out of the head and connects responses to the breath, helping sense of belief, conviction and assertion.

If we just think about what we should be doing, the voice will be empty and devoid of experiences. By connecting to the sense of 'I in the circumstances', the voice can be enriched with each moment. It becomes dropped in, rooted, on the breath, and resonates the experiences of the character within the whole pitch range.

EXERCISES

All the essential vocal elements represented by the symbols below apply throughout the chapter. To find relevant exercises for each symbol, go to the *Vocal Givens* in Symbols at the end of Chapter 8. We have added some key exercises in the following sections.

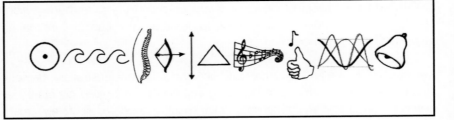

1. 'Me'

Let's revisit the 'Me' exercise from Chapter 5 – Centred onset of sound.

Wherever you are when reading this, go over your circumstances: who you are at this point in time, where you are, what time it is, why you're there, what you're doing.

Now say 'me' as a response to the circumstances and with full conviction from your core centre and spine. Express how you experience yourself through the word. Connect to your pelvic floor and the Elastic Band energy rooting you down and lifting you up. Allow your pitch range to respond.

Imagine your whole body as a stage, with the pelvic floor as the boards. Rather than just playing downstage in the front of your body, you should move into centre and upstage, towards your spine, the back wall of the stage, and then over the soft and hard palate in your mouth, the arc of the ceiling of your stage. The voice will become full and three-dimensionally expressive rather than thin and one-dimensional.

2. Imaginary given circumstances

This is suggested by an exercise in *Acting Stanislavski*.

I'm about to leave from work. I check my jacket for my car and house keys and they are not there.

Who am I? I am me as in everyday life at this point in time, with all my background, hopes and fears, ambitions and frustration, qualities and failings.

Where am I? I have come from acting school and have worked for three hours in a restaurant as a waitress.

Why? I work here because I need the money to pay for living expenses. I've only worked three hours instead of five but I'm leaving now because I'm coming down with a cold and get permission to leave early.

What time is it? It's 10pm, Thursday, 21 April 2012.

1. Simply respond to the situation.

You might genuinely check all your pockets and search your bag, maybe more than once, check around the room, retrace your steps and see if the keys have dropped anywhere. If you don't find them you might consider contacting the police, and work out alternative means to get into your home.

Focus on the problem and what you need to do. Do all your actions with belief and justification as if the imaginary situation facing you is totally real. Don't pretend or try to 'show' anxiety. A fifth 'W', the objective, what you *want* to achieve in the situation, comes through the action: *I want to find my keys or some other way to get into my home.*

2. Now try the improvisation while vocalizing your responses and thoughts.

Before you start, remind yourself of the elements in the receiving and responding process and make sure that you are rooted in your centred onset of sound; that you are on the breath (using the Elastic Band of the breathing energy connecting the journey of your breath to your spinal support); that your resonance areas are open and available; that your pitch range can respond freely and truthfully, and that you are in optimum pitch; and that your articulatory muscles are prepared to shape thoughts with clarity and ease: in short, that your vocal apparatus is free to respond to creative impulse.

As you imaginatively enter the circumstances, receive them by breathing them in through your solar plexus as each new event unfolds: getting ready to leave, checking for purse and keys, discovering the keys are gone, searching for them thoroughly, etc. Allow the circumstances to work on you, rather than pushing for results. *Really* search for your keys. Allow for a genuine moment of realization that you don't have them and the sensation that produces. Every impulse – thought, image, feeling – can prompt action and verbal action: a verbal expression of the impulses through the spontaneously responding muscles of voice production.

You might say 'Oh no!', 'Where the hell is my key?', 'Where have I been?', 'What am I going to do now?' You may, of course, be the sort of person who doesn't utter a sound, but for the purpose of this exercise speak your thoughts.

3. Now that you have found in-the-moment vocal responses, let's look at turning them into a script.

Establish some key sentences that you may have said in the improvisation, for example:

'Oh no!'
'Where are my keys?'
'This is not happening!'
'They've gone!'
'What the hell am I going to do now?'
'I can't take my car!'
'I can't get in!'
'Fxxxxxx brilliant!'
'Get in touch with the police – or the fire brigade.'
'I'll write a note and put it on the windscreen.'

Immerse yourself in the circumstances again, but this time with the script. Experience the discovery that your keys are lost and the decisions on what is to be done moment by moment *as if for the first time*. This is what we have to do on text as actors all the time. If I am in these circumstances what do I do and what gives justification for these lines?

Do this quietly initially: allow yourself to receive thoughts from the circumstances, to experience what needs to be done, and the spoken words and actions to achieve that. The circumstances are a pebble dropping into a pond and creating the ripples of thought, breath, word, action.

Now do it fully on the voice. When you receive the impulses to speak, feel how the muscular system kicks in and roots your responses vocally. You need to simply let this happen and not think about it.

Repetition of the sequence is a good way of discovering how to stay in the moment and not just repeat what you did before. It will help you to open yourself to the receiving and responding process. It will strengthen your imagination and prompt you to find new things, to *recreate*, to keep fresh. Most importantly it will help you to establish what acting and speaking on impulse means.

4. Now take three lines and only speak the vowels.

As mentioned earlier in Exercise 5 of Chapter 6, don't self-consciously articulate the vowels. They need to come out of the ripple that the impulse has created. The vocal muscles should respond to the need to solve the problem in the situation.

Do this as slowly as you need to at first – quite quickly it will become easier and flow. Your vowels will start to pick up the emotional response of what is happening in the moment. Don't emote or make it dramatic. Stay centred and allow your responses to do the work without mentally interfering.

Now communicate the whole lines again.
You should find that the vowels create spaces and a sense of flow, and a vibration of your experiences.

5. Now concentrate on rooting your consonants.
Do the lines slowly, focusing on all the consonants, but without losing the impulse behind the words. Imagine the spine as a magnet drawing the consonants into your core support to express the meaning and intent of the lines.

6. Now integrate the whole process and say the lines again as if for the first time in the circumstances.
The whole expression of thought, line, word, vowels and consonants should feel as one.

The *magic if* and belief in the imaginary circumstances allow us to receive them, to breathe them in through our solar plexus. This prompts impulses to action and to verbal expression, with the vocal muscles responding flexibly to the acting impulses.

Interacting and responding with others

Most situations we enter involve other people. We respond to each other according to many elements: personality, goals, relationships, status, class, attitudes, social customs and taboos, and crucially, according to what other people do to us. In everyday life we are in constant interaction with each other – looking, listening, touching, sensing, responding – and if that degree of what Stanislavski called communion or communication is not there onstage, we see disconnected and mechanical acting; this is neither enlightening nor entertaining because it lacks energy, dynamic and life.

Stanislavski insists on 'the first rule of dialogue: *limitless attention to your partner*' (*Stanislavsky Directs*: 318). Experience can only occur if we listen and respond, do actions that are reactions, adapt spontaneously to each new impulse. This doesn't mean deciding in advance how we will react to what someone says or does. It doesn't mean 'actioning' the text in week one of rehearsal, an invariably cerebral pre-programming exercise.

We need to make a two-way contact with the whole, living person in front of us, to experience their being fully and communicate our own. This applies just as much if we are playing characters. We are real human beings who are using our own tangible humanity to present new versions of ourselves, and we must continue to communicate as real people. The cast in the room *are* the characters. A different cast would make different versions of the characters.

The vital means for establishing this communication is through the eyes, governed by the right brain, not the mouth, governed by the left brain (see Chapter 2). We listen with the eyes as well as the ears. They create a continuous flow of contact and energy that prompts words, actions, thoughts and feelings, some of which may be expressed, some of which may only be experienced while the other person is talking: the process of genuine communication Stanislavski called *radiation* – one person *transmits* and the other *receives* without interruption – and what we're calling *receiving and responding*. There is an unbroken line of adaptation, with your senses taking in every nuance of what the other is saying and doing, every subtlety of intention, verbal intonation, physical movement and emotional expression. You react naturally and simply only to what has been done to you. As Sanford Meisner insists, you only do what the other person makes you do. Stanislavski described this communication as 'like an underground river, which flows continuously under the surface of both words and silences' (*An Actor Prepares*: 184).

Michael Chekhov also emphasizes giving and receiving: 'True acting is a constant exchange of the two. There are no moments on the stage when an actor can allow himself – or rather his character – to remain passive … without running the risk of weakening the audience's attention and creating the sensation of a psychological vacuum. To actually receive means to *draw*

> *toward* one's self with the utmost *inner* power the things, persons or events of the situation' (*To the Actor*: 19).
>
> Stanislavski says we must be like a bulldog and 'seize with our eyes, ears and all our senses' to achieve *grasp,* the strength of our ability to remain totally connected with each other, and which needs to increase in strength according to the power of a role and play (*An Actor Prepares*: 187).

The mutual receiving and responding in our communication creates an alive, spontaneous and dynamic interaction, which is so sensitized that it could go in different directions given a different thought, feeling or action at a particular time, and which consequently will create varied and subtle vocal responses from a prepared and flexible vocal apparatus.

As we've intimated, several things can block this process: externally driven characterization, cerebral choosing of actions, pushing for emotion, telling actors *how* to do something, forcing them into production 'concepts', absence of any exploration of the imaginary world by the actors themselves, and so on. Of course, there are also the common individual actor pitfalls that create a communication block and prevent experiencing: not listening, waiting for cues, trying to remember lines learned mechanically, thinking how to say the lines, speaking for effect or out of habit, imagining the person in front of you is someone else, not focusing on the action onstage, etc.

The vocal connection

EXERCISES

1. Throwing a ball

A simple exercise on receiving and responding involves throwing and catching a ball among a group standing in a circle. People often start by throwing the ball carelessly, tentatively or aggressively at someone else who may catch it – or not – and then immediately chuck it back to anyone as though it's a hot potato. So the exercise often brings actions such as dismissing, intimidating and apologizing in the way the ball is thrown or received. However, the essential nature of throwing and catching in this context is *responding by giving and receiving.*

* To achieve *real* giving and receiving we need to start from a position of alertness and ease in which we are open to each other and ready to receive. *And don't rush!* Someone gives the ball to someone who is *chosen,* and then continues to give, to radiate giving, until the other person has *fully* received the ball and decided to give it to someone else. They then resume the alert, open, ready to receive position, and so on. We never lose contact, *grasp*, with each other. Michael Chekhov also refers to this process as one of preparation and impulse, action and sustaining (*Lessons for the Professional Actor*: 69).

* Let's bring voice into this exercise. One person starts by throwing the ball to someone, really giving to them, but says their name with a chosen action, such as to cheer them. The receiver throws the ball to someone else with an action that is a reaction to being cheered, such as to encourage them. The receiver passes it on with an action/reaction of questioning, and so on. Each person responds not only to the last person's action but to their intonation, pitch range and resonance as well.

You receive and breathe in the situation created by the last person to throw, select someone new and then throw the ball. This physical action prompts the out-breath movement, which carries our psychological and verbal action towards the other person. Be careful not to tense as you speak and throw – let your verbal action ride the wave of the out-breath with ease. Root into the pelvic floor and spine.

* **This is a general pattern: impulse, in-breath, action, out-breath, speech.** Normally, we should only speak once this physical movement and out-breath has started to happen; otherwise, what often happens is the actor speaks too suddenly from a held position of tension, focusing only on the words and not the whole situation and action. We'll come back to this when we look at a piece of text.

* Now throw the ball using *word association*: one throws the ball and says 'tree', the next throws it and says 'leaf', etc., using a word and expressiveness responsive to what the other person gives them.

2. Word repetition

This is an exercise suggested by examples from *Sanford Meisner on Acting*.

One actor makes a simple observation about another sitting opposite. The other responds by *repeating the line from their point of view*. They continue to repeat the line until either person gets an impulse from the other to change the line: the other *makes* you change it by what they do. Everything is in the delivery; the line itself is not important.

Avoid pausing, consciously determining what to do, anticipating what the other might do, or doing line readings to create variety. Your delivery must be a truthful, spontaneous response to what the other is doing on the line, their intonations, actions, facial expressions, eye contact, feelings, body language and gestures.

For example:

A You have pink streaks in your hair.

B I have pink streaks in my hair.

A You have pink streaks in your hair.

B Yes, I have pink streaks in my hair.

A But you have pink streaks in your hair.

B Yes, I do have pink streaks in my hair!

A You don't have much taste.

B I don't have much taste?

A You really don't have much taste.

B I don't have much taste.

A No, you don't.

B You are very rude.

A I'm rude?

B Yes. You are *rude.*

A I am rude?

B Yes. You are really rude!

The other person gives you your line, as happens in everyday conversation and written dialogue. The other person determines *how* you respond by how *they* respond. In order to communicate this ping-pong quality in conversation the voice needs to be part of this free-flowing response and not fixed in a flat expressionless monotone. Every new line is a different action/reaction doing something different to the other person – for example, questioning, acknowledging, demeaning, praising, challenging, insulting, reassuring, etc. – all of which demand a different vocal expression with a different intonation, accenting, resonance and pitch range.

As always, make sure your responsive verbal action is surfing the flow of the out-breath, that you are rooted and engaged in spinal support.

3. Yes/no

A says 'yes' and B says 'no', with each word a response to how the last word was expressed, until a point comes organically when A takes over saying 'no' and B says 'yes'. You can give yourself a reason for saying 'yes' and 'no', for example, as a response to eating chocolate cake or going to a film. Also, you can each do a number of switches from 'yes' to 'no' in your exchange. As with word repetition, the voicing of the words needs simply to be a response to the other person.

4. Reading text

Now let's look at a piece of written dialogue, preferably a modern piece with sequences of duologue in the form of one-liners – Clare McIntyre, Pinter and Patrick Marber are good for this.

Here's a piece from Act One of *Total Eclipse* by Christopher Hampton. The two poets, Rimbaud and Verlaine, are discussing Verlaine's relationship with his wife.

RIMBAUD. Why don't you leave her?
VERLAINE. What?
RIMBAUD. Leave her.
VERLAINE. What do you mean?
RIMBAUD. Do you love her?
VERLAINE. Yes, I suppose so.
RIMBAUD. Have you got anything in common with her?
VERLAINE. No.
RIMBAUD. Is she intelligent?
VERLAINE. No.
RIMBAUD. Does she understand you?
VERLAINE. No.
RIMBAUD. So the only thing she can give you is sex?
VERLAINE. Well …
RIMBAUD. Can't you find anyone else?
VERLAINE. I …
RIMBAUD. You're not that fussy, are you?
VERLAINE. No.
RIMBAUD. Anyone within reason would do, wouldn't they?
VERLAINE. Within reason.
RIMBAUD. What about me?

Read the text with a partner and focus on reacting to each other's inflexions, meanings, actions, objectives, eye contact, pauses and body language. Let what the other person does affect you vocally and physically. Make sure you're integrating all the vocal elements represented by the symbols above.

After the first time through, do it again under different influences, allowing these to affect what you do in different ways, for example:

- start the dialogue with a different action on the first line – e.g. I mock you as opposed to I confront you;
- begin with a different overall attitude towards the other person – e.g. hostile instead of appreciative;
- work under the influence of a different personality quality – e.g. scornful rather than generous;
- try a different atmosphere – e.g. tense rather than friendly;
- adopt a different spatial relationship – e.g. close or distant, direct or indirect;
- use a different physical state – e.g. cold or hot, and so on.

Responding truthfully to these varied influences will reveal how differently any one piece of dialogue can be played, will free you from having a rigid interpretation of a text and increase your transformational ability and vocal versatility.

Objectives

As we receive and absorb the circumstances and the actions, words, feelings, gestures, expressions of other people, we act out *objectives* – or, as they are sometimes also called, aims, goals, motivations, wants, intentions or tasks. Objectives are the third element in a basic 'dynamics of action', constituted by *I in the circumstances*, *interaction with others*, and *what do I want?*, which provides the bedrock for character development in imaginary circumstances. We've already mentioned objectives, unavoidably, but now we'll focus on them directly.

We have objectives all the time through every day. Our behaviour has purpose. We act to satisfy some need or want, and though our objectives may be clear or unclear, simple or complex, weak or strong, conscious or unconscious, they are there, and as actors we need to identify those of our characters. Stanislavski suggested that *I want* creates the *impulse to action* when it is a subjectively experienced desire that is *active, achievable, specific, addresses the action onstage, stirs the actor, engages the will, and aims to change the other person and the situation.* Every objective needs to be expressed by 'I want' and in an active way, e.g. 'I want to *get* your support and trust' – rather than 'I want to *be* liked', which is passive and general, not aimed at changing another person and can't be played; or 'I want to convince you I love you' rather than 'I want to be with you.'

Objectives create the inner impulse which brings the action to solve a problem; but if objectives are formulated in a cerebral way, the actor will remain 'in the head', in the left brain-controlled reason and logic. Objectives become simply a tool for analyzing the text. If they are to be a means for *experiencing* the text and the action, we have to approach them with the right brain-controlled imagination and intuition: if I am in the circumstances of this character what do I want to achieve, to change in the situation? The want has to come from an experienced need: I lied to you, you now distrust me, I need to regain your love so 'I want to convince you I've changed and can be trusted.' What's at stake here is my whole peace of mind and future happiness. How important it is to achieve your objective, how high the stakes are, for example, life or death or not essential, determines how intensely you play it.

It is such impulses strung together which drive us on through the action of the play like fuel explosions in an engine. Objectives need to be physically experienced and engage our will. In performance we shouldn't be consciously thinking 'what is my objective, what is my action?', but we need the spark of a single word, image, thought, feeling or sense that launches us into the next attempt to change the situation. This acting on impulse offers both the security of an inner structure and the freedom of spontaneous improvised action on the lines, because we won't be thinking of the lines but pursuing what we want *through* the lines and the actions. Because objectives help us to engage with other people, they also release organic feeling through achieving or failing to get what we want. This all helps the integration of mind/body, feeling/action, speech/text.

Objectives such as those outlined above occur in small sections of a play, but when strung together they create a bigger objective running through a scene, or a larger episode, and possibly through the play as a whole. A character will also have a basic desire or *superobjective* in life, such as 'I want to get fame and fortune' or 'I want to achieve the highest standard in my art.' These bigger objectives can't be acted out in every line and unit of the text but will exercise an *influence* on how the smaller ones are acted out.

To achieve these smaller objectives we do *actions*, as outlined earlier. I praise, contradict, manipulate you in order to get you to lend me some money, for example.

Standing in our way will be the opposing objective of the other person, but also other *obstacles*: for example, something in our past (previous tension, favours rendered); external conditions (heat, wet, cold, time shortage); a physical state (headache, period pain); a psychological condition (fear of conflict, insecurity). These make it more difficult for me to achieve what I want, and set up an inner contradiction creating a deeper reality and a different range of actions to achieve what I want: for example, an obstacle may cause me to shift from pressing, instructing and educating someone, to imploring, soothing and manipulating them.

The vocal connection

Objectives are a central aspect of the actor's responding process. Whatever the initial impulse that gives rise to the objective – whether coming from mind, will or feeling – the objective can stimulate all three, e.g. if I'm rejected by someone and am in pain, I engage my will to get them back, and my intellect and imagination to find ways of dealing with the situation as it unfolds. Muscular, sensory and emotional readiness is necessary so that the impulses received and objectives pursued can be expressed immediately through a sensitized body and voice. The objective, if experienced imaginatively, can centre the body and connect thoughts, feelings and will to physical action and vocal action through sound and language.

So, through the objective we act on ourselves, if we're alone, or on other people to effect a change – and the voice needs to respond to this impulse in a released and spontaneous way.

A problem arises with the tendency to push – having the objective like a hammer drill in a jutting jaw rather than a spark in the eyes! The interplay between the receiving process and responding process, impulse and vocal production, is vital to avoid this.

In the following exercises, it is important that the connection between acting impulses and vocal expression is seen as a given. Only then will the actor respond vocally with skill and truth, because the vocal muscles will be reflexively engaged in the acting. Acting and voice become one.

EXERCISES

Here is a reminder of some key exercises from Chapter 3, Alignment: Exercises 4, 6; Chapter 4, Breath: Exercises 4, 8, 10, 11; Chapter 5, Centred onset of sound: Exercises 1, 3; Chapter 6, Pitch range: Exercise 5; Chapter 7, Resonance: Exercise 2; Chapter 8, Articulation: Exercise 1- 3 in Integration.

Through these and the following exercises we engage with a muscular and spinal movement that responds to the impulse of the objective voiced through the out-breath wave. We start to feel how mind, body, breath and voice connect within acting.

1. 'Come back, come closer ...'

* A person you love deeply is rejecting you and is heading for the door. Connect with the problem and what needs to be done. Your need and desire surges like an overflowing river, you have to hold them back and your objective becomes: '*I want to make you stay and win back your love*'.

Breathe the objective through your solar plexus and into your back and vocal root support muscles, enhancing your sense of conviction and identity.
Sense your pelvic floor muscles and lumbar spine in readiness and your impulse to breathe out.
Once the impulse has triggered the wave of your out-breath movement, follow the breathing movement and root to your centred onset of sound as you pursue your first action: '*Come back, come closer*'.

Follow the force of gravity against your spine and sense how the want comes through the words with strength and conviction as your spinal movement and Elastic Band energy roots you down and lifts you up through your balance line. The spine will connect your whole body to the objective.

* *Try working against an obstacle.*
The person is afraid of you, angry with you, torn between you and another person. You may feel guilty for your prior behaviour. There may be a time pressure.
Try different actions – I shame you, beg you, order you, bribe you.
Experience how these changes alter your pitch range and resonance.

* *Try the opposite objective, 'I want to make you go away.'*
Create the imaginary circumstances, the problem to be overcome, the need for this person to be made to go, and pursue the objective as above. Then explore the effect of obstacles and different actions, and allow your voice to respond.

2. Lumbar drive

To strengthen the spinal action and enhance the sense of rooting when acting out a strong objective with high stakes and against big obstacles, we can focus on the *lumbar* movement of the spine. This will give added drive to the out-breath movement that carries your objective. It will open the body's resonators and give strength, conviction and subtlety to the power and resonance of the actor's voice when responding to impulse.

We do this exercise with a broomstick to identify clearly the muscles around the lumbar area.

* Stand well aligned within your balance line, resting on the balls of your feet. Many people have the tendency to be balanced on their heels because it feels grounded and strong but it actually locks the back, and therefore your voice, and limits lumbar movement.

* Place a broomstick behind the lumbar area of your back and hold it with your elbows. With your weight on the balls of the feet, pull the stick towards your lumbar area and tilt your pelvis under. Feel your lumbar area engaging and driving your spine up and rooting at the same time. Your feet will grip the floor. Feel how this strengthens your breath support as well as opening all your resonators and how the body around the lumbar engagement frees up.

* Say 'Stay with me, please!' to a partner, with the objective of wanting to make them forgive you. After breathing in the person, let your spinal drive respond to this thought. You should feel the strength of your breath support and the released yet strongly resonant quality of your voice.

* Imagine your partner has really annoyed you. You respond to this by wanting to make them apologize to you, reprimanding them: 'It is *me* you are talking to.' You remain rooted, concentrating on carrying your objective to the other person through the lumbar drive, while your partner moves freely through the space. You need to stay connected with them by breathing them in wherever they are and reaching them through your spinal drive, which enhances the out-breath wave, without shouting or tensing up your upper body or throat.

* Next, explore a gentler action towards the person, like softening them, reassuring, teasing, or winning their trust without losing the strength of your response. If you truly respond to your impulse your voice will find the right quality to get what you want – but whatever the vocal quality and action you still need to drive with the breath from your back and stay fully on voice.

* Removing the broomstick, let's look at an imaginative way of getting the same result. Imagine that at the top of the lumbar area/bottom of the thorax there is a *coat hanger* with its hook between the shoulder blades. Again, play one of the above objectives, and this time on the in-breath when your lumbar/thoracic

area lifts back and up, imagine you are hanging from a coat hanger. Your back will open and your ribs will open like wings. When responding from your lumbar/thoracic area on the out-breath, let your whole body weight sink into the up/down pull of the Elastic Band, strengthening your vocal response triggered by the acting impulse.

If followed correctly, you will not think about your voice, but just respond with conviction to impulse. You will breathe in and energize the distance between you and acting partners, audience and periphery of the space, making an effective dynamic in this triangle – more on this in Chapter 14 on the space.

3. Making your point

You and a partner have conflicting views about something. For example, you are going to meet at a pub but disagree about exactly where it is:

A Let's meet at the Anchor on the left.

B No, it's on the right.

A The pub is on the left

B The pub is on the right

A No, it's on the left.

B It's on the right.

A It isn't, it's on the left, etc.

Visualize how you both see the pub's location, give it reality for yourselves, believe in the absolute truth of what you're saying, and assert your point with the objective *to convince the other person you're right.* See how your stresses change spontaneously in each new response in pursuit of your objective, trying to change the other person. Don't consciously predetermine how to say the lines to have a particular effect. Let them be a response to what you want and the resistance offered by your partner.

Make sure you apply the lumbar drive, as above. Keep rooted with the objective supported by the spine.

Objectives on text

We now apply the vocal connection to objectives explored above to a piece of text. Here, circumstances and language used are more detailed and complex

and we need a more finely tuned response through the voice. The same rules apply as above:
– breathe in the circumstances and objective through the solar plexus and into the vocal rooting and support muscles;
– engage the muscular and spinal movement through the out-breath wave;
– allow the pitch range and resonance to respond to each impulse as you play the objective.

We've chosen a speech by Blanche in Scene V of *A Streetcar Named Desire* by Tennessee Williams.

Blanche DuBois has arrived in New Orleans at the small and shabby apartment of her younger sister, Stella, to seek a refuge from her troubled life. Blanche has had to deal with all the deaths in the family and the accumulated debts, which have resulted in the loss of Belle Reve, their family home. Stella's husband, Stanley Kowalski, is an earthy and sometimes violent man who immediately distrusts Blanche. He rakes up rumours about her alleged sexually immoral behaviour in the town where she was a teacher and has just made insinuations about this to Blanche. Blanche is about to spend the evening with Mitch, a more sensitive friend of Stanley's, and hopes to develop a relationship with him. When Stanley leaves, Blanche wants to know if Stella has heard any gossip about her and Stella reassures her, followed by this:

BLANCHE: I never was hard or self-sufficient enough. When people are soft – soft people have got to court the favour of hard ones, Stella. Have got to be seductive – put on soft colours, the colours of butterfly wings, and glow – make a little – temporary magic just in order to pay for – one night's shelter! That's why I've been – not so awf'ly good lately. I've run for protection, Stella, from one leaky roof to another leaky roof – because it was storm – all storm, and I was – caught in the centre … People don't see you – men don't – don't even admit your existence unless they are making love to you. And you've got to have your existence admitted by someone, if you're going to have someone's protection. And so the soft people have got to – shimmer and glow – put a – paper lantern over the light … But I'm scared now – awf'ly scared. I don't know how much longer I can turn the trick. It isn't enough to be soft. You've got to be soft and attractive. And I – I'm fading now!

We'll tackle this speech in step-by-step stages:

1. Given circumstances

The essential given circumstances for Blanche, giving rise to this speech:

Who am I?	I'm Blanche DuBois.
Where am I?	I'm in the bedroom with Stella.
Why am I here?	Stella is getting ready to go out with Stanley. I've been writing a letter to an old admirer, who I hope may help us both out, and I'm shortly to see Mitch for a date. Stanley has just flown through and made disturbing insinuations about my sexual conduct.
What time is it?	It's summer, around seven in the evening, some weeks after my arrival.

2. The objective

The fifth W we can add to the above four is:
What do I want, what is my objective?

Place yourself imaginatively in Blanche's situation. If I'm in these circumstances, saying what Blanche says, what do I want, what do I do? So, getting the objective comes from imagination, empathy and intuition rather than the calculating left brain, but it has to be justified by the text we're given. So, the objective could be:

I want to get Stella's understanding and sympathy for whatever I had to do.

3. The stakes

What is at stake for Blanche here? Whether Stella and Stanley will allow her to stay with them, at least as a temporary refuge. Whether she will be able to find some comfort, peace and kindness here. She has no money and no other place to go. Her whole mental and physical well-being are at stake.

4. Explore quietly

Before launching into a fully voiced and performed rendition of this speech, first speak it quietly on your feet, taking your time, and exploring the objective and the different thoughts and experiences that may be coming through the words. Get the impulse of the objective – what I need to achieve, how I need to change the situation – and flow it through the thoughts, words, measures (phrases marked by commas) and sentences of the speech, like an electric current flowing through a wire. Allow each impulse to move you physically in however small a way.

5. Mark the beats

Now look at each impulse, beat, thought change within the objective in more detail, and the actions Blanche may be doing to get what she wants. These beats are usually marked by a full stop, dash or semi-colon, but a change could occur with a comma in a sentence as well. Here is our suggestion for where they occur, and what actions Blanche may be doing to herself or Stella or someone else:

1 I never was hard or self-sufficient enough.

   I judge, excuse, or reproach myself

2 When people are soft – soft people have got to court the favour of hard ones, Stella.

   Soften Stella

3 Have got to be seductive – put on soft colours, the colours of butterfly wings, and glow – make a little – temporary magic just in order to pay for – one night's shelter!

   Disarm her

4 That's why I've been – not so awf'ly good lately.

   Exonerate myself

5 I've run for protection, Stella, from under one leaky roof to another leaky roof – because it was storm – all storm, and I was – caught in the centre …

   Confront or alarm her

6 People don't see you – men don't – don't even admit your existence unless they are making love to you.

   Resent men or defy her

7 And you've got to have your existence admitted by someone, if you're going to have someone's protection.

   Educate her

8 And so the soft people have got to – shimmer and glow – put a – paper lantern over the light …

   Charm her

9 But I'm scared now –

   Arrest

10 awf'ly scared.

   Worry

11 I don't know how much longer I can turn the trick.

Warn

12 It isn't enough to be soft.

Alert

13 You've got to be soft and attractive.

Enlighten

14 And I – I'm fading now!

Implore

A word of caution here! People can get very prescriptive about *actioning*, as though there is only one valid way of doing it. A common way of tackling Stanislavski's emphasis on the importance of actions is to spend considerable time at the beginning of rehearsal intellectually choosing an action for every line of text, and only allowing transitive verbs (which have a direct object) such as 'I order you', as opposed to intransitive verbs (which don't have an object) such as 'I grovel'.

Many of the actions fixed by actors and directors in early rehearsals are in fact what Stanislavski called *adaptations*, actions that are in fact *reactions* to other people and events as they occur in the moment. These need to be discovered intuitively in practical rehearsal – using objectives, for example, as a stimulus (as in the invented dialogue in Exercise 3 above). Although some character qualities and actions may be very evident early on in repeated forms of behaviour (e.g. Blanche does a lot of justifying, imploring and deceiving), it's not helpful to the actor's creative process to try to determine all actions/reactions/adaptations in week one of rehearsal, before actors have started to connect with each other and explore the world of the play together imaginatively and on their feet.

This view is in line with Stanislavski's later rehearsal process of *active analysis* and *method of physical action.* This replaced his earlier approach of extensive round–the-table discussions, which he found made actors too much stuck in the head. If actions are not clear and defined enough as a result of an interactive, organic process, then a more conscious and rational consideration may be used *later* in rehearsal. Done too soon, actors will walk through rehearsal consciously thinking about what action they should be playing, cutting them off from genuine interaction with each other and preventing spontaneous, imaginative and richer discoveries and flexible vocal responses – in other words, they won't be playing *the action*!

As for transitive verbs, generally they offer the most specific and connected actions, but sometimes you may not be able to express something in one word because of the complexity of human behaviour, so … let's not get too anal and controlling about it all. Whatever helps you get to the truth of you-as-the-character-in-the-situation and to communicate the writer's themes and imaginary world is useful.

So, the breakdown we've suggested above is there to indicate impulse changes and a possible range of actions in the speech, and not to prescribe what you should consciously do – you need to discover that through your own imagination and commitment to the circumstances of Blanche. In the early stages, the most important thing is to intuit an objective and know where the impulses change.

6. Move the beats and voice the speech

Having made clear where each new impulse is, we're going to speak and move the speech, and make a physical movement to really mark each beat and allow it to affect you physically and vocally: initially try substantial moves like sitting, standing, turning, walking, stopping.

This is not the well-known voice practitioner exercise where you move deliberately to a different chair or walk across the room *after* a beat, and then resume speaking once you get to the new position, thus physically but mechanically marking the changes. This is a *psycho-physical* approach and involves moving *with* the new impulse, so that a specific thought or feeling determines the type of movement spontaneously.

Speak the speech now with full vocal support, committing to the objective and using each new impulse and action to achieve what you want: *to get Stella's understanding and sympathy for whatever I had to do.*

* Imagine the circumstances through your five Ws and 'If I am in the circumstances of Blanche what do I do?' and let the objective launch you into the speech.

* Explore each new impulse, breathe it in, then find the responsive physical movement and verbal action. This is only what we do in life: *impulse, breath, action.*

It's now thought by some that language evolved from music, gesture and imagistic thought associated with the right brain, and that an impulse will *first* give rise to a movement *followed* by the spoken word, produced by the left and right brains in partnership (see Chapter 2, and *The Master and his Emissary*: 190, and D. McNeill's *Hand and Mind: What Gestures Reveal about Thought*: 25).

Anybody accustomed to doing or observing responsive, organic acting will know that this is what invariably occurs, however small the initial physical movement prior to speech may be, and reflects movement and speech in everyday life. We rush into speech through nerves, tension and time pressure, instead of allowing it to come naturally from experiencing the impulse and circumstances in our whole body.

* For example, physical and verbal actions could be as follows: on beat 1, I turn away and judge myself; on 2, I walk away and soften Stella; on 3, I walk in a circle back to face her and disarm her; on 4, I sit and exonerate myself; on 5, I stand and confront her; on 6, I walk a step to her and defy her; on 7, I turn away and educate her; on 8, I walk to the back of the chair and charm her; on 9, I sit and arrest her; on 10, I sink down over my knees and worry her; on 11, I turn to her and warn her; on 12, I stand and alert her; on 13, I move towards her and enlighten her; and on 14, I walk away and implore her.

* Now do the speech again without feeling you have to do such large physical movements:

- Prepare as above, and make sure you breathe in the impulse (the thought, feeling, image) and let it ride on the movement of the breath.

- Support the out-breath with the pelvic floor and the lengthening of the Elastic Band through the spine.

- Let the sense of Me/I in the situation create a clear onset of sound and articulation. These points are important even when we play a gentle and emotional character like Blanche in order to bring clarity to her intentions and to avoid emoting and playing a general vulnerable state. Her feelings need to emerge through her circumstances and needs, through a conflict between what she wants and what she has.

- The spine speaks: engage your lumbar drive as you play your objective and actions, the need to change the situation, through your out-breath.

- Let rhythm, intonation and pitch range flow as a spontaneous response to situation, impulse, objective and action.

7. Mind, feeling and will

Let's now look at how the impulses to speak are informed by where they are coming from in our psycho-physical make-up.

Stanislavski referred to three key *inner motive forces* or *inner psychological drives* – mind, feeling and will – as a defining aspect of character (see Chapter 12 in *An Actor's Work* and *An Actor Prepares*; and also Chapter 11 of *Acting Stanislavski*).

Mind here means intellect, reason and imagination and is centred in the head.
Feeling is all our passion, feeling and emotion and is centred in the chest, or, more specifically, the solar plexus.
Will engages you on a path of action, whether aspirational, mundane or habitual, and whether initially prompted by thought or feeling. This is centred essentially in the pelvis and legs and also engages the arms.

* So, let's look at the speech and its beats from this perspective.
In Blanche's opening three beats she is arguably using her *mind* primarily to undercut any criticism that may be coming her way.
In 4, 5 and 6 she focuses on her vulnerability and is drawing on her *feeling*.
In 7 and 8, she talks of what she's got to do, so engages her *will*.
In 9 to 14, she is full of fear and warning, so drops into *feeling* again.

Of course, all the three forces are interconnected: Blanche will have feeling under her mental calculations, thought alongside her feeling and will, and will running through her whole speech, but in the sections identified above one may be predominant.

* Try the speech again under this influence, still keeping aware of each change of beat, but see how each force affects your verbal and physical action, e.g. the main influence of mind might make you more careful and indirect (e.g. 'Have got to be seductive – put on soft colours'); feeling might prompt you to sit for longer focusing on the past (e.g. 'it was storm – all storm'); or the influence of will might drive you round the room more (e.g. 'you've got to have your existence admitted by someone').

* As you do this, you *will* find yourself connecting with different aspects of your character and body. This influence may well alter the actions you used earlier and, providing you keep open and responsive, will affect your pitch range and intonation.

* The key element that will be influenced, though, is resonance: it can switch from head to chest to pelvis as the predominant force of mind, feeling or will shifts. Try the speech again with this specific focus.

8. Other influences on the objective

* **Try the speech with an obstacle, as mentioned above.**
For example, Blanche may have to overcome the fear that Stella and Stanley think of her as a whore and side with her detractors; that they may turn her out onto the street with nowhere to go; she may make herself more vulnerable by saying anything in her defence; she may damage her chances with Mitch; she may feel guilt over what happened; she may feel resentment against Stella for not helping more at Belle Reve; it may be too hot for her; she may be feeling faint and panicked.

Any of these obstacles will make it harder for Blanche *to get understanding and sympathy from Stella*, and will, therefore, strengthen or moderate the type of actions you use, e.g. Blanche may reproach Stella more at one point and beg her more at another.

* **Try a different objective with a different obstacle.**
For example, *I want to get Stella to do her duty by me now*, and the obstacle could be that she feels faint. See how this affects the range of actions and vocal response. Note how it contrasts with, or sheds new light upon, the first objective and obstacle. You might find useful elements in a range of different such attempts.

* **Now use a friend to provide a silent response to each of your beats.**
They sit or stand opposite you, for example, questioning, censuring, affirming, contradicting, comforting or shaming, so that each of your impulses and actions is a reaction to a possible response from Stella.

* **Look at the key words in the speech.**
The key words

- give emphasis and clarity to the literal sense;
- channel the thought and feeling;
- convey the objective and make your point.

So, for example, Blanche's key words might be:
beat 1 – self-sufficient
beat 2 – soft/hard (an antithesis, opposites in the same sentence – as we see later in Chapter 15)

beat 3 – seductive, magic
beat 4 – good
beat 5 – protection/storm (another antithesis)
beat 6 – men/love (another possible antithesis)
beat 7 – existence, someone
beat 8 – shimmer, lantern
beat 9 – scared
beat 10 – awf'ly
beat 11 – longer, trick
beat 12 – soft
beat 13 – attractive
beat 14 – fading

These words convey the needy, fragile and vulnerable state of Blanche, who has had to seduce men to get support and now fears she's losing her ability to turn on the magic. If we had to choose one key word, it might be 'scared'.

First, use just these key words to play the objective *of getting Stella's understanding and sympathy* – make sure your voice responds to the need to change Stella through these words. If the words develop a set pattern, for example, falling inflexions, it means you're getting into cerebral mode, attempting to describe the word rather than respond through it with all Blanche's need and intention.

Allow each key word to fill out the span of your out-breath entirely. Every word should sound active, alive and different.

Now only respond through the vowels of the key words. This will help you to find a flow through your emotional response to the situation and to vibrate your experience through the resonance of the vowels. Make sure that your voice is rooted into the pelvic floor and the spine.

Focus only on the consonants. Glue the consonants of the key words to your spine and drive them from the lumbar area in order to get what you want. Your spine should transmit the energy needed to play your objective through the out-breath.

Go back to the whole speech focusing on the importance of these key words. You will sense that your objective is strengthened and vocally expressed with greater clarity and resonance.

Now look at the alternative objective *to get Stella to do her duty by me.* Some of the key words may change – for example, you might emphasize 'hard' and 'protection' more.

* Try the speech for a final time, just focusing on the circumstances and objective and a strong sense of 'Me/I' vocally. What you've explored should automatically feed in without consciously thinking about it now, so just allow release and ease.

All such influences will reveal how flexible you can be in acting a piece of text, providing you don't decide how it should be said come what may, and remain open and flexible, with your body and voice responsive to each inner creative impulse. All the essential vocal elements have to be in place for each exploration, but should adapt like water flowing into different-shaped vessels to convey the psychological, physical and vocal truth of a character in a situation.

9. Stanley's perspective

For male actors, here's Stanley's assessment of Blanche two scenes later:

It's now mid-September. Evening. Blanche is in the bath, preparing for her birthday party, and Stanley arrives eager to relate news he's gathered about her to Stella:

> STANLEY: Honey, I told you I thoroughly checked on these stories! Now wait till I finished. The trouble with Dame Blanche was that she couldn't put on her act any more in Laurel! They got wised up after two or three dates with her and then they quit, and she goes on to another, the same old lines, same old act, same old hooey! But the town was too small for this to go on forever! And as time went by she became a town character. Regarded as not just different but downright loco-nuts. (*Stella draws back*) And for the last year or two she has been washed up like poison. That's why she's here this summer, visiting royalty, putting on all this act – because she's practically told by the mayor to get out of town! Yes, did you know there was an army camp near Laurel and your sister's was one of the places called 'Out-of-Bounds?' Well so much for her being such a refined and particular type of girl.

So, work out:
* The given circumstances for Stanley and the objective, which could be something like: *I want to convince Stella that Blanche is a fake (to justify getting her out of our lives).*
* What is at stake: possibly his contentment and whole future relationship with Stella.

* His beats and possible actions: for example, he instructs and disillusions Stella and demeans and scorns Blanche.
* His obstacle: maybe he wants to avoid seeming brutish, and he knows how attached Stella is to Blanche.

* Find the vocal support and responsiveness as above, and try the speech moving the beats; under the influence of mind, feeling and will; with an alternative objective and obstacle; with someone responding to you; and finding the key words.

It will, of course, help to absorb and integrate all this work and make it believable and natural if you take in the text as you work on it, so that you don't need to look at the page or try to remember lines.

To sum up:

To act truthfully as a character and vocally express it we need to:

- **Create and enter imaginary circumstances through the 'magic if' and the 5 Ws and breathe them in through the solar plexus to create a full vocal response.**

- **Interact spontaneously with others by really seeing them and listening and responding to them. Allow the voice to respond flexibly and speak each word and line as if for the first time. Vocally root responses in the pelvic floor and spine.**

- **Follow objectives, pursued by actions, and mediated by obstacles and what's at stake. The drive of the actor through expressing a want needs to be complemented by the breath and spinal action working together.**

12

SEEING, SENSING AND FEELING

Here we develop and enrich our sense of the character and the world and themes of the script through creating sensory and emotional experience. We examine the creation of images, both visual and relating to the other senses; sense memory; means to stimulate feeling indirectly through the text and action; and specific vocal responses to all these stimuli expressed in the manner described in the previous chapter.

For all the explorations described in this chapter, the vocal response will only be able to express these stimuli clearly if the *Vocal Givens* are in place:

- Receive the impulses through the solar plexus on your in-breath (Chapter 4, Exercise 4).

- Transmit your response through rooting into the pelvic floor and engaging the spinal support, drive and Elastic Band (rooting plays a particularly important role here because you need to stay grounded and controlled when you work with emotional responses – see Chapter 4, Exercise 8).

- Allow rhythm, intonation, pitch range and resonance to flow as a spontaneous response to situation, impulse, objective and action.

Images

In Chapter 10, Awareness, Ease and Focus, we looked at creating strong vivid images for words like 'sea'. Instead of trying to *illustrate* the word, physically and vocally, by working out *how* to say it to convey 'sea-ness', we imagined specific elements of colour, movement, sound, smell, taste and touch, and breathed in those images and sensations, letting the experience into our solar plexus, in order to find a responsive and unself-conscious vocal expression. This involved allowing the right brain and old brain to function freely without controlling interference from the left brain.

We need to see images and draw on our other senses in order to bring to life a character's given circumstances and previous circumstances (as in the previous chapter), to create imaginatively the surroundings which may not actually be there in performance, and to summon up experiences from the character's past.

Antonio Damasio emphasizes: 'In short, the process we come to know as mind when mental images become ours as a result of consciousness is a continuous flow of images many of which turn out to be logically interrelated. ... *Thought* is an acceptable word to denote such a flow of images.'

And the images are a 'mental pattern in any of the sensory modalities, e.g., a sound image, a tactile image, the image of a state of well-being'. They also relate to the 'obsessively repeated feelings that constitute the self in the act of knowing ...' (*The Feeling of What Happens*: 9, 318–9).

EXERCISES

1 For example, the speech of Blanche above contains references to her past:

I never was hard or self-sufficient enough. When people are soft – soft people have got to court the favour of hard ones, Stella. Have got to be seductive – put on soft colours, the colours of butterfly wings, and glow – make a little – temporary magic just in order to pay for – one night's shelter! That's why I've been – not so awf'ly good lately. I've run for protection, Stella, from one leaky roof to another leaky roof – because it was storm – all storm, and I was – caught in the centre ... People don't see you – men don't – don't even admit your existence unless they are making love to you.

To give this section an experienced quality, *as if* you the actor have been through what Blanche is talking about, in order to make the audience believe in you, you need to imagine specific experiences which the words describe:

• When was she not 'hard or self-sufficient enough'? What had happened and what did she do? Did she let a now-dead relative spend too much of the estate's money because she felt sorry for them, and then need to offer sexual favours to 'hard ones' who could give her money? Who were they? What did they look like?

- Who paid for 'one night's shelter' and when?

- What happened when she was 'not so awf'ly good'? Did she collapse in the street drunk?

- What are the 'leaky roofs' she mentions? Belle Reve and the hotel where she ended up? What did they look like?

- What is the 'storm' she refers to? All the deaths of relatives and the accumulating debts? You need images of the relatives and solicitors she had to deal with.

* What is one example of men who 'don't see' her until they are 'making love' to her?

- What are all the sensory elements associated with these images?

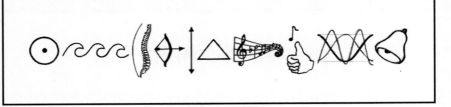

These vocal symbols apply throughout the chapter.

* Go through the speech seeing, hearing, smelling, tasting, touching and feeling these images before and during the lines. Of course, we can't hold up the momentum of a speech while we spend time conjuring up images, although the punctuation here does indicate a fragmented, broken delivery providing some space for reflection. We need to prepare all our images for present and past circumstances and our surroundings during the rehearsal process, so that they pop up onto an imaginary screen in front of our eyes, and register in our other senses, before and during the relevant words describing them.

* What we experience and what it means to us will then inform the expression of the lines, how we act out our objectives, and the range and intensity of the actions. The images need to be *specific, detailed and vivid* so that we and the audience are affected: *we need to see with our speech so that they see*

with their ears, as Stanislavski emphasized. This means avoiding playing a state and emotion and allowing the images to work on us as we pursue the objective. This keeps us rooted, and keeps emotion balanced by our minds and wills.

* Vocally, our in-breath energy should be like an umbilical cord connecting us to the imagined sensory images, while with our out-breath we find both responsive flexibility in expression of the images and pelvic and spinal rooting for their clear communication – otherwise, we may see in an introverted manner rather than really connect with our partners and the audience.

Again we start with the text, go to the subtext of imagined experience that also connects with us psychologically, physically and emotionally, and then arrive back at the text with the spoken word describing our experience. As Linklater makes clear, in this process 'the spoken word reveals rather than describes the inner content. It is *the word made flesh* rather than *the word as symbol* (*Freeing Shakespeare's Voice*: 35). This is another differentiation between the organic and the representational schools of acting. In the former we *experience* the sea, the mountains, brutality or pleasure as ourselves as the character in imaginary circumstances; in the latter, we *describe* the words and the character, with the text working *parallel* to the action rather than being an intrinsic part of it.

2   Here's a vivid speech from Scene 19 of *A Warwickshire Testimony* by April de Angelis, which involves images of the present scene, the past and the future. The character, Diggie, has no work and sometimes sleeps in the woods, where he is now. He switches focus between seeing what the woods used to be like and a murder he thinks he sees in the future.

DIGGIE: It's peaceful here. Except when he comes. I don't like to see him. I don't like to see him with the girl. He has her by the arm and he pulls her. She is talking to him all the while but he's not listening. She's a pretty girl. I found an orchid here that's very rare. You don't see them much. Like a white flame balancing on its stalk. Things have gone. Things you saw every day. Flowers. Primroses. They used to be everywhere. Birds have gone too. It's quieter in the woods. Maybe they all flew away one winter and decided not to come back. I might have done that if I was a bird. She's saying to him to let her go. But he's not. She's white. Her face is white and her hair is stuck to it dark like weeds. He has her by the arm and he's not letting go. He has a coat on like a soldier's so it's harder to make him out, but her white face sticks out.

* From the words, create the images, and let these impulses flow through the words describing what you see. Re-experience rather than make a report.

- Look at the huge contrast between violent and peaceful images.
- See how they may create an opposing tempo and rhythm.
- Create specifics:

  What do the man and girl look like? See her white face and dark hair and the man's army coat. What is the weather as they struggle? What flowers and birds is Diggie seeing from the past? What does he see now in the 'quieter' woods around him?

* For an image passage to be real and alive we must know it *by heart* – that is, literally absorbed into our body and feeling – so that we can 'run the film' without breaks and allow the words and our voices to respond.

* As we see images more clearly, so we become more responsive, and how we communicate them will develop. For example, we will respond physically to the impulse of specific images: 'He has her by the arm and he pulls her' might provoke a physical impulse of retreat. Rather than play fear, shock or awe, we should breathe in the images and allow an organic response to take place in our emotions, physicality and vocal expression.

* We will *focus* on different areas in the space. If something is very difficult to admit – as with Blanche's 'That's why I've been – not so awf'ly good lately' – focus may be towards oneself. If you're looking into the past, it may be downwards – as with Diggie's 'Things have gone. Things you saw every day.' Different images – for example, the flowers and the violence – may be seen in different areas of the space. Seeing into the future might bring the focus up and to the right. These adjustments will, hopefully, become automatic and spontaneous. We'll look at this in more detail in Chapter 14, The Actor in the Space.

* The images will also develop a distinct mode of progression, forming patterns, as with Diggie's switch between nature images and the acts of violence.

* There will be an obstacle – the obstacle to the objective – that will create a resistance to the images.

All these elements will change and colour our vocal response. We can tackle image passages any time. They don't have to be from written text. We can make them up: for example, describe a painting or landscape you know, or a journey, accident or wedding you've experienced. The more we work from images, the more we break the pattern of seeing words on the page and cerebrally illustrating and telegraphing them.

Sensing

EXERCISES

Sensory score

Imagine a *sensory score* for where you might have been reading a book: what do you see, hear, smell, taste and touch? Let's say you were sitting outside a park café in May. You will see the book, and possibly a table, other people and toddlers, dogs running, grass, trees and flowers. You may hear birdsong, the clatter of crockery, music, a hum of voices. You may smell hot coffee, cut grass, wisteria from the café walls, and sun on your skin. You may taste coffee and the remains of a sandwich. You feel your bottom on a wooden chair, arms on the tabletop, collar against your neck. Now imagine you are back in that situation by recreating those sensory elements. Breathe and receive them. Take in how your breathing is affected.

Respond with a sound to each sensory experience, whether a sound of surprise, release or amusement; then respond to the whole situation with a sound. Try this with other circumstances, such as being at a party, on a snowy mountain, or in a castle.

Sense memory

This leads us on to how we are vocally affected by specific physical sensations that we can recreate through *sense memory*.

Sensations from outside

* Let's look at a few examples, beginning with *heat*. To be truthful and organic we need to avoid *indicating* heat through mechanical use of cliché, such as lots of face-fanning or brow-wiping – although these actions may be acceptable if they come from a genuine experience and impulse.

* First, recall a time when you experienced intense heat. Imaginatively recreate

the situation and place yourself back in it. Where were you? Why were you there? What were you doing? When was it? For example, you might have been on a coach in South America in the August of 2008.

Now think of the specific sensations created by that heat – wet armpits, dry mouth, sweat on the back of the neck, swollen feet, headache?

Thirdly, how did you deal with the symptoms? Did you put a hanky round your neck, drink a lot of water, shade your eyes with a hat or sunglasses? We will feel the sensation most when trying to deal with it, as Uta Hagen points out (*A Challenge for the Actor*: 80).

Finally, you should be aware of the sensory score in the situation. Do you hear a straining engine, traffic noise, chatter in Spanish? Do you see the back of a straw hat and a battered seat? Do you smell stale sweat and diesel fuel? Do you feel rough cloth against bare thighs and the window against your arm? Do you taste warm Coca-Cola?

In this way you create truthful responses to heat because they are based in reality and will inevitably be richer, more varied and interesting than an attempt to describe heat through stock gestures. What you discover in such an exercise can then be transferred to creating heat in the situation of a performance and developed according to the requirements of the specific character and circumstances.

* Vocally, what is happening? What is your breathing pattern – slow and shallow, for example? Are your mouth and throat dry? Are you relaxed, floppy, and energy-less? Explore the sound which sums up this state. How is your resonance affected? Do you use a lower resonance area? Is your pitch range wavier? Is your onset softer and articulation a bit blurry on the consonants?

* Now look at the opposite sensation, *cold*. Place yourself back in a situation of extreme icy cold. Recall the circumstances, your symptoms – chattering teeth, frozen joints, watering eyes? – and how you dealt with them. What was the sensory score? What is happening vocally now? Is your breathing deeper and more energized because the cold is taking it away? Maybe your alignment is a bit shortened and tight as you hold your arms and body in? Your onset may be more explosive, resonance higher, pitch range flatter, and articulation crisper.

* And if you're *drunk*? Deep, slow breathing? Floppy posture? Released, strong onset? And maybe resonance in the throat, unpredictable pitch range and slurred articulation?

* With *flu* you may find difficulty breathing, the body is closed and aching, onset is weak, resonance is nasal, pitch range non-existent, and articulation a major struggle.

Sensations from inside

* A truthful expression will only be found for other physical occurrences if the right physiological basis is created. For example, a believable sound for a *yawn* will only happen if we recognize we yawn when the brain needs air: so we need to prize open the upper jaw, suck in air, allowing the wind-rush sensation to occur, the eyes to press closed and water, and then the air and yawn sound to come through a closing jaw.

* We'll only get a truthful *gagging* sound if we imagine stuff rising up from the stomach into the throat and contract the uvula and soft palate and raise the tongue.

* A panicky, fearful, shocked sound from *losing balance* and staggering will best come if you defocus your eyes and let the legs wobble as though the bones have disappeared suddenly.

* A credible cry of *surprise* will come if we don't anticipate an unexpected event or appearance, and allow the impulse to come from the solar plexus, a nerve centre: the rib cage jerks upwards, a sudden sharp sound will happen, often followed by recovery, an intake of breath and a sigh of relief, possibly with a hand placed over the solar plexus.

Whatever the vocal response, make sure that you transmit it through rooted out-breath energy and share it with the audience.

Feeling

The essence of vocal responsiveness to our feelings is in avoiding effort and self-consciousness. *Feeling* encompasses a wide range of experiences. We have a feeling, intuition or sense about something – we feel uneasy or distrustful; we have feelings in the sense of an attitude towards people – we feel love, respect, hostility. We also have passions, a strong commitment and intensity of feeling for something or someone: a lover, football, or theatre. We have emotions that arise from our memory bank reminding us of past joy or loss. Very often emotions are created by pursuing our objectives against obstacles and either failing or succeeding to get what we want. I can't get what I want so I burst into tears or throw plates in anger; or I get what I want and laugh or shout in relief. I try to change or encompass reality through the emotion, by a means that isn't rational, conscious and controlled, but is coming from the subconscious, memory, and from our will with a touch of attempted magic.

What is clear is that feelings come out of real concrete circumstances. Stanislavski advised actors to 'Direct all your attention to the "given circumstances". They are always within easy reach', and to 'forget about your feelings, because they are largely of subconscious origin, and not subject to direct command' (*An Actor Prepares*: 44). *Not subject to direct command* is the key insight here. Actors are human beings, we have the same basic make-up as every other human being on earth. We feel empathy and compassion for people suffering earthquake, flood and famine on the other side of the world, whom we don't even know. We all need air, food, shelter, clothing and human contact to survive. We all feel the same range of emotions, which are stimulated in the same way. So, when we come to recreate these feelings in performance, we need to trust we're human, and trust in the reliable stimuli for the emotions: believing, imagining we are the character in their circumstances for the duration of the performance; reacting to other people spontaneously; pursuing what we want against the other person's objective and a range of obstacles, and knowing how important it is to get what we want. If we commit to this recreation of how we act in everyday life, then feelings will flow automatically and freely.

The worst thing we can do is to endgame and think about results: to think about what emotion we should be getting; to anticipate when and how it should happen; to try to repeat what we did in the last performance or rehearsal; to work for an effect or squeeze the emotion through physical tension; to enter a private bubble to summon up a remembered emotion while cutting off from other actors.

So, as with experiencing images and responding to sensations, we need to have a free vocal response to feeling. This has to come from ease as the actor, and be controlled artistically and not indulged or excessive. The above mistakes would produce self-consciousness and premeditation, and either heady vocal descriptions of emotion or something tense, strangulated and disconnected from the action. Even if the character is tense, the actor must always be at ease. This is a hard one to learn for student actors, but we are recreating reality artistically and not imitating it. Without ease, as we stressed in Chapter 10, our creativity will suffer.

EXERCISES

Emotion memory and empathy

In performance, if we strip away blocks to our impulses and believe in the circumstances, we will draw unconsciously on our emotion memory. This may take the form of tapping into an accumulated experience of feelings of pain, loss, anger, relief, joy or jealousy, rather than a feeling associated with one specific incident. Stanislavski referred to these accumulated feelings as 'distilled into a single, wider, deeper memory ... This is a synthesis of all like feelings.'

The emotion we then experience will not be some new emotion, but what he called a *repeated* or *recurrent* emotion, 'analogous to the one you experienced before', but it is undeniably *your* emotion as the actor and not the writer's or anybody else's (*An Actor's Work*: 206, 218).

As an exercise to connect with our common humanity and our past feelings stored in our old brain, body and nervous system, we can look back at a range of circumstances in which we experienced particular basic emotions.

* Imagine:

  * events of great excitement and happiness, like a wedding or reunion;
  * events of sadness and loss, like a funeral;
  * situations prompting success or failure, jealousy, guilt, fear, indifference;
  * times when you were nervous, depressed, or hopeful and full of anticipation;
  * relationships that created anger and hate or tenderness and love.

* See if analogous feelings arise from the memory and give it a spontaneous expression: like a whoop of excitement, a wrench of grief, a growl of anger, a sigh of depression or a love-filled laugh.

* Use words that express the recreated circumstances – 'I was so tense about everything', 'she was gorgeous' – or that put you back in the situation as if it's happening again – 'I've had enough of you', 'I'm so happy for you.'

* Look at *other* people and what they're experiencing: war victims in Afghanistan or Syria, a friend who's lost a relative, a neighbour who's had an amazing holiday. Our empathy can translate into a more direct experience. You identify with someone else's situation so much that you start to feel what the other person feels.

* Again, find a vocal expression through sounds and words for the emotional states of others, and then speak as though their experience is yours. For example: go from 'God, these poor people, how can they survive all this?' to 'I've lost everything, how can I recover from this?'; and from 'Lucky Jack, he had such a great time' to 'It was fantastic!' Michael Chekhov believed that creative consciousness itself is innately compassionate because it observes characters and seeks to identify, so you suffer for Hamlet and cry with Juliet. Compassion

'severs the bonds of your personal limitations and gives you deep access into the inner life of the character' (*To the Actor*: 100).

* If you find it hard to identify with the predicament of others, you can always use 'as if'. I've no conception of what it's like to be bombed and made homeless, so I think of it *as if* a gas main has ruptured and blown up my house, completely wrecking it. Or I can imagine something real which has actually happened to me, like a ceiling falling down, and multiply tenfold how I feel about it, with the appropriate vocal response.

Sensation of feeling

Michael Chekhov's technique for arousing truthful feeling was first to create a sensation of it through simple physical action – through gestures and movement. This opens the way for development of a genuine feeling, of associated feelings and qualities, and a stronger sense of the character as a whole.

* So, let's look at a feeling of *impatience*. I start by moving my arm or foot impatiently, so the simple action is filled with a psychological quality. I then move through the space under the influence of impatience, finding the gestures, movement and physical actions associated with it. I also think impatient thoughts. This is easy because we've all experienced impatience or observed impatient people. We have a knowledge of it and can respond intuitively without having to make conscious decisions. As I move creating this sensation of impatience, I now start to feel genuinely impatient. Also, other qualities may develop, such as irritability, resentment, dismissiveness, frustration. These qualities will affect my physicality and tempo and rhythm, and how I occupy the space I'm in and relate to other people.

* They will also, of course, affect my vocal response. What are the sounds and words of impatience – for example, 'tah!', 'Why do I always have to wait?' – or of caution, anger, generosity, suspicion, or any other quality we might explore in this manner? If we get accustomed to making believable voiced responses to such imaginative impulses, we will find it easier to make believable textual responses to our characters' impulses.

Atmosphere

If emotions are our *individual* feelings, atmosphere is the *objective* feeling, created by the actors' sense of circumstance, interaction, objectives, qualities, and all the external elements like light, set, temperature, music and sound. The atmosphere binds actors together and draws the audience deeper into the imaginary reality of performance. It will affect every aspect of our behaviour: our movement, speech, thoughts, feelings and relationship to others.

* Try working under the influence of different atmospheres (similar to the last exercise): for example, *fear, tension, hostility, joy, relief, relaxation, suspicion*. You need to work with others collectively for this. Just imagine that each new atmosphere pervades the space like smoke so that you can draw on it as a tangible thing. For this exercise, you needn't create detailed circumstances. The particular atmosphere can come from whatever situation enters your imagination first. Just go with it and respond, relating to the space and other people under the influence of a collective awareness.

* Again, find the spontaneous vocal response in sounds and words. For example, a *joyful* atmosphere will open you up to the space and others and prompt an open released sound from rooted breath support, lifted alignment, strong onset, full body resonance, free pitch range and confident articulation. A *suspicious* atmosphere will close you down and create a tighter response: you still need to keep rooted as the actor, but there may be a less emphatic onset, a resonance more in the cheekbone area, and flat pitch range and slower speech rhythm.

To sum up:

- **Create images from the text, then use the words to experience them.**

- **The voice should respond to every nuance of sensory experience via breath, alignment, onset, resonance, pitch range and articulation.**

- **Feeling comes indirectly through the action, not through 'direct command', and the voice must respond to feeling rather than illustrate it externally, while still remaining under control.**

13
CHARACTER VOICE

In the previous three chapters we've looked at the importance of ease and focus to prepare your mind and body for creativity; at the foundation of circumstances, interaction and objectives for the creation of character; and at the role of senses and feeling in enriching and filling a characterization with life. We now look at the physical embodiment of a role, with our main focus on the voice.

As always when acting, the *Vocal Givens* should be in place so that the voice responds spontaneously and expressively to acting impulse. Make sure that:

- your alignment is easy and centred;
- your breath is ready to receive;
- your pelvic floor muscles and spinal drive are ready to root and drive your response through the out-breath wave of every moment;
- your onset is centred and clear;
- your pitch range is ready to express your responses freely and musically;
- your resonance spaces are open and the voice can resonate freely through your whole body;
- your articulators are ready to react with clarity and muscularity.

A character's voice, like every other aspect of character, can only come from you, from your basic resources, but these resources can be transformed into an enormous range of permutations. Every actor wants to transform really, but we need to do that with belief and a sense of truth. While 'going to' the character we have to remain rooted in the reality of *our* physical, emotional, sensory and mental nature – a nature that hopefully will be expanded in scope and potential through our training and eagerness for knowledge and experience.

So, we have to start with our own voice and train it, not just to produce a good clear easy voice, but to extend its possibilities – in flexibility of alignment, ease and control of breath, clarity of onset, range and quality of pitch, accessibility to resonance areas, and in different types of articulation – so that the whole quality of the voice can change as a response to creative impulse and become *anyone's* voice. We can see the potential range of the actor's voice in the work of extraordinary impressionists like Rory Bremner and actors like Meryl Streep, who can switch from a Danish farmer to Margaret Thatcher. Have a go at creating the vocal quality of the different people you know, of either sex and regardless of age, and get a sense of your versatile possibilities and present limitations. It's great fun and increases your awareness!

When we come to develop a specific character voice, it needs to be a total response to all the influences coming from the text and the imaginary world of the play. It should be a unique vocal aspect that fits the actor's whole characterization. Its tempo and tone may come from personality qualities; its pitch, placement and resonance may come from external factors and be part of an accent. It should be an organic, natural response, not superimposed on a character like a funny walk: you are your voice, the character is their voice.

We've covered a lot of imaginative impulses behind physical and vocal action and shall revisit some of them now and look at some new ones. Don't forget your essential *Vocal Givens*:

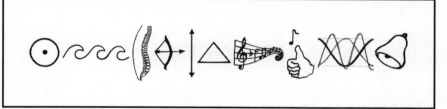

Background and given circumstances

The voice we have changes throughout our lives according to what we do with it and where. If we were to move from quiet office life to work as a cattle auctioneer, or from a steel mill to work on a farm, the environmental change and demands of the job will exert some influence on how we sound. So consider where the character was born and brought up, in country or town, their family background, class, education and occupation: a lawyer educated at Westminster School and living in Surrey will not sound like a car worker educated in a comprehensive school and living in Coventry. This is an obvious point, but we need to identify all those elements that make us different, and discover through research, observation and imagination how they affect the voice.

Accent and dialect

A part of the effect of circumstances on voice will come from accent, and also dialect, the specific nature of speech and language in a particular area or job. These are often seen by actors as the only elements changing the voice, but clearly people with the same accent and dialect have different vocal range, intonation, resonance, articulation and so on. Accent and dialect are important, though, and make an immediately noticeable impression of character, and if not done well will break audience belief in your acting.

When working on this area of the voice there are numerous points to consider: geography, history, culture, climate, class, occupation, gender and education, for example.

How is our own accent different from our character's? What is the tune, tone, tempo rhythm and energy of the character accent? How is it stressed and how loud is it? How do the vowels and consonants work? Where is the placement in the mouth? What shapes do the tongue, lips, cheeks, soft palate and lower jaw make to produce sound? In what direction does the accent travel in the mouth, and how does the whole body respond?

EXERCISE

You've probably worked on a number of accents before, so just try out a few and observe the changes that take place in the above elements, and how they differ in your own accent.

Developing a good 'ear' – an intuitive feel for accent – is indispensable for accent work, but there are many helpful resources to draw on, from local recordings and CDs in accent books to the Sound Archive at the British Library and various websites such as the BBC's, YouTube and IDEA – the International Dialects of English Archive; these and a good accent coach should be consulted if you need assistance.

Interaction

The nature of our social interaction with others also affects how we speak. Again, this will be affected by environment, culture, climate, history and class. Two English accountants may appear quite calm, controlled and contained when speaking to each other. On the other hand, two Greek café owners may get so agitated and physically expressive that to people from a northern European culture they appear to be having an argument.

The energy and tempo, volume and range with which we speak also changes with the situation, revealing different aspects of character. For example, one of the accountants may transform into a loud, abusive and demonstrative person at an England–France rugby international, whereas one of the Greek café owners may become romantic and playful with his new, younger girlfriend! The voice is specific to a character, but also to all the different manifestations of a personality.

EXERCISE

Look at how your own voice changes in different situations, e.g. with parents, at a party, on holiday, in arguments, or with close friends or lovers.

Imagine yourself in each of these different circumstances, and try to reproduce the particular vocal quality that occurs, e.g. calm and laid-back, excited and higher, forceful with chest resonance. Take note of what changes occur and why.

Drives

Superobjectives

We've talked about superobjectives in Chapter 11, and these can be a Life Superobjective, or one running through the play, or just through a main episode of the play.

Possibly the key influence on our vocal quality is the Life Superobjective, our objective in life before the play starts, understood from everything that happens in the play. It may change completely during the play, for example, if you're Othello, who goes through a major transformation, as we'll see later; or stay the same, if you are, for example, Desdemona in the same play.

We express this superobjective like this: *What do I want in life, why, and to what lengths would I go to achieve it?* For example:

- I want to make a load of money, because I love all the material things of life, and I'd go to the length of breaking the law and moral codes.

- I want to find real love, because life is meaningless without it, and I'd go to the length of patient searching without compromise.

These Life Objectives can't be acted out in every line and section of the text but will exercise an *influence* on how the smaller objectives are acted out. They also define the essential drive of your character, their attitude to life and the parameters they set themselves. They get to the core of who you are and of your vocal quality.

EXERCISE

Focus on your own Life Superobjective: What is it? How has it developed? How does it affect your voice and mode of expression?

Say the above superobjectives out loud with conviction and see what effect they have on your vocal quality, including onset, pitch range, resonance and volume.

Inner motive forces

Objectives, however small or all-embracing, also contain elements of Stanislavski's *inner motive forces*: the *mind, feeling and will* we all possess in different combinations and which affect our whole psycho-physical make-up (see Chapter 11).

Each force has a different physical centre:

- *Mind* – intellect and imagination in the two hemispheres of the brain – is centred in the head.

- *Feeling* – our passions, emotions, intuitive feelings – is centred in the solar plexus, the energy and nerve centre at the core of our breathing.

- *Will* – derived from both mind and feeling, engaging us on a course of action – is centred in the lower abdomen, pelvis and legs.

One of these, as Michael Chekhov makes clear, can be predominant in a character's life, or in particular scenes, and may change at different points in their life. For example, Hamlet starts the play surging with discontented, disturbed feelings; then, after learning from the ghost of his father about his murder, his mind takes over to assess how to proceed; and arguably at the end he follows his will and a determined course of conduct.

The character with the first superobjective above might be will-led. The second one, feelings-led.

These forces can take on different qualities. Thought can be cold and sharp, slow or lightning fast, light or weighty. Feelings can be intense, humorous, obsessive or sunny. Our will may be fiery and passionate or cold and steely.

EXERCISE

What is your own balance of forces? Which one predominates and in what circumstances? What are the specific qualities of your thinking, feelings and will? How do these factors affect your own voice?

* Take any speech you're familiar with and say it under the influence of each inner force; as a predominantly thinking, feeling or will-driven person. What does that do imaginatively to your voice?

Qualities

So what we want will be expressed with a range of thought, feelings and will – and also a variety of qualities.

The first superobjective above, *I want to make a load of money, because I love all the material things of life, and I'd go to the length of breaking the law and moral codes*, reveals a clear intellectual assessment, a lack of relationship to human empathy and feeling, and a ruthless will.

Possible personality qualities in such a character are materialistic, acquisitive, calculating, affable, gregarious, shallow, hedonistic, enthusiastic, exuberant, positive, ruthless and disrespectful: a character more led by the left brain.

You can also see here contradictory qualities – like affable and ruthless – which we all have and which make us human. There will also be ones we ourselves do or do not possess. We need to find a connection with the ones we don't have – normally. For example, there might have been some point somewhere when we *did* reveal an element of them, or we can use the *magic if* to effect an imaginative transformation: if I were in this character's circumstances, with their background, at this point in their life, with this particular attitude and relationships, etc., *what would I do and become?*

The second superobjective is *I want to find real love, because life is meaningless without it, and I'd go to the length of patient searching without compromise.* Here we have an opposing sort of character. They are motivated by a feeling justified by a philosophical position and personal experience, and they will pursue their goal with commitment and integrity. Possible traits in this character might be aspirational, idealistic, frustrated, lonely, generous, loving, empathic, patient, dismissive, rigorous, uncompromising: a character more present in the right brain.

EXERCISE

What are your own qualities and what specific effect do they have on your voice? Take the same speech as before and speak it under the influence of a main quality, e.g. as an acquisitive or generous person. How do the changes manifest vocally?

Psycho-physical expression

What voice and physicality can we imagine from the combination of elements in the two characters above? The first character might be someone who is predominantly will-led, who leads from the lower body and swaggers a bit with the chest out and chin up, and makes sudden, strong movements, or they might be leading from the head, a plotting, calculating type, revealing nothing through a contained and indirect physicality.

Vocally, in the first option, the posture might be pulled up, creating a forceful, even loud, barked onset, with chest resonance, a pitch range in the mid to low area, and clear emphasized articulation. In the second option, the character might sit more and lean to the right, take slower breaths, use an economical onset, with head resonance, a limited and higher pitch range, and a tighter, clipped articulation.

The second character, who wants love, might physically be open, lifted, light, alert, leading from the solar plexus, steady and direct. Vocally, their breath might be easy, slow and deep, have a clear but gentle onset, full body resonance and a pitch range varied by their emotions, with a slow, deliberate articulation.

You may have completely different ideas, and that's as it should be – but the key thing is that we use our imagination and experience to prompt these types of transformations: whether they are slight or grotesque depends on the form and genre of the script, but we must allow them to happen and also be believable.

A note of caution: when you're out of optimum alignment as a character and use a forceful voice, you need to make sure that it is still healthy, endurable and sustainable in performance. It is essential to counterbalance anything that might create tension, e.g. if the chest is out and chin up, we need to make sure that the neck is long and not crunched, the shoulders are dropped, and that the lumbar and pelvic area strongly support the raised chest, so that the larynx is unrestricted and the breath can flow easily, releasing a free vocal response. A barked quality can be created, but through open channels rather than grinding the vocal folds.

Michael Chekhov developed some character creation exercises to give full psycho-physical expression to character objectives, inner motive forces and qualities. These can be discovered in more detail in his *To the Actor* and John's *Acting Stanislavski,* but here they are in brief.

Psychological gesture

This is an active gesture made with the whole body to physicalize in a non-naturalistic, expressive way the essence of a character. The character's superobjective in life is the basic stimulus for this. The gesture, like objectives themselves, connects to our will initially, and triggers the other elements of mind and feeling.

EXERCISES

Let's work with *I want to make a load of money, because I love all the material things of life, and I'd go to the length of breaking the law and moral codes* or *I want to find real love, because life is meaningless without it, and I'd go to the length of patient searching without compromise.*

1   You can start by just exploring these desires with one hand and arm, finding an archetypal gesture for reaching and grabbing or yearning and aspiring. We then include the other arm, the legs and trunk. We take a clear starting position, possibly one that expresses where the character is coming from, their life situation at the start of the script, and execute the want physically, and finish cleanly.

As with the Chekhov basic movements we did in Chapter 10, the PG is about integrating mind and body, making the body responsive to a creative impulse, and creating a clear, communicable psycho-physical action. We start with an impulse and run it through a physical action in a way that can give us an imaginative and physical sense of the whole character.

Anne Dennis, in *The Articulate Body – The Physical Training of the Actor* (27), calls this 'the physical feeling' of the character, which needs to be sustained through a whole performance. Inspired by Etienne Decroux, the French actor, teacher and director, she also emphasizes one of our running themes: '*We are looking for an external physicality dictated by an internal source*, and reflecting the very essence of a character – his thoughts and feelings. We are *making the invisible, visible'* (39).

So the PG is inspired by what we intuitively grasp of the character but, through its physical expression, it will also inspire a feeling of the whole character:

The *kind* of gesture will awaken a specific desire.
The *strength* of it stirs the will.
The *quality* evokes particular feelings.

2   Below is a possible PG for the grasping character. The desire is a grabbing acquisitive one, the will is strong, and quality and feelings are exuberant and ruthless, sweeping aside opposition.

Figure 52 Psychological gesture

* Start legs hip-width apart. Arms are bent alongside the legs, and fingers are splayed, palms to the floor. The right hand thrusts forward as the right knee bends, and grasping, forms a fist, which bends towards the right shoulder. At the same time, the left hand is open, moves across the front of the chest, and then sweeps to the left side of the body and forms another fist with the arm extended.

3   The PG should be:

   • strong in conception and execution, even if you're not playing a strong character;

- simple, in the way it grasps the essence of a possibly complex and contradictory character;

- clear in form, with a sense of ease and wholeness;

- and definite in tempo.

* A quicker or slower tempo can change the nature of mind, feeling and will in the gesture. The tempo in the above gesture is fast with a sudden, thrusting feel to it. If we were to do this PG in a slow, sustained way the quality and feeling might become more deliberate, calculating and gloating.

Try it out and feel the difference.

4   Keep making attempts at the above gesture until you're satisfied you are really physicalizing the want, main qualities and will of the character and grasping a psycho-physical feeling of it.

Try saying the superobjective before the gesture to see if they really match. Then just say *I want to make a load of money* through the gesture as you do it. Then say it without the gesture to see if that embodied sense is retained in your vocal delivery, which is what we have to achieve in performance.

5   Now find a sound that expresses this character essence and run it through the gesture: a guttural, visceral roar of triumph perhaps.

6   Having vocally responded above to a sense of the character according to superobjective, inner motive forces and qualities, take note of how doing the PG has affected you: you may well find that you become vocally more defined, muscular and embodied.

Make up a few lines this character might say, and speak them with the feel of what you want in life and of the PG running through them.

We can use the PG to get a full sense of a character before a performance, and also use it to express a particular speech or line or moment to discover new life and clarity. The PG is part of the process of acting and so shouldn't be shown to an audience, but it can inspire how we stand, move and gesture, and speak.

Imaginary centre

We can all become aware of where we live in our bodies, where we *experience* ourselves to be. It might be in one of the main centres, head, chest or pelvis; it might relate to other energy areas (*chakras, tan tiens*); but it could also be in your eyes, nose, fingers, back, feet or even outside the body. This is an imaginative idea – there are no limits. For example, if I am a sharp, clear intellectual I might have a very focused centre in the middle of my forehead. If I'm very inquisitive and thoughtful I might be centred in the tip of my nose. If I'm very languorous and sexy I might be in my pelvis.

We can then embellish by defining the centre more specifically. What is its size, colour, shape, texture, mass, temperature, mobility? So, for example, a confident, integrated person, connected to the world, might have a solar plexus centre that is a round, soft, warm, revolving, radiating, golden ball of fire the size of an orange. An unfocused and uncontrolled person who is always chasing themselves might have a centre above their head, a cold, flashing ice-blue light, zig-zagging from side to side quickly in front of them.

EXERCISES

1 Start by walking in your space and get a sense of where *you* are centred.

Then try out a whole range of different centres, working from head to toe. Imagine each strongly and walk through the space, allowing it to affect your movement and how you feel. It's an imaginative influence to which we simply respond. Don't make intellectual decisions about how you should act.

Each centre can affect our tempo, rhythm, length of pace, posture, hand movements, head angle, and whether we move directly or indirectly, lightly or forcefully, in a flowing or jerky way. Each can also make us feel we have a different predominant quality. And each may prompt a different vocal sound.

2 *Resonance areas*

A centre may shift during a script as a character's main objectives, predominant inner motive force and qualities are changed by events. We can see such major shifts in characters like King Lear, Hamlet, Ophelia and Lady Macbeth. Vocally, we may shift from one main resonance area to another, from chest to head to pelvis.

* Remind yourself of the Exploring Resonance exercises in Chapter 7 and make all the sounds we worked on: *YOO, YOE, YAW,* etc. Listen to how the sounds fit and resonate in particular areas.

* As you experiment with a range of centres, find the resonance area and sound that match up.

Find the optimum pitch for each centre and the corresponding pitch range. See how each affects the tone of your onset of sound, possibly shifting from crisp and bright to warm and rounded to dark and gruff: it's through this that the audience hears the identity of the character.

3 Now consider the two characters above.

The character who wants to make money might have a centre in the lower gut or pelvis, with a *YOE* sound. It could be a round, hard, shiny, red disc, cold and spinning, and the size of a saucer.

The second character, who wants love, might have a centre in the solar plexus, with a *YAW* sound: large, oval, soft, warm, green and still.

* Try these two different centres. See how they affect normal everyday movement: walking, running, stopping, turning, sitting and lying. Don't be tempted to caricature and represent the character. This is you moving with a different centre – just let it change you.

* Vocally, try tuning yourself, for example, into the *YOE* sound of the first character: imagine you pass a shop window displaying diamonds and watches. See an expensive watch you want and respond through *YOE*. Make sure you start from your optimum pitch, allow your out-breath wave to vibrate on *YOE*, and root your response into the pelvic floor and lumbar drive.

You can access your whole pitch range while resonating through the pelvis – you needn't be trapped in one range. Respond by saying: 'This is me: YOE. I can speak high and I can speak low', exploring your high and low pitch. Say 'I love this watch' through your resonance.

* Work with all the objects in the room: put on a coat, drink some tea, close a window under this influence.

* Invent an activity or task these characters might do during any day of the week, for example, checking bank statements or cleaning shoes, writing an email or brushing the hair, and allow the centre to work on you, affecting how you perform these actions.

4 While you're doing the activity, allow sounds, words and sentences to come through as a direct vocal response, so that a particular voice is suggested by the centre.

Imaginary body

Each influence we look at will exert an effect on physicality and voice, like adding colours to a painting rather than bricks to a wall. The overall vocal picture will gradually emerge through all the various imaginative influences we use and a growing understanding and experience of the character. So, again, don't rush. Use a rehearsal period to the full and allow for organic, natural development.

The idea of imagining a character body complements the imaginary centre.

EXERCISES

1   Walk in your space again and make yourself very aware of the nature of your body – height, weight, build, posture – and of how you move, the space you fill and the energy you radiate.

2   Now take the characters above, or a character you would like to play, and imagine what sort of a body they might have as a result of their superobjective, qualities and balance of inner motive forces. See this body and imagine that it now exists *in the space of your own body* – not thrown on like a coat. It's as if it's grown out of your own flesh and bones.

* You can start by imagining one arm or a leg, then extend into the whole body. Note how you need to imagine your body grow thinner or fatter, taller or shorter, straighter or more bent – adapt your body to the imagination, while avoiding creating tension. A flexible, easy body is again vital. It's amazing how imagination and belief in yourself as someone else can actually make you look much bigger or smaller in performance. Once you've made this imaginative step in transformation you can start to think about make-up and padding and suchlike, but not before – it will just look fake. For example, never wear a pregnancy pad until you've got a strong imaginative sense of what pregnancy does to your body and how it makes you feel.

* The first character might have a solid, weighty build, be of medium height, generate a lot of energy and walk with a thrusting movement. The second might be tall, light and slim, have a contained energy and walk with a gliding movement. Imagine their posture, and also their hair, eye and facial colouring.

* Move through the space under the influence of these bodies, and check to see if the imaginary centre you chose fits the new body.

* As with the centre, explore everyday movements, objects and an activity.

3 Again, what sounds and words are prompted as you do your activity? What is the vocal quality suggested by this specific body influence?

Sensation of feeling

In Chapter 12, we already looked at this Chekhov technique for arousing truthful feeling by first creating a sensation of it through action and gesture. It also prompts associated feelings and qualities, and a stronger sense of the character as a whole. It's best to do this exercise with others, but you can do it alone.

EXERCISES

So let's focus on the main quality in each of our two characters: let's say acquisitive and generous.

1 We start by moving under the influence of acquisitiveness, finding the movement, physical actions, gestures and thoughts associated with it. We can do this intuitively, rather than control things intellectually, because most of us have been grasping at some point or have observed it in others. As we fill ourselves with this main quality, we may also start to become aggressive, calculating, exuberant and disrespectful. All this affects our physicality and relationship to the space; we may adopt an open but confrontational bearing, impose ourselves on the whole space, possessing it, and move in a direct, strong and sudden manner, thrusting forward.

2 If we move under the influence of generosity, we may also become friendly, affectionate, supportive and joyful. Physically we are open and reach out to others in the space. We glide through the whole area in an easy, flowing movement, but in order to share it with others, only settling on the sides to form sociable groups.

So much happens as a result of working intuitively under this influence of a particular quality, and far more than could be gained from consciously deciding how an acquisitive or generous person would act and then representing the idea.

3 What words and sounds come through spontaneously, and what voices emerge from these qualities? Do they fit what was developing from the other influences?

Tempo-rhythm

As we do the above exercises we inevitably come across tempo and rhythm. Tempo is the speed of movement, speech or music. Rhythm is the pattern formed by the number, length and stress of beats of sound, stillness and movement.

We saw with the psychological gesture how a change of tempo can change the quality and feeling in an action, for example, from fast and thrusting to slow and calculating. We've also seen how imaginary centres and bodies and different qualities will also prompt different tempo-rhythms. For example, our acquisitive character has a sudden, explosive, fast tempo-rhythm, and the generous one has a calm, sustained slow one. So tempo-rhythm can create a quality or feeling, and be created by them.

We also have an outer tempo-rhythm and an inner, which could be different. I may move very slowly and deliberately, but think, sense, feel and absorb information very quickly. So, I have a conflicting internal dynamic, which might be dramatically more interesting than, say, a slow outer and inner or fast outer and inner tempo. I could also be slow inside, a bit dim, and quick on the outside, with my energy channelled into unfocused fidgeting.

Stanislavski makes the point that 'Tempo-rhythm cannot only prompt the right feelings and experiences intuitively, directly and immediately, *it can help create characters'* (*An Actor's Work*: 476). All of us have a particular set of tempo-rhythms that define us and which will change according to circumstances.

If I am a time-stressed, anxious, insecure person with an imaginary centre outside my body and led by my emotions, I may panic if I'm late for work, hurtle towards the underground, dive through the closing doors and sit fearfully sweating that I'm going to be late, both my tempo-rhythms fast, jerky and frantic.

If I'm a calm, ordered and confident person with a centre in my chest and led by my mind, I get to the train quickly but without rushing, and sit, controlling my breathing, while I quickly but calmly think through my chances of getting to work on time and how to deal with matters if I were to be late. My tempo-rhythm is basically slow and steady on the outside and quick but even on the inside.

EXERCISES

1   Move through the space, experimenting with different inner and outer tempos, e.g. fast/fast, slow/moderate, quick/slow, moderate/quick.

2   As you walk slowly, moderately or quickly, say a line of a nursery rhyme (e.g. Mary had a little lamb …) in different and contrasting tempos.

3   Imagine you are in the above situation of being late for work and rushing for the train. Create the circumstances and act out the situation: Where are you, where have you come from and where are you going to? What time is it and how late are you? Why are you late? What will happen if you're late? What do you do once on the train? What do you want to achieve – e.g. to get some work done, or work out how you'll be punished?

* Now try it with the opposing tempo-rhythms of the two people above, or of the materialistic and love-seeking characters from earlier.

* Speak some words out loud to yourself or to someone else on the train. What sort of vocal qualities come through?

Here's our suggestion:

Frantic person: forward-leaning alignment, clavicular chest breathing, with breathy onset, a resonance in the cheekbones (*YEH* from Chapter 7), thin tone, fast and jerky vocal tempo-rhythm, a high and fluctuating pitch range, and inconsistent articulation.

Calm person: balanced alignment, deep breath, with clear centred onset, a resonance in the sternum area of the chest (*YOH*), rounded tone, measured and sustained vocal tempo-rhythm, a lower and smaller pitch range, and clear and consistent articulation.

> We reiterate here what we've said before, that whatever the defects of a character the actor has to communicate those defects with clarity and ease within an artistic recreation of reality, unless indicated otherwise by the writer.

4   If, when playing a role, you find the voice you're using doesn't feel right with the text and the action, experiment with different tempo-rhythms.

You may find your character needs to speak with a quicker tempo – if they speak in short sharp sentences, like Mick in Pinter's *The Caretaker*, or in a 'stream of consciousness' style, like Lucky in Beckett's *Waiting for Godot;* or a slower tempo – if they have long, reflective speeches, like Trigorin in Chekhov's *The Seagull.* The different tempo and rhythm will effect an immediate change in the feel of the character and can open doors for you.

* Have a read of text examples such as these, and get a sense of what character qualities the tempo-rhythms suggest and what vocal qualities are fitting to them.

Laban effort actions

The above exercises lead on to complementary techniques devised by Rudolf Laban, the Hungarian movement and dance theorist, around the same time as Michael Chekhov was creating his own. You will recognize some of his definitions of movement from terms we've used earlier. Laban broke down all movement into various categories, the basic ones being *space, weight and time.* We move through space in a direct or indirect/flexible way. Our weight is strong (or heavy) and forceful, or light and buoyant. Our timing is quick, sudden and broken, or sustained and steady. All movement involves a combination of these elements to produce what Laban called *efforts.* There are eight actions, placed below in pairs of opposites, and with their different elements:

ACTION	SPACE	WEIGHT	TIME
Pressing	Direct	Strong	Sustained
Flicking	Flexible/Indirect	Light	Sudden
Punching or Thrusting	Direct	Strong	Sudden
Floating	Flexible/Indirect	Light	Sustained
Slashing	Flexible/Indirect	Strong	Sudden
Gliding	Direct	Light	Sustained
Wringing	Flexible/Indirect	Strong	Sustained
Dabbing	Direct	Light	Sudden

He adds the concept *flow,* which can be *free* or *bound*. An action is *bound* if it meets resistance or is controlled, e.g. moving a piano. It is *free* if it meets no resistance and can be done with no worry, e.g. whitewashing a wall. The actions of pressing and wringing clearly have a *bound* flow. Gliding also has a bound flow, although to a lesser degree, because of some resistance from, say, ice or air. The actions of flicking and slashing have a *free* flow. Punching or thrusting, dabbing and floating can be performed with a bound *or* free flow. (See Laban's own books, and *Laban for All* by Jean Newlove and John Dalby.)

EXERCISES

1   To get a grasp of these efforts, try performing them in the sequence of opposite pairs in the table. Use your whole body – hands, arms, legs, feet, shoulders, head, pelvis, back and bottom – to create the action of pressing, floating, wringing, etc.

Laban intended these actions specifically for movement analysis, and actors can use them to define their character movement, but also to identify the character's *inner* action.

We can see how these actions apply to some of the characters we've looked at above. Our acquisitive, thrusting person is primarily direct, strong and sudden: clearly a *punch or thrust.* Our love searcher is direct, light and sustained: a *glide.* The frantic, insecure person is probably indirect, strong and sustained: a *wring*, and maybe indirect, light and sustained: a *float*. The calm, controlled traveller could be either a *glide*, or direct, strong and sustained: a *press*. Every character will have a main effort action, but they will have more than one, which will appear according to the nature of the action at different points in the script.

A character may have different or contradictory inner and outer efforts. The calm, gliding traveller might have many interests and projects to plan and she flits from one to another in her head, *dabbing*. The love-seeker may glide outwardly, but be full of inner doubts and unresolved conflicts, a *wring*.

2   This is another influence on our character voice. Try speaking some lines with different actions:

Say 'Please stay with me' using:

- a verbal action of commanding, an effort of punching

- a verbal action of begging, an effort of wringing

- a verbal action of urging, an effort of pressing

- a verbal action of teasing, an effort of dabbing

Say '*I'd like my book back*' using:

- a verbal action of castigating, an effort of slashing
- a verbal action of reassuring, an effort of gliding
- a verbal action of dismissing, an effort of flicking
- a verbal action of admonishing, an effort of floating

Try saying these lines with conflicting efforts revealing a subtext of feelings that contradict what's being said:

- a punch on the line while wringing inside because you're in love
- a glide while really wanting to slash the person away
- a flick while pressing away at another activity

So, as you see here, these effort actions can also inform our psychological and verbal actions. They affect how we operate as characters through a script, and so help to define who we are. A punching or slashing person will have a different vocal quality from a floating or gliding one.

3   Take a piece of text and try reading it as a dab or a wring, a press or a flick, and then look for a mixture of different efforts within the speech. Experiment with how the different efforts create different types of onset, resonance and pitch range.

Of course, other techniques might be used in rehearsal to prompt the development of your voice as the character, including improvisation and the sort of spatial exploration to be found in, for example, the Viewpoints approach devised by the US practitioners Mary Overlie and Anne Bogart. Whatever influences are used, the new transformed voice should be a response to the forming of the whole picture of the world of the script.

Create a character voice

Here is a chart summary of all the influences discussed in this chapter, with our suggestions on how they may possibly relate to the two characters we invented. Have a go at creating each of the characters and their voices by *receiving* and absorbing the influences, and then *responding* to them with all the *Vocal Givens* in the symbols below firmly in place.

Also, try the *opposite* vocal qualities to the ones you first invent, e.g. in *Sleepy Hollow*, Miranda Richardson plays a ruthless stepmother, but with a softly spoken, controlled and quiet manner, hiding her true self. The influences can affect different people in different ways. Let your imagination take off within the limits of circumstances and credibility, and create your own individual voice. Then make up a short speech the character might say and express it with this new voice.

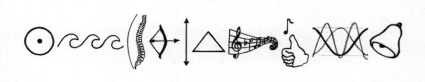

Influence	Character 1 Money Grabber	Character 2 Love Searcher
Background and Given Circumstances	Jack. 38. City trader. Educated at an independent school in Surrey and Sussex University	Juliet. 25. Musician. Educated at a school specializing in music in Verona, and University in Rome in 1930
Accent and Dialect	Well-off middle-class London but affecting working-class vowels and idioms	Cultivated standard speech, deriving from a family of teachers
Interaction (culture, climate, history, class)	Influenced by the financial milieu in 2012 England	Influenced by the fascist period of C20th Italy and opposing moral values
Drives: • Superobjective	I want to make a load of money, because I love all the material things of life, and I'd go to the length of breaking the law and moral codes	I want to find real love, because life is meaningless without it, and I'd go to the length of patient searching without compromise
• Predominant inner motive force	Will	Feeling

Influence	Character 1 Money Grabber	Character 2 Love Searcher
Qualities	Materialistic, acquisitive, calculating, affable, gregarious, shallow, hedonistic, enthusiastic, exuberant, positive, ruthless, disrespectful	Aspirational, idealistic, frustrated, lonely, generous, loving, empathic, patient, dismissive, rigorous, uncompromising
Psycho-Physical Expression	Body: Will-led, leading from the lower body, swaggering a bit, chest out, chin up Voice: Thrusting emphasizes secondary spinal curves; forceful breath and loud, barked onset; pelvic and chest resonance; pitch range mid to low area; clear, emphasized articulation	Body: Physically open, lifted, light, alert, leading from the solar plexus, steady and direct Voice: Balanced alignment; easy flowing breath and clear but gentle onset; full body resonance; pitch range varied by emotions; slow, deliberate articulation
Psychological Gesture	Based on an archetypal gesture for reaching and grabbing	Based on an archetypal gesture for aspiring and yearning
Imaginary Centre	Lower gut – round, hard, shiny, red disc, cold and spinning, saucer-size	Chest – large, oval, soft, warm, green, still
Resonance Areas	Pelvis – YOE	Solar plexus – YAW
Imaginary Body	Solid, weighty, medium height, generates a lot of energy, walks with a thrusting movement	Tall, light, slim, contained energy, walks with a flowing movement
The main quality/feeling (sensation of feeling)	Acquisitive	Generous
Tempo/Rhythm	Steady inner, quick outer	Quick inner, steady outer
Laban Effort Action	Punch and press	Glide, with a wring inside

The character voice, of course, is not just the individual vocal elements, as described under psycho-physical expression in the chart above, but is the overall quality of sound and dynamics, that unique aspect every voice has, and which will only come from imaginatively experiencing all the influences.

Do's and don't's for character voice

Do	Don't
Choose a quality you can sustain: that is easy to release and free from constriction.	Adopt an uncomfortable, tense voice, stressing the vocal folds – such as a growl in a pitch that is too low.
Find a pitch range that can communicate the character with ease, e.g. if your character has a lower pitch and resonance than you, find a centred note (Yes, I like holidays!) within the new character range, from which you can still go up and down and use the resonance quality.	Get stuck in a restricted high or low pitch, using one area of resonance: every voice, to be expressive, needs range.
Find a centred, voiced onset. Even if the character may have a breathy quality, this needs a voiced sound supporting it at its core. For example, in the extreme case of the 'stage whisper', we need to balance the convincing quality of a whisper with the need to be heard and understood; so, we need some body in the tone, lots of support, as well as clear articulation.	Use an unsupported breathiness: while a microphone may pick up whispering, a theatre space won't, and it's not a healthy choice (it dries out the vocal folds).
Always support the voice, even in quiet, tender, intimate moments.	Fall into the 'naturalistic' trap of giving up support when playing shy, introverted, insecure, sick or dying people.
Maintain ease and flexibility in your alignment, even when playing a tense character or one out of balanced alignment (in commedia dell'arte, for example). Find vocal support so that you can keep channels of breath and resonance open. Try to enhance primary curves, keep your neck supported, shoulders loose and larynx released. You need to counter-balance the areas out of alignment.	Let the tension and posture of the character make you tense and constricted, since this can harm your voice. We are not speaking in reality, we are recreating reality as if it is actually happening within imaginary circumstances in a performance. Actors have to convey reality through their art, not through a literal and naturalistic imitation of all the defects we may encounter in everyday life.

To sum up:

- Character voice is created by all the influences in the text and imaginary world of the play.
- It should be a unique and organic aspect of characterization.
- Influences include:
  - background and circumstances, accent and social interaction;
  - what drives us in life and how;
  - psycho-physical expression: psychological gesture, imaginary centres and resonance areas, imaginary body, sensations of qualities and feelings, tempo-rhythms, Laban efforts.
- The character voice should always be safe, supported, and free from tension and constriction.

14
THE ACTOR IN THE SPACE

Previous chapters in this part have dealt with character creation and communication of the writer's themes. We now look at how the actor needs to relate to the audience within different performance spaces and the response of the voice.

The space – centre and periphery

The transfer from rehearsal room to larger theatre space can be tricky.

As soon as the actor performs in a theatre space, a dynamic is created between the triangle points of the *actor's vocal centre*, *other actors*, *and the audience and the periphery of the space*. Actors now share their performance with an audience in spaces of different sizes, with different stage formats and acoustic qualities, and this demands extra awareness and acting and vocal skills. We need to understand how physical and vocal choices will be read by the audience. When receiving the acting impulses, we cannot just deal with the distance between ourselves and other actors but need to expand and embrace the whole space with our awareness and presence.

The actor lays the basis for this dynamic through the *breathing process*. To reach the audience within the space, as we receive and transmit impulses between each other, we need to root into the vocal centre, the core muscles and spine, and produce a centred onset of sound. We also need to *breathe in* the periphery of the theatre space.

Spaces, large or small, will have their own plus factors and problems but there are two great, common traps for the actor in relating to the space:

- *Pushing with the voice*, through trying to fill the space by act of will, and resulting in tension, shouting and a barking sound, and possible loss of voice: we lose connection with organic acting impulses, produce a lack of vocal responsiveness and authenticity, and the audience may feel bombarded and under attack.

- *Devoicing*, often through trying to keep 'truthful', caused by lack of breath support, articulatory clarity and resonance: we produce under-energized, undefined and dull voices that don't communicate the text or the action.

The more demanding the space we shall need:

- greater breath and rooting in the pelvic floor and spine;
- clearer articulation and greater energy of thought through the lines;
- sharper clarity of action, psychological, physical and verbal;
- careful assessment of the optimum resonance, vocal onset and pitch range required.

The best actors are at ease with their voices within the space. Filling the space seems effortless, released, resonant and clear – their voices seem to flow easily into the audience's ears. The audience will feel confident and open themselves to the experiences created. If actors struggle with the space, seeing and hearing a performance becomes hard work.

Acting spaces

First we shall look at different spaces and their requirements in order to become more aware of the challenges.

Greek theatre

The earliest form of theatre developed in Greece, emerging from religious ceremonies, and was performed as a community experience to educate and confront issues. The theatres had to be large to accommodate thousands. They were built into hillsides, sometimes looking out to sea, and were eventually made of stone. The audience seats rise up like an inverted cone and surround the actors in a semi-circle, reflecting their voices.

One of the most famous surviving theatres is Epidaurus in the Peloponnese, an amazing space holding an audience of 15,000, which we visited in 2009. Large it is, but when you walk into the centre of the playing space it feels remarkably intimate. You need only turn your head slightly to left or right and raise the eyes for you to encompass and breathe in the whole space and feel a close contact with the audience. You feel rooted, strong and easy, and drawn into the periphery of the space, welcomed and wanting to embrace it. The acoustic is wonderful – no need for stage mics here! A coin dropping on the stone centre can be heard on the back rows. This is a space ideal for actor and audience alike and is both freeing and demanding. Energy, clarity, breath rooting, resonance, pitch range and awareness of the whole space at all times will be vital, but whether actors wear masks or not, the connection with credible human experience and the psycho-physical life of the characters has to be kept – the smallest falseness in impulse and execution, any pushing or devoicing will be immediately evident.

Medieval and community theatre

In the fourteenth and fifteenth centuries new theatrical spaces developed. Religious plays based on Bible stories and morality plays such as *Everyman* centred on abstract notions of vice and virtue and were played throughout Europe. They were acted on raised, portable, wooden platforms, which toured from village to village and usually played in the open air. The later Italian *commedia dell'arte,* arriving in the sixteenth century, was also itinerant and toured from village to noble hall to palace. These forms of indoor and open-air theatre have much in common with the sort of street, community and political touring theatre that proliferated in Britain in the 1970s. Stages and set would be fitted up and taken down for each show, which could be played anywhere from outside in a park to a community hall, a trades club or a tent at a miners' gala.

The vocal demands are considerable, since the actor has to overcome weather and traffic noise, the chat of the audience, and the sounds of daily business going on around you, e.g. the ringing of a cash register and crash of breaking glasses in a working men's bar. This requires great vocal and physical energy, the confidence to focus sometimes directly on the audience to grab their attention, muscular articulation, soaring resonance and undaunted clarity of thought and will!

Elizabethan and other open-air theatre

James Burbage built the first permanent London theatre, known as the Theatre, in 1576, in Finsbury Fields. It was most probably like the later Curtain, Rose, Globe and Swan, the drawing of which from around 1596 is the only surviving contemporary drawing of an Elizabethan theatre. The structure, like the recon-structed Globe of today, was of wood with a raised platform for a stage with doors at the back plus a raised gallery for musicians and actors, standing space on the ground and two or three galleries of benches circling the stage. Shakespeare calls it a 'scaffold', 'cockpit' and 'this wooden O' in the Chorus speech in *Henry V*, which we'll look at later. Although these theatres were open to the air, the circular nature and hard wooden reflective surfaces used onstage and in the audience would have created a vibrant acoustic – this would be handy for overcoming the London street and air noises, even more present today.

The modern Globe resonance works well as long as the actors know how to focus their sound to include the whole house. This requires a centred onset and optimum pitch and resonance. Due to the circular shape of the theatre, the audience will not always see the actors' faces and read their thoughts, so actors need to focus on reaching the whole space with vocal clarity. Also, imaginary focus points should include all parts of the audience. Some parts of the Globe, such as under the first tier, are difficult to reach; and when the stage is extended into the yard, voices can spiral up and out of the 'wooden O'. The actor therefore needs clarity of thought, objective and articulation to communicate clearly to the audience. Often female voices can sound shrill and male voices too loud. Thoughts will sound disconnected and pushed, so the actor needs to find their centre and 'vibrate the experience'.

Some pointers relevant here are even more relevant to modern open-air theatres. Unlike the Minack in Cornwall, a neo-Greek theatre built from stone into a hillside and facing the reflective power of the sea, open spaces like the Regent's Park Theatre do not have a hard periphery to reflect sound. There is also no cover at all so the audience may get cold and rained on. Speaking quietly and quickly in an underpowered and poorly supported way will disperse the sound and lose the audience. You need full body resonance and strong and flexible rooting of the breath, like an opera singer. Keep in optimum pitch and focus the sound above the audience so that they see your eyes rather than the top of your head. Fill the moments of each thought by riding the wave of the breath.

However, you don't need to stand facing out to the audience at all times like old declamatory actors from the nineteenth century; being aware of the problem and understanding the space and keeping focused on where the sound needs to reach will offer a solution – but open positions and directing sound outwards may be necessary. A crucial point here is that to retain belief in the action and a truthful expression we must keep the contact with our fellow actors and play our objectives so that the audience receive real sense and not just an out-front recitation. We should also explore where the strong places are onstage, where we can be seen and heard with least effort, and where the problematic places are and what to do about them. Many stages have dead spots, the Globe included.

The proscenium arch

This format first appeared in Renaissance Italy in the sixteenth century, and is probably the most common in theatre buildings even today. It developed as a framed, raised stage with elaborate curtains, classical pillars, painted scenery and side entrances. After the ban on theatre during the Puritan Commonwealth in England, Charles II encouraged the development of this European style of theatre in the Restoration period.

The format was well suited to the nineteenth-century realist drama of Ibsen, Chekhov and Shaw, out of which came the notion of the imaginary 'fourth wall' through which the audience saw the action.

As with any stage space, the audience are all focused on it, and unfocused action or dropped energy will be immediately noticeable and suck the audience's attention as into a black hole. Perhaps because we view proscenium arch theatre 'end-on' and through a frame, it's a bit like looking into a tunnel or through a telescope, and so nothing escapes our notice. Thoughts, actions and articulation must be energized and clear.

Standing for too long in closed positions or facing upstage will cut off the audience, and when we move upstage and speak we have to keep aware of the audience behind us and throw our voice over the head. Equally, speech directly into the wings will get lost. In realist plays usually done in this format, actors, particularly students, tend to stand close to each other instead of finding a *realistic* social distance determined by relationship, status and the circumstances. Even intimacy will need some distance to be communicated in most theatre spaces. Again, we don't need to stand facing out all the time, but open positions allow the audience in more and enable the actor's face and all-important eyes to be seen.

Another issue is the auditorium seating. Proscenium arch theatres have stalls with a circle overhanging them at the rear. The actors' sound can get trapped under this so that it doesn't rise to the circles and balcony, or conversely, the sound flies up to the circles but doesn't reach the rear stalls. The actor has to be aware of all areas of the audience and not channel the sound down to the stage floor, particularly when sitting, or just focus on 'the gods'.

Thrust stage

This literally 'thrusts' the actors and action into the audience, connecting the actor more directly and physically to the audience and bringing the audience closer to the play. It removes the barrier between the audience and a framed arch and creates a more egalitarian experience for them, more in line with the radical drama appearing from the 1950s.

A large space can still feel intimate – witness the old Elizabethan theatres with which the thrust has a basic similarity. For example, Chichester Festival Theatre, built in 1962, seats nearly 1,400 people but no one is further than 65 feet from the stage. The new Royal Shakespeare Company thrust stage in Stratford replaces a proscenium arch, and the Young Vic in Waterloo has often used a semi-circular audience format as in the Greek theatres and is a wonderfully intimate and friendly space to play in.

However, the more you move down the thrust to the 'front', the more of the audience is placed behind you – so, vocally we have to reach behind us and to the sides. We can't allow the voice to drop into devoiced intimacy when talking around the front rows because the majority of the theatre will not then hear us – the people at the front won't worry if you are speaking in a louder volume than you would use in secrecy in a corner because they know they are in a large theatre too. We also have to be available to physically include everybody, because everybody at some point will see our backs. Vocal awareness and reach is all the more important at those times, as is our physical energy and presence as the character. You can still be eloquent with your back! So, don't drop the breath energy, articulation and ends of words and sentences, and keep alive psychologically and physically at all times in all positions.

Theatre-in-the-round

This takes the principle of inclusivity even further. As the name suggests, it means that the stage is round or square and the audience is seated all around the actors. Entrances are from four or more aisles or 'vomitories'. You can only be seen by the whole audience when standing at the opening of one of these. Again, this means that we often show our backs to some part of the audience at some time, so we need to radiate the performance and voice through the whole body and the spine, being aware of the space all around us, and finding the optimum vocal energy suited to the space.

Famous examples of theatre-in-the-round are the Stephen Joseph Theatre in Scarborough, run for many years by Alan Ayckbourn, and the Royal Exchange, Manchester, both of which John has played. Both theatres have the feel of being in a large living room; you are embraced by the space but need to breathe in the whole area, around and above, especially at the Exchange, which is high-tiered. The actor's vocal energy needs to fill the space from the floor to the ceiling. Movement away from sections of the audience needs to be accompanied by clear articulation and onset, energy, rooted breath and resonance – it's easy to lose syllables and line endings.

Also, because the audience is all around there is an intense *shared* focus – the audience can see not only the actors but each other. The experience is more collective than any other in theatre. It's like focusing into an operating theatre: as such, our movement, actions and thoughts need to be clear, defined, motivated and fully expressed, but we also need to be free and energized and keep a flow of movement going, both inner and outer – too much stillness will appear lacking in dynamic, and the audience will hear better when they see us.

When we are standing still, we again need to be aware of the need for social and artistic distance between others and ourselves. If you stand directly opposite and close to someone in this format you will obscure them from most of the audience; it will also help to take a position at a diagonal to the other, rather than square on.

Traverse theatre

The audience is on two sides of the stage running like a path between them, as at the Traverse Theatre in Edinburgh. If we stand at either end of the stage everyone can see us. Further into the space we experience the same challenges as with the above two formats, and must use the same awareness, vocal and character radiation and energy to reach the people behind and above us. Speak through the whole body and especially the spine, find optimum pitch for the space, reach with the voice from the floor to the ceiling and beyond the walls, articulate clearly and keep the breath rooted in the thoughts and actions.

Small-scale theatre

This may be a small studio theatre attached to a larger repertory theatre, such as at the West Yorkshire Playhouse and Bristol Old Vic; independent arts centre studios, as in the Battersea Arts Centre; fringe theatres such as the White Bear and Old Red Lion above London pubs; or spaces in non-theatrical buildings such as libraries, retirement homes or swimming baths, used by touring companies. The theatre spaces are often 'black boxes' with the audience end-on or on two adjacent sides. What they have in common is their small size.

This means you don't have to worry about the challenges of a large space, the open air or the audience on different sides. However, it raises other problems. The major one is to do with perception: the idea that because we're in a small space we don't need energy, sustained breath and clarity.

Any space, however small, demands performance energy and focus that lifts us out of everyday reality and puts us into a theatrical reality. We're not at home flopped in front of the TV. We mustn't be too big for the space but we still have to fill it, reach all the audience and radiate beyond the walls of the theatre. The Japanese actor, Yoshi Oida, makes a comparison between martial arts and the stage:

> If you are trying to hit someone, and you only focus on that person, then your action becomes very small … It is better to imagine that when you strike, you are reaching to the horizon … Actors should maintain this wide imagination in all their work on the stage. In this way, even small gestures become

imbued with vast power. Also, the relationships between characters become a symbol of a wider world, not merely a moment between two individuals. For example, when you perform Chekhov, the play seems like small incidents in daily life, but they should be able to represent the whole of existence. (*An Actor Adrift*: 149)

If we don't root our breath and breathe in the circumstances and space we block emotional connection and experience; the voice becomes flat and lifeless; we lose vocal identity; the text becomes dulled and dropped. Finding a vocal quality that fits small spaces and is believable, audible and intelligible can be a difficult task; but we believe the key is in acting energy, sustaining the presence of the character and wanting to communicate to the other actors and the audience. It's an acting issue and we must never lose touch with our psycho-physical technique.

Trying to be small and 'naturalistically' truthful will stifle credible emotional expression, clear and definite actions and strength of will, and the thoughts and their articulation will become self-conscious and fuzzy as words are swallowed and lines delivered monotonously. All the vocal essentials – easy alignment, breath, onset, articulation, resonance, pitch range – are just as vital in a small space as a large one, and for that matter, on TV, radio or film as on the stage.

So:

- play the action, not a style suggested by the space;
- fit the level of projection to the size but reach beyond the audience;
- play your objectives and interact to produce the necessary energy for the play.

Non-theatre spaces

As we mention in small-scale theatre above, we sometimes perform in spaces that have not been designed as theatre performance spaces, e.g. factories, school halls, churches and community halls. These create vocal challenges for actors, especially when we have to do a get-in and assemble the set and may have little time, if any, to warm up and test the space. John remembers one touring venue where he was rigging lights only a few minutes before going on stage. At East 15 Acting School, BA third-year students tour their Christmas shows to various schools and community halls and need to be ready to perform at 9.00 or 10.00 in the morning. They have to get there, set up and go. This can be a real learning curve for young actors, who need to be aware of how to deal with problems arising – e.g. when the space's acoustics are too live because hard surfaces reflect the sound like an echo; or too dead because the space is full of carpets, curtains and polystyrene ceiling tiles, which remove any sense of vocal resonance because no sound is coming back to the actors. Traffic and number of shows permitting, try to schedule so that you can drive to the venue, get-in *and* have time to calm down, warm up and test the space before performing (see Preparation, below).

Problematic acoustics

* Lively acoustics

The acoustic of churches or castles with stone walls and high ceilings is often very live. Churches are designed to make the sound huge and resonant. While the acoustic may accommodate a choir or a priest delivering a sermon – as long as they speak slowly and clearly – a company of different voices moving around the space may encounter a blurring echo. Employing soft sound-absorbing materials to baffle the sound could really help the actors here, but we need strong rooting into the spinal and core support and crisp clear consonants to give resounding vowels more definition. Pushed sound and speaking too quickly will create a blur: we need a clear onset of sound and a tempo that suits the space, and to focus the sound with an optimum pitch, resonance and tonal energy for actor and space.

* Dead acoustics

At East 15 Acting School the dance studio is often used as a performance space. Black curtains are hung all around to block out the light from the windows and to cover the mirrors. While the space is too live when empty, when the curtains are up the space becomes dead. It will help to put in some hard reflective surfaces, but essentially actors need to speak with the right tonal energy. We need a clear onset of sound, strong body resonance, optimum pitch that carries the voice effortlessly through the space and use of vowel energy through the text.

Preparing for the space

In preparing for the move from rehearsal space to performance space, actors need to adjust acting choices and stagecraft so that the triangle between you, other actors and the audience is created in a way suited to the space. If we have little time in the space before performance, it will still be possible to prepare imaginatively, but we should try to fully explore it physically and vocally as well.

Exploration of the space

- We suggest *walking the space* before each performance until you're used to it. This involves walking around the whole stage area *and* the audience seating area and getting a tangible physical sense of the dimensions of the space, touching the walls, walking between the seats, going up into any circles and balcony. Sense the audience's perspective and how far away the stage is from the furthest seat.

- Stand on the stage, legs apart and rooted, and breathe in the whole space. It's not enough to simply identify different areas where the audience sit. Open out the arms in a backward, circular motion so you feel your body lift up and out to *embrace the space* as you breathe in. Make a mental and physical connection with every bit of the audience area and the stage area. How does it feel to *breathe the space* – not just in front, but also behind you and to each side?

- Do a *sound test*, speak and listen to each other from the stage and the audience, run some lines.

- Where should your *eye level* be for the audience to feel contact with your thoughts and feelings?

- Where are your *imaginary focus points* so that you can reach the whole audience with different sections of your speeches and dialogue?

- What does it feel like to breathe into the solar plexus the problem that arises for your character in the circumstances, and to respond on the out-breath through the action into the space?

- Where are the strong points on stage from which you can reach the whole audience with ease?

- What are the *acoustic demands* of the particular space? Where are there dead spots onstage and in the audience?

- How strong an onset is needed? A breathy onset is to be avoided at all times.

- Which *pitch* and *resonance* carries in the space?

- Do I need to engage more *vowel* or *consonantal* energy?

- Are my thought/word beginnings and endings energized and articulated clearly?

- What particular *stagecraft* is needed for the stage and audience format and the action of the play?

The Vocal Givens

We remind you here again of the vocal foundations we explored in Part Two:

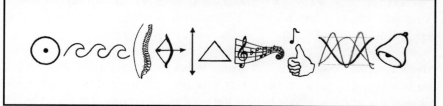

These are constants that enable the actor to produce a clear, supported, resonant voice and to fill all the different kinds of space. Just as the *Given Circumstances* are a constant factor within which the actor responds, the *Vocal Givens* are the means through which the actor shares their experience with the audience through voice and language while remaining released yet rooted.

Tackling the space

EXERCISES

The following exercises apply the Essential Vocal Six to the space.

1. Tonal energy

* The actor's tonal energy is achieved by activating the vibrations of a sound like *yyyyy* – Lessac's Y-buzz – voiced with a centred onset all along the spinal support's Elastic Band operating within the balance line of the body. The lumbar area of the spine, which makes the C-shape/primary curve on the out-breath, drives the breath into the Elastic Band rooting us into the earth and lifting us into the sky at the same time. This sound focuses the voice in the hard palate and front of the mouth and is excellent for achieving a clear supported onset and reaching through the space (see Chapter 7, Resonance).

* Stand in the middle of the space and focus on an imaginary vertical column rising from the floor to the ceiling and fill it with a *yyyyeeehhh* as you glide up and also down, allowing your pitch range and resonance to respond.

* Introduce yourself to the audience saying: 'This is me!' Make sure you engage into the Elastic Band while doing this.

* Sound *yyy-away, away, away*, getting the tonal energy through the Elastic Band with intention and a forward voice. This is what Lessac terms *calling energy.*

* Now visualize the golden ball of energy within your solar plexus. Imagine you are receiving the sun's rays and that your solar plexus radiates them back. Imagine that the spinal area behind the solar plexus drives and transmits the rays into the space.

* Open your solar plexus and your breath to take in the impulse for the sound. Sense your muscular and spinal support engage, ready to create a platform of support for the centred onset of sound – it helps students to see this support as a tray from which you offer things.

* Next, release the sound *yyyy* as if it is the rays of the sun. Engage the spinal drive and *radiate* the sound along the Elastic Band, creating a pillar of sound energy along the spine, and out into the space – *the spine speaks*.

Useful mottos:

* *To make things mine, I use my spine* (as coined by one of Christina's students, Lewis Mann).
* *Whatever you say, speak on your tray!*

We become centred and able to reach through the space when our core centres work together: the spine, the vertical centre; the pelvis, the gravity centre; and the solar plexus, the impulse and emotional response centre.

The centred onset of sound will radiate out if the pelvic and spinal support offers a firm platform combined with a psychological sense of commitment and conviction.

If you are doing this correctly you will have a released larynx. It's important that you breathe your impulse into the places you need for support, and that you don't sound until your breath is truly in its out-breath movement.

2. The spine speaks

We shall now do some exercises to activate the sense of 'the spine speaks', and the lumbar drive explored in the Objectives section of Chapter 11.

Growing bigger and smaller

(see Chapter 10, Ease and Focus, for the physical actions)

* Apply the same principles as above when sounding on *yyyy*.
Make sure you radiate, growing bigger beyond your out-breath/sound movement, completing the action in its entirety before releasing and coming back to neutral.

* Synchronize the sound and the physical action so they begin and end together and the body's and voice's execution of the intention are one and the same.

* Sound out on 'Me' while growing bigger.
You should be left with an increased awareness of your centre and the space around you. Your breath should feel wider and your core and spine stronger.

* Next say 'Me', really connecting to your sense of identity, without the movement. Don't drop the end of 'Me'. Sense if your voice feels more rooted.

* Grow bigger again, and after the height of the movement go into growing smaller, closing down, while keeping the voiced energy of the *yyyy* sound.
Do it on 'Me'. Then without the movement, say 'Me', keeping the sense of being smaller but retaining the identity, onset and space awareness.
This is of particular relevance for when we are doing quiet, intimate scenes in a space.

Cat

* Kneel on the floor in a table position, ready to explore the primary curve of the spine (see Chapter 3, Alignment – 5. Primary Curves). Imagine you are on a bridge, and underneath you is someone you know. You recognize them, breathe them in through your solar plexus and respond by greeting them with: 'It's you!'

* Once you get the impulse and feel your spinal support engage, hook your response into the vertebrae of the spine and drive from there into the primary shape of the cat position as you say 'It's you', elongating the *yyyy* and *ooooouuu* sounds. The drive is strongest when your spine is fully extended into the arch

of the cat. Drop your neck into the curl of the back and look through your legs. Release your jaw and lift the soft palate, thus creating an optimum resonance space in the oral cavity.

* Next put your forehead on your hands and keep your bottom in the air with your toes against the floor for support. This time when going into the cat position on 'It's you', you need to let your lumbar area rock you forwards, which will in turn curl your neck and release your jaw as well as lift your soft palate. This will drive the breath and sound through your open body resonators and ease the release of your response.

* Moving into the cat position again, breathe the other person and respond through your pelvic area *to seduce* them with 'You make me feel so *YOE*' (see Chapter 7, Exercise 2).

* Give the person a vocal hug in order *to embrace* them from your spinal drive on *YAA*, released through the chest area.

* You can go through the whole resonance scale inventing actions to respond to, releasing the different vowel sounds with the 'y' sound in front of them. This will open your whole body and activate the different resonance areas of legs, pelvis, torso and head.

As we said before, we place a 'y' before the vowels because it is created in the hard palate and vibrates from this central placement through the entire balance line of the body.

These exercises should always be done incorporating an objective. We see someone, get an objective towards them, breathe and respond with the lumbar area of the spine. This way, the in-breath is active and has purpose within the present moment and can adapt to the spatial distance between you and the person you are connecting with – it will serve as a measuring device for how strong the spinal response needs to be; the out-breath will respond back and release the voice spontaneously rather than push it out technically. We sense the space rather than endgame for the voice to be loud.

Soft palate

K, G, NG are velar sounds that connect well with the spine because they are formed at the back of the tongue as it meets the soft palate. Hook these consonants into your spinal support and make them strong. Now say:

Cleave then carve the crystal rock as if urging on a lazy apprentice in a fairytale to get him to work. Fill the space with this.

Or say:

Those groaning tree trunks in the ghastly dark are grievously tricky in order to warn someone before they enter a threatening forest. Really go for the initial consonants and dig them into the ground like a spade.

3. Expanding the breath into the space

Swinging on vowel sounds for release

To get into the swing and bounce of your breath, try this exercise based on one of Cicely Berry's.

Rock side to side from the hips, with the arms and head hanging loosely, then swing your arms from the floor to the ceiling and back to the floor of the theatre space in a circle. On your way up, breathe in the distance from floor to ceiling, and on the way down release a fully voiced sigh on the wave of the out-breath as it follows the weight of your body.

Throwing the ball

* Stand at opposite sides of the space and throw a ball to your partner/s. Throwing and catching needs to be done with the sense of *giving and receiving,* rather than chucking the ball in an unfocused way. In Chapter 11 we did this with the focus on interacting with others – now the focus is on the space.

* Breathe in the other person and throw the ball silently to them in an underarm arc, matching movement and breath. Now get the impulse for an action such as to welcome, embrace or recognize them. Let the impulse trigger the throwing action and the out-breath and, once the ball has reached your partner, respond vocally with 'It's you!', so that your voice releases its verbal action on the wave of the breath.

* Don't throw the ball and speak at the same time, in a way that can cause tension in your upper body and larynx, but throw the ball and then speak once it's reached the other person, so that your voice releases together with the ball going into gravity, riding the wave of your breath.

* Now increase the distance between you and sense how this changes your breath and voice. You will elongate the vowels. You can do this on the resonance scale sentences in Chapter 7, for full release of your body resonance through the vowels and their corresponding body parts. You should always aim to play actions so that you practise the connection between receiving acting impulses and responding vocally in a reflexive manner.

* Play also with 'Come closer' and 'Go away' or lines from a speech or play you are working on.

Throwing the discus

This is an extension of the ball exercise and is particularly useful for following through the energy of a whole thought: the body spins in and back when it prepares, and spins out and forward with greater dynamic and releases breath and voice as the imaginary heavy discus flies to its goal. This and the next exercise are based on Steiner exercises.

* Take aim at a focus point in the space. Imagine you have a weighty discus in your hand. Stand strongly with feet hip-width apart. On the in-breath, if right-handed, swing your body and arms round and backwards to the right and let your left heel rise from the floor with the ball of the foot rooted. On the out-breath, spin your imaginary discus out towards its target, and once it's hit its target release a vowel sound.

* Now do the movement with an objective. For example, attract attention: 'Hey, you, over there!'; get rid of someone: 'Get out of my space'. Then do it with a line from a play. You can also do a whole chunk of a speech on one breath to explore the drive through it, having aimed the discus at a clear focus point in the space. The movement and the sensation of gravity will fully engage and extend the wave of your breath. Rather than chopping lines through interrupted breath, you will gain flow and expansion of breath.

Throwing the spear

This exercise is great for taking a clear focus and breathing in through the back to release the voice through an arc in the space. The release created by the spear flying towards its target will expand your out-breath and voice into the space.

* Stand strongly with legs apart, one foot behind the other. On the in-breath, take aim with the imaginary spear and extend it backwards while your other hand and arm point at the target, and shift your weight onto the back foot. On the out-breath, throw the spear along your aim, transferring weight to your front foot, and once it has reached its goal release your voice towards it.

* Do it playing a verbal action: command someone to 'Sing a song!' Throw the intention silently with your imaginary spear; sense the gravity when the spear hits the target and keep your mind focused on the target; allow yourself another in-breath (if necessary) and on your out-breath wave command the other person to sing.

Bow and arrow

The bow and arrow exercise in Chapter 4, Breath, gives you a real sense of integration of your mind's intention, breath and spinal support.

* On the in-breath, take aim while drawing your imaginary bow and breathe in someone across the space and prepare to give them a command, e.g. 'Sit down', 'Get up', 'Leave the room'. When you feel your out-breath and spinal support are ready to respond, release your arrow and speak once it has hit its target. If you speak and release the arrow at the same time your voice might get trapped. Be aware of your spine doing the supporting and the speaking.

4. Expanding into the vertical space

This is best done with a whole cast.

* Imagine you have a beautiful silk sheet or parachute. Throw it up towards the ceiling on your collective in-breath. It will float up and once it reaches the ceiling and starts to float down, on your out-breath release a sigh, *haaahhh*.

Now play an objective as the sheet falls, e.g. make someone aware that there is a bird on the ceiling: 'A Bird!'

5. Focusing on the audience

Imagine you are market fruit sellers and while focusing on different areas of the audience within the space, sell them fruit.

* Breathe in the seat/imaginary audience member you focus on and make them buy your delicious fruit: 'Bananas, madam?', 'What about some lovely apples,

sir?' Make it big but real and use all your charm. This will really connect you to the audience rather than simply identifying them.

6. Energizing as a group for performance

Any game that makes you concentrate on others is good for voice and acting because it makes you react while playing a clear objective.

* For example, play a game of tag. Try to keep your breath centred and deep. Do it with lines from a speech playing an objective or action.

* Or play tennis with lines from your dialogue. Make sure that you don't get tighter as you become more energized. Rather, let your breathing movements be energized as you surf the wave of the breath while playing actions with strong movements.

Receiving and sending Samurai-style

Christina learnt this from Maria Alexe, a student from Romania, who used it in her training there. This is a good group focus exercise that will energize responsive breath and voice.

* Stand in a circle. Put your hands flat together and be open and alert.

* One person sends a sound to another, e.g. 'ha!', while gesturing with the closed hands. The other makes a receiving movement with their closed hands and repeats the sound towards themself. The two people to left and right now give the same sound 'ha' back to the receiver as they do a simultaneous 'sword stroke' with their closed hands towards the ribs of the receiver (but no touching!).

* The receiving person then sends another sound to someone else and the whole procedure starts again. This should be done without hesitations and as regularly as one breath leading into the next.

Concentration and rooting – the hunter

Christina learnt this from Shannon Howes, a Canadian student. This roots and engages the core muscles and creates awareness of the space.

* Stand for at least five minutes in the hunter position in your space: feet hip-width apart, knees bent, upper body slightly leaning forward with a straight back and your coccyx tail released into gravity while your spine stretches up to

the sky. Make sure that you can breathe through the solar plexus freely. Imagine you are hunting an animal and need to be absolutely still. Become aware of the space around you and any noises or movements. The longer you stand the more you will find your muscles engage and if you do it long enough you will probably start to tremble. This is a good thing since it will release superfluous tensions. You may also sweat a bit.

* Having done this for a time, you suddenly view the animal you are after in the distance. Now you need to strike. Focused on the spot, find your moment to rush towards the animal and catch it.

* Release a line from the play with this focus and with an objective or action.

1 to 7 – contracting and expanding through the breath

This is a Eurythmy exercise that will unite you as a group in rhythmic breathing and physical movement.

* Stand in a circle. Breathe together. Without anyone taking the lead but by sensing each other through your breath, do the following:

* On one in-breath, move out taking 1 step. On one out-breath, move back in taking 1 step. Physically expand and contract your arms and body as you move out and in, like a sea plant responding to currents.

* Then expand the number of steps taken on each single in-breath and out-breath.
    Move out taking 2 steps. Move in taking 2 steps.
    Continue until you take 7 steps out and 7 steps in.

* Then do the reverse until you end up with just one step.

Running and jumping

Christina learnt this exercise from Martin Porteous, one of her teachers in Stuttgart.

* Run as if a flock of birds. Imagine your group are geese that migrate from one continent to another. One of you tries to break away from the rest but you try to embrace them back into the flock.

* Run around and make sure there are no gaps – so that the space is evenly balanced.

* Jump as a group, all at the same time without anyone taking the lead. Allow the dynamics of the group jump to develop. This will get your blood pumping and will also give your diaphragm a good bounce, wake it up and make it responsive.

* Now 'jump' as a group without actually leaving the floor – root your feet firmly into the ground while your diaphragm alone engages in the jump.

7. One cast, one space

It is really important that the whole cast breathes and vocally tunes into a space together. Sometimes one witnesses performances where all the actors seem to be playing in a different space. One is overloud, one too quiet; one is too small, one too big. It is essential to do warm-ups together in order to avoid this, to meet as one, to tune the voices together and share the same energy, breath and voice.

8. Tuning your articulation into the space

When filling a large space your articulation needs to be stronger and more muscular. You get the idea when listening to opera singers. They use strong consonants to shape the vowel energy of their singing voice; otherwise they won't be understood.

Try one of these exercises inspired by Steiner.

* Draw the sound *huuh* out of the floor gently with an expansive and upwards gesture. Then mould it with a *mmm* sound by bringing your hands close together as if the breath is clay being moulded into a ball. Use different vowels with the consonants: *huumm, haamm, heemm, hiimm*. First do every sound formation individually. Then say all of them on one breath and mould them into one huge ball of clay. You can do this small at first but then make it as big as the space.

* Say: 'Warm waves move over foam washed pebbles', strongly accentuating the consonants and riding the wave of your breath. Picture what you are saying and paint it with the sound vibrations. After doing this for a while, you should feel a sensation of buzzing around lips, face and articulators.

Make sure that your onset of sound meets each consonant at the start of each syllable. Let the 'w' be rooted and feel its resistance when sounding through the following vowel sound.

* Now try: *Ha, forceful rush. These showers of chaff from threshers flail.*

Give it an objective of hustling someone to be faster with what they are doing. Because of the nature of the fricatives, we are challenged to root the consonants as the breath escapes. It will really get your breath going and shape your articulation.

Make sure that your word endings also are clearly articulated and carried into the space. Dropping endings of thoughts/words will create inaudibility.

* Combine playing actions with clear articulation, paying attention to thought and word endings:

- Order someone to 'Fetch my hat!' Send the action through to the final 't'.

- Charm someone to 'Buy me a drink.' Make sure you still use clear onset and articulation when the actions are gentler.

- Challenge the audience with 'What's he then that says I play the villain?' Although the last syllable of 'villain' is unstressed, the energy and the action need to be sustained through to the end of the line.

Sustaining thought through the breath

To flow a thought through a line successfully requires the actor to stay in the full movement of the breath and to hold the energy of the intention beyond the physical breath. Collapsing the breath and dropping energy can be a real disease, especially among acting students: if the actor doesn't breathe – *inspire* – the play, true inspiration cannot happen and the play cannot fly.

EXERCISES

1 To get a sense of the distances you have to travel on the breath, try the following exercise of Dr Colin Sell, former Head of Music at East 15 and Rose Bruford College. To avoid doing it mechanically, we will add simple circumstances.

* Your partner doesn't believe you can speak a long sentence on one breath. Breathe the problem of their doubt into your solar plexus until you feel affected by it and need to prove that you can do it very well. Respond with wanting to

convince them you can do it, and flow that thought through the whole line as it increases in length, as below:

I am now working.

I am now working on a very important exercise.

I am now working on a very important exercise for breath support and breath control.

I am now working on a very important exercise for breath support and breath control and my aim is to control the breath.

I am now working on a very important exercise for breath support and breath control and my aim is to control the breath through this very long sentence with ease and clarity.

I am now working on a very important exercise for breath support and breath control and my aim is to control the breath through this very long sentence with ease and clarity and now I am going to count to five: 1, 2, 3, 4, 5.

I am now working on a very important exercise for breath support and breath control and my aim is to control the breath through this very long sentence with ease and clarity and now I am going to count to five: 1, 2, 3, 4, 5, and I still have enough breath left to sigh out like this: ah!

Through using a simple objective and taking in the whole arc of each increasing length of thought with your mind and your in-breath, your breath will perform its task and you will speak in a fluid way and with the right tempo to avoid gabbling.

2   Let's now do this on some lines from a play.

Here is a dialogue between Garry and Joanna in Noel Coward's *Present Laughter*, Act 2, Scene 1.

Joanna claims to have lost her key and comes to Garry, a famous romantic comedy actor, at midnight knowing he has a spare room; but she really wants to start an affair with him. Garry gently mocks her and doesn't hold back in saying what he thinks of her. Joanna is annoyed and starts to telephone for a taxi. Garry tries to hold her back:

Joanna dials a number and waits a moment.
Joanna: "Hallo – hallo ... Is that Sloane 2664? – Oh, I'm so sorry it's the wrong number."
Garry collapses on to the sofa laughing.
What are you laughing at?
Garry: You, Joanna.
Joanna *(dialling again):* You're enjoying yourself enormously, aren't you?

Garry *(jumping up and taking the telephone out of her hand):* You win.
Joanna: Give me that telephone and don't be so infuriating.
Garry: Have another drink?
Joanna: No, thank you.
Garry: Just one more cigarette?
Joanna: No.
Garry: Please – I'm sorry.

Joanna's problem is that Garry is disdainful. Her objective in this little piece is to convince him she's had enough of his mockery and wants to leave in order to change his conduct towards her. Garry's problem is that Joanna is the wife of a friend and doesn't respond positively to him having fun or admit honestly to him why she's come. His objective here is to make her stay and find out what she really wants.

* The thoughts in the scene are short and the tendency could be to think one doesn't have to breathe. So, breathe in the problem and respond with your objective – but make each thought longer by counting 1, 2, 3, 4, 5 at the end of the line so that you carry your objective *beyond* the line.

Joanna dials a number and waits a moment.
Joanna: "Hallo – hallo … Is that Sloane 2664? – Oh, I'm so sorry it's the wrong number 1, 2, 3, 4, 5."
Garry collapses on the sofa laughing.
What are you laughing at 1, 2, 3, 4, 5?
Garry: You, Joanna 1, 2, 3, 4, 5.
Joanna *(dialling again)*: You're enjoying yourself enormously, aren't you 1, 2, 3, 4, 5?
Garry *(jumping up and taking the telephone out of her hand)*: You win 1,b 2, 3, 4, 5.
Joanna: Give me that telephone and don't be so infuriating 1, 2, 3, 4, 5.
Garry: Have another drink 1, 2, 3, 4, 5?
Joanna: No, thank you 1, 2, 3, 4, 5.
Garry: Just one more cigarette 1, 2, 3, 4, 5?
Joanna: No 1, 2, 3, 4, 5.
Garry: Please – I'm sorry 1, 2, 3, 4, 5.

Now, do it again without the 1, 2, 3, 4, 5 but keep the sense of sustaining and radiating the thoughts beyond the actual words. Sense how your lumbar drive gets a feel for this and keeps the ball of action in the air.

Focusing the voice – focus points

We looked at focus points in Chapter 12 (see the Seeing section), and how particular images and thoughts take your attention to particular areas of the space. Stanislavski's object of attention (see Chapter 10) is a thing or person on which we focus our attention – e.g. a door, a lover, a book – and which acts as a stimulus to action. While dealing with this object and our objective towards it we may have a variety of focus points on which we focus our senses and energy and to which we speak. This may particularly be the case with long speeches full of images.

Focus points bring more detail, clarity, release and contact with the space. By focusing on specific areas we:

- focus the breath and energy on a single area in time and space: we breathe in each new point and root into the pelvic and spinal support necessary to contact it;

- release resonance;

- gain variety of expression through a stimulated pitch range and intonation and use of different volumes;

- find a stronger sense of identity in the Me/I in the moment.

Some of the focus points we mentioned in Chapter 12 were:

- oneself – we may focus on a hand or a personal object like a ring or key when something is very difficult to talk about;

- the past – if we look into the past, focus may be downwards;

- the future – seeing into the future might bring the focus up and to the right;

- different images – images of flowers, people or violent action, may be seen in different areas of the space.

The choice of these points comes from our belief in ourselves in the circumstances: *If I'm in these specific circumstances here and now, what do I do – and where do I focus in pursuing my objective and actions?* What is intuitively suggested by the text and the images and thoughts imaginatively giving rise to it?

EXERCISES

We'll now look at this in more detail using the Chorus speech at the beginning of Shakespeare's *Henry V*.

O, for a Muse* of Fire, that would ascend   *goddess of poetic inspiration*
The brightest heaven of invention;
A kingdom for a stage, princes to act
And monarchs to behold the swelling scene!
Then should the warlike Harry, like himself,
Assume the port of Mars;* and at his heels,   *demeanour of the god of war*
Leash'd in like hounds,* should famine, sword and fire   *coupled together like*
Crouch for employment. But pardon, gentles all,   *three dogs*
The flat unraised* spirits that hath dar'd   *unimaginative*
On this unworthy scaffold* to bring forth   *platform*
So great an object: can this cockpit* hold   *theatre arena*
The vasty fields of France? Or may we cram
Within this wooden O the very casques*   *helmets*
That did affright the air at Agincourt?
O, pardon! since a crooked figure may
Attest in little place a million;*   *one zero makes a small number big*
And let us, ciphers to this great accompt*   *nothings in this great reckoning*
On your imaginary forces work.

Given circumstances

The actor playing the Chorus has the task of transporting the audience into the scene of battle between France and England in 1415. Henry's exhausted and diminished army has fought in France and wants to return to England. The French army blocks the way to the coast and Henry is held up at Agincourt. The story goes that the two armies meet head to head on open land between two woods so that an escape isn't possible. It had been raining overnight and the field is muddy. The French army waits with heavy armour and weapons on horseback and foot. Henry doesn't have the same heavy weapons – but he has bowmen. The French attack but are hampered by the weight of their weaponry in the thick mud. Henry orders his bowmen to fire arrows and the French are slaughtered although they outnumber the English.

The Chorus has to create this story and the vast armies and fields of France on a bare Elizabethan stage, 'this unworthy scaffold', 'this wooden O' – only imagination can transport the audience into the scene.

We can call this unit of action:
The Chorus sets the scene for the battle of Agincourt and appeals to our imaginations.

The 5 Ws for Chorus

Who am I? I am the Chorus – the storyteller/commentator for the play.

Where am I? I'm in the Globe theatre where I address the audience and *imaginatively* I'm in France.

Why am I here? To transmit the story of the battle to the whole theatre space so that the audience can experience the events.

The Chorus is the link between the physical reality of being in a bare theatre with a limited number of actors, and the magic that will happen by letting 'imaginary forces work'.

What time is it? We have two time frames. The time of the performance and the time before the battle of Agincourt on Friday, 25 October 1415 – Saint Crispin's Day.

What do I want? I want to arouse the imagination of the audience to create our scene.

The obstacle for the Chorus is obviously the bare stage and lack of numbers in the cast – and in this day and age it's possibly an audience preference for grand spectacle and their great distance from this period of history.

Focus points in the speech

The text gives us subtextual thoughts and images. They provide the impulses to bring the lines to life.

The impulses are *received* through the solar plexus and breathing centre and directly communicated by the muscles of the *responding* system.

How they are radiated to the audience depends on the *magic if.*

Let the image prompt a particular focus point, and breathe them both in: this will give us the support, resonance and clarity needed to reach the point and fill the space (see also *Mastering Shakespeare*, Scott Kaiser, Scenes 2 and 3).

Each measure of the text may have a separate image.

Remember the umbilical cord connecting our breath energy to the images you're now planting in the space: we should experience a physical link between our body, breath and the image. On our out-breath we need to find both responsive expression of the images and pelvic and spinal rooting to communicate them.

So, looking at the speech:

* See the image of a fiery goddess of inspiration, focus its centre above the audience, breathe in that point, then say the line

O, for a Muse of Fire,

* See the Muse rise up into the skies over the audience and create, like a film, the battlefield of France to transfix the audience; receive into the solar plexus and respond with

that would ascend
The brightest heaven of invention;

* See the palace of the French king, Charles VI, to the left over the audience and respond with

A kingdom

* See the stage beneath your feet

for a stage,

* See an image of princes charging on horses and focus to the left of the stage with

princes to act

* See an image of monarchs watching the battle and focus to the right of the stage for

And monarchs to behold the swelling scene!

* See Harry, armoured, mounting his horse for battle as you look out centre for

Then should the warlike Harry, like himself,

* See Harry leading the attack on the French with a thundering of horse hoofs for

Assume the port of Mars;

* See forces of destruction in the form of three snarling dogs to the left and down in the pit

and at his heels,
Leash'd in like hounds,

* See villages desperate with hunger

should famine,

See swords drawing blood

sword

See looting and burning of homes

and fire
Crouch for employment.

* Focus on the whole audience, from left to right

But pardon, gentles all,

* Focus on you and other actors

The flat unraised spirits that hath dar'd

* Focus on the stage

On this unworthy scaffold to bring forth

* See Henry V victorious out centre

So great an object:

* Focus on the stage

can this cockpit hold

* See a panorama of French countryside at circle level, from left to right

The vasty fields of France?

* Raise your focus to the upper periphery of the Globe's roof

Or may we cram
Within this wooden O

* See numbers of soldiers' helmets, focusing into the pit

the very casques
That did affright the air at Agincourt?

* See one soldier in the audience

O, pardon! since a crooked figure may
Attest in little place a million;

* Focus on yourself or the whole company of actors

And let us, ciphers to this great accompt,

* Sweep the entire audience

On your imaginary forces work.

Although this may seem fragmented, it is worth going through the text as described, breathing in each image and focus point. This will no doubt slow delivery down to begin with. Feel free to do images and focus points of your own invention – this is about finding your own organic connection to the text.

Once you're achieving this, connect the images and lines without pauses (except for breath on a line ending) so that you flow your thoughts and images through the iambic pentameter metre of five unstressed/stressed beats to the line. We cover this in more detail in Chapter 15, but here are a few lines with the regular and irregular stresses marked:

> O, for a **Muse** of **Fire**, that **would** ascend
> The **bright**est **heav**en **of inven**tion;
> A **king**dom **for** a **stage**, **princ**es to **act**
> And **mon**archs **to** be**hold** the **swell**ing **scene!**

To sum up:

- In a theatre space, a performance dynamic is created between the actor's vocal centre, other actors, and the audience and periphery of the space.
- The tougher the space, the more the voice needs to be rooted, energized and articulated and have the right resonance, onset and pitch range for the space.
- Actors should always:
  - prepare in order to adjust to every new space, both individually and as a group.
  - focus on the audience and how to contact them.
  - find focus points for dialogue and especially for soliloquies.

*   *   *

Overview of the *Acting Givens*

Element	What is it?
Receiving and responding	The core of the approach: breathing in the circumstances and changing them.
Awareness, ease and focus	Opening to the world and creating a focused ease to allow receiving and responding to happen.
Action	*Given circumstances*: where we are, prompting what and how we are, and what we can become. *Magic if*: the impulse into imagination and action. *Interaction*: reacting and adapting to others. *Objectives*: what do I want? what's in my way? what do I do to get it? what's at stake?

Element	What is it?
Images	Images seen, and created through the other senses, of past and present circumstances.
Sensing	Creating a sensory score and recreating sensory experience.
Feeling	Tapping into emotion memory, empathy, intuition and atmosphere.
Character	*Background* – what has made me? *Superobjective* – what drives me in life and through the play? *Inner motive force* – what is my balance of mind, feeling and will? *Qualities* – what characteristics come through my words and actions? *Psychological Gesture* – what gesture sums up who I am? *Imaginary Centre* – where do I imaginatively live in my body? *Imaginary Body* – how is my character body different? *Tempo-rhythm* – what are my inner and outer tempo-rhythms? *Space, weight, time* – what are my effort actions?
Space	Preparing, adapting to the space, and finding focus points.

PART FOUR

INTEGRATING VOICE IN REHEARSAL AND PERFORMANCE – PUTTING IT ALL TOGETHER

INTRODUCTION

In Part Four, we go through a process of rehearsal and performance of a scene from Shakespeare's *Othello*, following Stanislavski's approach, and integrating voice at every stage. We aim to bring together all the processes from the rest of the book and focus them into one scene.

This is intended as a guide for rehearsal and performance in the future – but you can clearly benefit now by working on elements of the process alone and with a partner.

We look at:
- First meeting with the play and character, and the actor's vocal preparation.
- Active analysis and connecting vocally to improvisation.
- Connecting vocally to each objective and thought.
- Vocal expression of images, and of sensory and emotional experience in the scene.
- Character voice for Othello and Desdemona.
- Relating to the space and finding focus with the dialogue.
- Formal analysis of the language: rhythm, accenting, figures of speech and sound.

HOW TO WORK

1 Work with ease, openness and positivity.
2 Warm up before doing exercises.
3 Work in an undisturbed and unpressured environment.
4 Apply what you've understood and experienced in Parts Two and Three:
   - integrate the exercises and skills;
   - experience as you act – find continuity, coherence and entirety in the process.
5 Keep the muscles responsive in order to make a vocal connection to each impulse.
6 Work for a left and right brain partnership, so that you go from analysis to spontaneous expression, from conscious to subconscious.

15
MEETING THE PLAY AND THE CHARACTER

We now arrive at the point where we put everything together – integrating all the previously examined vocal and acting elements within a piece of text for rehearsal and performance.

In this chapter, we begin with our first impressions of the text and an initial personal exploration of character, narrative and theme.

We'll look at a classical play, Shakespeare's *Othello*, and the scene between Othello, Desdemona and Emilia at the start of Act 4, Scene 2, because this will clarify well the approach we map out through the book.

Stanislavski's approach starts with the text – the essential given of the author; goes to the subtext – all the circumstances and character life that create the imaginary world of the play and give rise to the text for the actor; and then back to the text, to clarify and express more fully the formal nature of the language, particularly prominent in classical theatre. Concentrating on the formal nature of the language in a detailed intellectual or purely physical way at the beginning of rehearsals might be as blocking for the actor as not dealing with it at all. As Linklater says: 'The practice of form must be plugged into an electrical outlet of thought/feeling impulses or it will leave a mechanical imprint on the brain, and the actor will end up "speaking the verse" but not "acting Shakespeare"' (*Freeing Shakespeare's Voice*: 121).

John Barton, in *Playing Shakespeare*, outlines an attitude to Shakespeare in line with an organic acting process. While Shakespeare's verse must be appreciated and respected, he makes these points:

An actor has to get on top of the thoughts before he thinks about the tune … the vague idea of 'the poetic' can lead to … playing a mood rather than specific thoughts and intentions. (23)

Ask yourself how you would naturally stress the line in everyday speech because of the meaning of what you are saying and try saying it without thinking about scansion. (29)

So although it's up to us to analyse the verse as well we can, in the end we must treat it intuitively. We must trust it and let it be organic rather than conscious. (46)

In the end, it [the poetry] may well be the most important thing of all, but I don't believe in rubbing an actor's nose in it at the outset. To do that blocks and inhibits him …' (52)

Here's a quote from Dame Peggy Ashcroft in the book:

Only when you have found the character are we able to say the line as it should be said. Not by everybody, or anybody, but by us, because we've made that particular character. (209)

This is all about trying to 'marry the two traditions of heightened language and naturalistic acting', naturalistic in the sense of sounding natural, human, organic; of being 'rooted in nature', to quote Ben Kingsley (20, 19). This is the opposite of drilling the verse, exploring the figures of speech, caesuras and line endings, alliteration, assonance and sounds at the start of rehearsal. This is an academic and literary approach, possibly suited to a sixth-form classroom, but not suited to the actor. Once we get into our stride in rehearsals, though, we find we can organically respond to these formal elements to enhance the meaning and richness of text and subtext.

First meeting with the play

INTEGRATING VOICE

The actor should be prepared vocally and physically before starting rehearsal, establishing a regular routine of exercises on the Essential Vocal Six to bring ease, flexibility and focus.

The breath and the voice should become ready to respond to an imaginative grasp of the text before rehearsals begin.

Warm-up and integration exercises
- Your body needs to be free, flexible, grounded, centred and ready to support
  - see Chapter 3: Exercise 2 – Spine roll; 3 – Grounding; 4 – Elastic Band;
  6 – Spinal movements when breathing; and Integration into acting. Also, do

exercises to energize, warm up, stretch the body and integrate acting impulses into physical movements, as in Chapter 10 – Opening the channels of your body, and the Chekhov movements.

- For receiving acting impulses, you need to be tuned into your natural breathing movement – see Chapter 4: all the exercises in Exploring the breathing movements, especially Exercise 4 – The solar plexus – breathing in acting impulse.

- For transmitting your responses to acting impulse, get in touch with your reflexive muscular support (pelvic floor, abdominals, ribs, spinal and back support) – see Chapter 4: Exercise 5 – Pelvic rocking; 6 – The diagonal stretch; 7 – The back roll; 8 – Exploring the root of your voice; 10 – Shooting the arrow; 11 – Strengthening the objective by engaging the Elastic Band; 12 – Exploring the ribs; 14 – Breath control; and Integration into acting.

- Ground the identity of your character and centre your onset of sound: use the exercises from Chapter 5.

- For colourful and musical response, warm up your pitch range – see Chapter 6: Exercise 1 – From relaxing into sirening; 2 – The y-buzz; 4 – Connecting your pitch range to the balance line of your body; 5 – The responding voice through the vowel energy; and Integration into acting.
  - Activate your resonance – see Chapter 7, all exercises.
  - Limber your articulators – see Chapter 8, all exercises.

Do daily 20–30-minute warm-ups before rehearsal and work through key exercises in each area, while keeping the aims in mind. Gradually you will get to know the exercises, make your body and voice responsive and find your own warm-up routine. As with learning any new skill, repetition is the key.

Here are the symbols for all the *Vocal Givens* to remind you they need to be applied throughout this chapter's work.

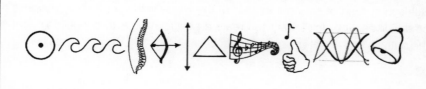

Before the first day of rehearsal, the actor should be prepared, and below are some points that we ought to consider when reading the script on our own (for a more detailed account, look at Stanislavski's *Creating a Role* (trans. Hapgood) or *An Actor's Work on a Role* (trans: Benedetti), and Chapters 10 and 11 of John's *Acting Stanislavski*).

Openness

When we first read a script, we need to be open, receptive and focused. So, don't read it in a rush on a train. Don't come to it with preconceptions or prejudices, created by a particular view of the author, the style or period, or productions you've seen before. For example, don't assume that Othello is a jealous man, or the play is or isn't partly about racism, or that the play itself is racist. Take it in without making early judgements.

INTEGRATING VOICE

Even though you may not speak at this stage, allow yourself to receive and breathe in the world of the play and the nature of all the characters. Put yourself in the situation and observe them living; and then place yourself in their circumstances, seeing the action through their eyes.

Remind yourself of the role of the imagination, the breath and the solar plexus, as described in Chapter 9 on receiving and responding and Chapter 11 on the action.

So, even at this early stage, we can start to create a psycho-physical connection between image and breath, and their effect on senses and emotion.

Only after two or three objective readings should we start to look at it more subjectively, from the point of view of our particular character.

We don't advise highlighting your part in the text: this places *your* part in isolation instead of seeing it as part of the whole with your lines a response to others' lines. You don't want to create a possible block to connection right at the outset.

Facts

Now we start to do systematic work on the text. First, note down all the facts the author gives us: for example, the age and relationships of the characters, which might appear in the list of characters, followed by any information given during each scene. We are told that Desdemona is 'wife to Othello, and daughter to Brabantio', and we discover in Act 1 that Othello was once a slave and comes from 'men of royal siege'.

Facts about time, place, description of surroundings and previous events will give you your *previous* and *given circumstances* for each scene, and will inform your imagination to create whatever is not made explicit; for example, why you enter a particular situation, what you're doing as you enter, and what you want with your first objective.

So, these facts are not dry and academic, but a mining of the resources of the text to feed your knowledge and imagination, creative intuition and feeling. And for Stanislavski, *to know means to feel* (*An Actor's Work on a Role*: 103).

Questions

The facts will raise a number of questions, which you can try to answer. How did Othello and Desdemona get married? It was in secret – was there a priest? What sort of ceremony was it, and where? When was their betrothal – an event more important in this period than the formal wedding ceremony? Did Iago know about the wedding? If not, why not? How much was Cassio involved in the secret elopement? What does Iago come to conclude? Does this add to his numerous motives for resentment against Othello and Cassio? How did Iago come to exploit Roderigo? Roderigo is described as 'a gentleman' – what does this mean in this period? Where does his wealth come from? Do Othello and Desdemona ever actually have sex? If not, does this add to Othello's jealousy? What created Iago's jealousy over Othello and his wife, Emilia? Have Cassio and Bianca had a relationship before the play starts – if so, in Venice, in Cyprus? Was Cassio with Othello on his previous trips to Cyprus – because the Duke says that Othello knows it well, indicating he's been there before? And so on – and more questions come out of each answered question. This *appraisal of the facts,* as Stanislavski called it, builds up a detailed imaginary picture that takes on a reality for us.

Research

Assessing the facts will often necessitate research, for example, about coinage, the army, government, agriculture or customs, if we are fully to understand a text. Stanislavski did thorough research for Othello (see *Creating a Role* and *Stanislavsky Produces Othello*): this covered the nature of the Venetian state and its imperial ambitions, attitudes to race and class, and the competition from the Turks. We need to focus on the general historical background to a play, whether sixteenth-century Italy, ancient Greece or nineteenth-century Russia; on the social, political, religious and economic climate; specific subjects arising from the play, such as life on a Russian estate or civilian life during the Second World War; and subjects specific to your character: nursing, teaching, football, mining, alcoholism, etc.

We can also discover audiovisual resources such as paintings, photos, video and film records, and recorded interviews with accents and dialects, and maybe even visit the places which appear in the action. We need to understand everything that is said and done in the play: we can't believably do verbal and physical action if we don't understand the meaning of what we're saying and doing. This sort of research is wonderfully stimulating and enriching and helps to create what Stanislavski called *artistic enthusiasm* for the play and the role, so that not just our minds but also our feelings and will are engaged in exploring and committing to the play.

Theme

Why has the writer written this play? What issues concern and drive him or her? Identifying the themes of a play is important, not just to understand what it's about, but to inform characters' objectives and relationships, because the themes will be revealed through them.

Chekhov writes of dissatisfaction and displacement in a pre-revolutionary society, and his characters are often seeking some sort of fulfilment and release; Beckett looks at the absurdity of life and the comedy and pain of human endurance; Shakespeare often focuses on lack of self-knowledge, the nature of free will and exercise of power, and the conflict between appearance and reality. Certainly, *Othello* examines how the prejudice of Venetian society and the deceit of Iago can exercise a corrosive power on the narrow experience and self-knowledge of Othello.

We can see how theme comes into the title of a play: *Othello* is actually *Othello, the Moor of Venice,* revealing his contradictory situation from the start. *Hedda Gabler* is a title that reflects the unresolved attitudes of its leading character, the unhappily married Hedda Tesman. Character names may also reflect theme: in *Othello*, Desdemona, in Greek, means unfortunate; Bianca, the courtesan who arguably acts purely, means white.

Write down all the themes that come to mind as you keep reading the play.

The *primary event*: This is a concept used by some Russian directors – it establishes the event in the circumstances prior to the beginning of the play that initiates its action and story. In *Othello,* for the play as a whole, the event is Othello's secret marriage at night to Desdemona. For Iago though, it might be Othello's appointment of Cassio as his lieutenant instead of him. For the Duke, it would be the advance of the Turks towards Cyprus, Venice's colony. All of these events launch us into the action and themes of the play.

The *Ruling Idea* or *Superobjective* of the play: This is the main theme, the message, the reason why the writer wrote the play, and which needs to be uncovered by the actors and director together, often drawing on the writer's whole body of work. So a possible Ruling Idea for *Othello,* relating to the nature and actions of Othello and other leading characters, could be: *Narrowness of knowledge and outlook make us vulnerable to malevolent forces that can destroy innocence, order and love.*

Try to sum up the Superobjective in your own words.

Genre and form

One of our first impressions of the play will be how it is written. Is it tragedy, comedy, farce, drama, etc.? Is it in prose or verse, in acts or scenes? The style and form will carry and intensify meaning and theme, and will make different demands on the actor to communicate content in a manner that is appropriate and truthful for each. The reality required to play Winnie in Beckett's *Happy Days* is different from that required for Willie Loman in *Death of a Salesman* or Emilia in *Othello*. We have to start with 'If': 'If I am in these circumstances as this character what do I do?', and the circumstances and language tell us how to be truthful in each style of writing.

Othello is a five-act tragedy written in blank iambic pentameter verse and prose, through which means the love, pain, despair, brutality, buffoonery and pathos of the characters is heightened to fit the extremes demanded by the tragic genre. But we cannot play form alone without being shallow and mechanical; we have to bring the content to life and express it through the sometimes complex formal rigour of the language.

Meeting the character

As we get a sense of the play as a whole, we also start to develop a sense of our character, imagining it, seeing it, maybe feeling with it and understanding what drives it. Whatever the degree of our intuitive understanding of the character, it will help to gather all the information that can offer a comprehensive overview of it.

Four lists

We do this by writing down four lists:

1 *What the author says about the character, the facts.* For example, Othello is a general in the service of Venice.

2 *What the character says about himself or herself.* This, and the information in the next two lists, is word for word, and not a summary or an opinion on it. For example, in Act 1, 3, Desdemona says: 'I do perceive here a divided duty.'

3 *What the character says about other people.* For example, in the same scene Othello says: 'Her father loved me, oft invited me.'

4 *What other people say about the character.* For example, if I'm Othello, Brabantio says of Desdemona and me: 'She is abused, stol'n from me, and corrupted / By spells and medicines bought of mountebanks.'

Write down a few examples of each list for yourself.

This process draws together everything relating to your character and will stop you making wrong turns and missing information. You will very often grasp their age, birthplace, class, education, viewpoints, relationships, sexuality, ambitions, temperament and physicality, all of which have an effect on your vocal interpretation of the role.

Life Superobjective

Like the *primary event,* the character's *Life Superobjective* gives us an imagi-native launch pad into the action of the play. As we saw in Chapters 11 and 13, this is what they want in life before the play starts (discovered from the whole play, of course), a motivating force which can be expressed as *a basic desire, the reason for it, and the length the character would go to in order to achieve it.* Here are suggestions for the three characters in the scene:

Othello: *I want to find happiness with my fair warrior as an accepted part of Venetian society* – because I've felt alone and alien in serving it, and without her now all would be chaos – I'd go to the length of investing this love with the commitment I give to my service.

Desdemona: *I want to create the perfect family life with my lord, Othello*

– because he means all the world to me and gave me escape and adventure – I would go to any length of risk, loyalty and commitment.

Emilia: *I want to win appreciation from Iago and society* – because I want stability, comfort and respect – I'd go to the length of complying with all his demands.

These Superobjectives can't be played on every line and action – that would create generalized states – but they are an *influence* on all the smaller specific objectives running through the play. They are drawn from the actions and circumstances of the characters and incorporate similar words to those they use in the text. They should embody one's sense of the whole character, including their feelings, needs and will, so that a vocal and physical response is an organic one, not a purely intellectual one.

Inner motive forces

How do the forces of mind, feeling and will relate to each other in the character and what is the predominant one at any given point? (See Chapters 11 and 13.)

Othello may start the play predominantly guided by mind; he then becomes overpowered by his emotions; and finishes driven by will.

Desdemona is dominated by feeling in the first part of the play; and then events force her to use her mind more to search for answers to Othello's behaviour.

Emilia is driven by will, first to do what Iago wants, then to expose his treachery.

All these shifts will have an effect on the actor/character's physicality, onset, resonance and pitch range, as we'll see shortly.

Qualities

The character's qualities or personality traits come through their words and actions: verbal, psychological or physical. The initial exploratory work above and subsequent rehearsal will reveal these. We can identify:

- qualities from different aspects of the character's make-up;
- conflicting, contradictory qualities;
- qualities similar to and different from our own;
- and a *point of sympathy* through which we identify with the character in some respect, through a common quality, experience, relationship or objective.

What qualities do you perceive in each of the three characters?

Attitudes

By now the character's attitudes and relationships to other people should be revealed. Often contradictory, they affect our objectives when we enter a situation because they come from past experience: we don't *play* suspicion, but suspicion towards someone will determine what we want with them and how we get it.

Othello loves Desdemona in a romantic way but doesn't know her well enough as a complete person to have real trust in her. In the throes of jealous passion, he trusts 'honest' Iago but hates what Iago's told him and threatens him. Emilia will do anything for Iago, but resents the unfaithfulness of men.

Meeting the scene

Here is the scene from Act 4, Scene 2 of *Othello*.

Enter DESDEMONA and EMILIA

DESDEMONA   My lord, what is your will?
OTHELLO   Pray, chuck, come hither.
DESDEMONA   What is your pleasure?
OTHELLO   Let me see your eyes.
                    Look in my face.
DESDEMONA   What horrible fancy's this?
OTHELLO [To Emilia]
                    Some of your function, mistress:
                    Leave procreants alone and shut the door;
                    Cough or cry 'hem' if anybody come.
                    Your mystery, your mystery! Nay, dispatch!

                                                            Exit Emilia

DESDEMONA   Upon my knees, what doth your speech import?
                    I understand a fury in your words,
                    But not the words.
OTHELLO   Why? What art thou?
DESDEMONA   Your wife, my lord; your true and loyal wife.
OTHELLO   Come, swear it; damn thyself;
                    Lest, being like one of heaven, the devils themselves
                    Should fear to seize thee. Therefore be double-damned:
                    Swear thou art honest.

DESDEMONA	Heaven doth truly know it.
OTHELLO	Heaven truly knows that thou art false as hell.
DESDEMONA	To whom, my lord? With whom? How am I false?
OTHELLO	Ah, Desdemon, away, away, away!
DESDEMONA	Alas, the heavy day! Why do you weep?

Am I the motive of these tears, my lord?
If haply you my father do suspect
An instrument of this your calling back,
Lay not your blame on me. If you have lost him,
I have lost him too.

OTHELLO   Had it pleased heaven
To try me with affliction, had they rained
All kinds of sores and shames on my bare head,
Steeped me in poverty to the very lips,
Given to captivity me and my utmost hopes,
I should have found in some place of my soul
A drop of patience. But, alas, to make me
The fixed figure for the time of scorn
To point his slow unmoving finger at!
Yet could I bear that too, well, very well;
But there where I have garnered up my heart,
Where either I must live or bear no life,
The fountain from the which my current runs
Or else dries up – to be discarded thence
Or keep it as a cistern for foul toads
To knot and gender in! Turn thy complexion there,
Patience, thou young and rose-lipped cherubim;
Ay, there look grim as hell!

DESDEMONA   I hope my noble lord esteems me honest.

OTHELLO   O ay: as summer flies are in the shambles,
That quicken even with blowing. O, thou weed,
Who art so lovely fair and smell'st so sweet
That the sense aches at thee, would thou hadst ne'er been
born!

DESDEMONA   Alas, what ignorant sin have I committed?

OTHELLO   Was this fair paper, this most goodly book,
Made to write 'whore' upon? What committed!
Committed? O thou public commoner!
I should make very forges of my cheeks
That would to cinders burn up modesty
Did I but speak thy deeds. What committed!
Heaven stops the nose at it, and the moon winks;

The bawdy wind, that kisses all it meets,
Is hushed within the hollow mine of earth
And will not hear it. What committed?
Impudent strumpet!

DESDEMONA   By heaven, you do me wrong.
OTHELLO   Are not you a strumpet?
DESDEMONA   No, as I am a Christian.

If to preserve this vessel for my lord
From any other foul unlawful touch
Be not to be a strumpet, I am none.

OTHELLO   What, not a whore?
DESDEMONA   No, as I shall be saved.
OTHELLO   Is't possible?
DESDEMONA   O, heaven forgive us!
OTHELLO   I cry you mercy then:

I took you for that cunning whore of Venice
That married with Othello. You, mistress,
That have the office opposite to Saint Peter,
And keeps the gate of hell! You, you, ay, you!

Enter Emilia

We have done our course; there's money for your pains.
I pray you turn the key, and keep our counsel.   *Exit*

We shall examine this scene in a similar way to how we looked at the speeches in Chapter 11.

Previous circumstances

Othello, a Moor, is a general hired by the Venetian state. He has secretly married Desdemona, the young and white daughter of Brabantio, a senator. Brabantio accuses the black outsider of witchcraft but Othello is needed to fight the Ottoman Empire in its advance on Cyprus, a Venetian colony. He leaves for Cyprus, with Desdemona, Iago, his ensign, Emilia, his wife and Desdemona's maid, and his new lieutenant, Cassio. Cassio has been promoted over Iago, who is bitter and vengeful. To bring down Othello and Cassio, Iago engineers Cassio's disgrace and dismissal and convinces Othello that Desdemona is unfaithful with Cassio. Othello wants them both dead, but cannot suppress his loving feelings for Desdemona. Iago constantly feeds his doubts until Othello strikes her in public. The scene begins shortly after this event.

Given circumstances

Lodovico, a noble Venetian and kinsman of Desdemona, has arrived with a letter from the Duke for Othello, summoning him back to Venice and appointing Cassio in his place (the Turkish fleet has been destroyed by storms, and Lodovico doesn't know about Cassio's disgrace for drunken brawling). Othello has struck Desdemona in front of him, to his great surprise.

Desdemona retires to her room. Othello now summons her, perhaps a couple of hours later, in their lodgings on Cyprus, having probed Emilia about Desdemona's conduct with Cassio.

The 5 Ws for the actor playing Othello might be:

- *Who?* I am Othello: with all that now means as a changed and tormented man whose dreams have been crushed.

- *Where?* I'm at our lodgings: the rooms assigned to him as new governor of the island, possibly decorated in an Ottoman style; he might have come from an isolated tower in the fortress, where he has brooded alone over developments; and after he's seen Desdemona, he might be planning to find Iago to get details on their plans to kill her and Cassio.

- *When?* It's 6pm: at the end of Act 4, Scene 2, the trumpets sound for the meal with the Venetian messengers; let's say it's Sunday; it's a stormy season, possibly November; and it's around 1569 – the Turks actually succeeded in taking Cyprus in 1570.

- *Why?* I struck Desdemona for her open support for Cassio, my suspicion and torment are overpowering and I need to prompt a clear confession from her.

- *What do I want?* I want to get confirmation that Desdemona has whored herself and betrayed me.

INTEGRATING VOICE

You will launch into the scene with this partly experienced and partly imaginary set of circumstances, and with the prompt of 'If I am in Othello's circumstances what do I do?' This will help to give you the sense of I am Me/Othello in the circumstances, with your voice rooted in a deep emotional need for satisfaction of your suspicions *and* fear of them being confirmed.

▶

Othello is being driven by his emotions at this point. Whereas he may have started the action of the play with a centre in his chest, he may now be centred in his gut or a seething knot of nerve endings in his solar plexus.

This is likely to intensify his breathing, lower the resonance area used, but make the delivery and pitch range unpredictable and more extreme and the onset potentially explosive. Your voice will need to be rooted and ready to respond in any of these ways.

Objectives

As we suggested above, Othello's Life Superobjective could be *I want to find happiness with my fair warrior as an accepted part of Venetian society.*

Then there are character Superobjectives *within* the play. There could be five major *episodes* that mark a significant shift in the development of the narrative of the play and of Othello's own journey. In the past, it was customary to look for one Superobjective running through the whole play, and sometimes that occurs, but more often than not it doesn't, particularly in Shakespeare where characters may go on lengthy and tortuous journeys.

- In Act 1, he wants to make his bond with Desdemona secure.
- In Act 2 up to Act 3, Scene 3, he wants to establish order, calm and joy in their life in Cyprus.
- From Act 3, Scene 3 to the end of Act 4 – and this is the main objective affecting the scene we're looking at – *he wants to work out if Iago's suspicions of Desdemona's infidelity are true and what's to be done.*
- From here into Act 5, Scene 2, he wants to avenge her crime.
- Finally, from where he discovers he's been deceived and has committed the appalling murder of Desdemona, he wants to make amends.

In the Scene of Act 4, 2 as a whole, there are a number of smaller *scenes* marked by the major entrance or exit of a character: Othello, Emilia, Desdemona, Iago, Roderigo.

Othello is in two of these small scenes, one with Emilia, and one with Desdemona and Emilia (Emilia actually leaves the stage at one point, but is still around listening, and is then summoned back in). This latter is the one we're looking at.

From his entrance to his exit, Othello's Scene objective is: I *want to get confirmation that Desdemona has whored herself and betrayed me.*

In this scene, as in most, there are smaller *units* or *bits*. A *unit of action* contains an identifiable event, dynamic and piece of thought and action taking place between the characters. Within these units there are smaller objectives, as we saw in Blanche's speech in Chapter 11.

To achieve these, a character uses a range of often simple actions: psychological and physical, verbal and silent.

So there is a form of pyramid spreading down from the character's Life Superobjective at the top to the episode Superobjective, to the scene objective, to the unit objective, to the actions – all of which provides a *through line of action* for you as the character.

What is at *stake* here for Othello is literally everything: his peace, happiness, trust and love, his hope to be accepted into society, his career as a soldier. Nothing can be salvaged from this sudden shipwreck of a life unless he proves Desdemona a strumpet and takes the action believed justified in this sixteenth- and seventeenth-century society: to kill his wife for adultery.

We suggested that Desdemona's Life Superobjective may be *I want to create the perfect family life with my lord, Othello.* In the episode of the play prior to the one in which the scene occurs, she wanted to bring reconciliation between Othello and Cassio. Now, in a new episode created by Othello's strike at her, her Superobjective might become *I want to find out my alleged fault and convince Othello of my innocence.*

Events change people, and Desdemona has retired to her rooms and no doubt discussed matters with Emilia. Her world has turned upside down. What is at stake is her future happiness, trust in Othello, and whole understanding of life, which up to this point has had a very limited scope. These, then, are the circumstances for the actor playing Desdemona before entering the scene.

How we put these discoveries into action is the subject of the next chapter.

16
FROM IMPULSE
TO ACTION

Real action begins when there is no character as yet, but an 'I' in the hypothetical circumstances. If that is not the case, you lose contact with yourself, you see the role from the outside, you copy it.'

(*Stanislavski in Rehearsal*: 110)

In Chapter 15, we made a basic study of the play and character, using our analytical, organizational and imaginative faculties, both our left and right brain (see Chapter 2). We now focus on bringing the play to life through a partnership between left, right and old brains: going from conscious preparation to intuitive and imaginative response.

Although integration of the voice and acting process is ultimately the responsibility of actors themselves, we believe the best results will be achieved by actors, directors, movement and voice teachers working as a unified team, an ensemble, rather than as separate elements in a fragmented process, as can happen. Stanislavski's later rehearsal approach, presented in part below, can certainly offer a good framework for unification.

Analysis through action

When Stanislavski worked on *Othello* (1930–3), he introduced his 'new and unexpected method' of starting rehearsal by physicalizing the action of the play (*Creating a Role*: 131) Below, we'll look at elements of this process, as we apply them, and as they directly affect voice in work on the scene.

This is what we know as the *method of physical action, active analysis* or *analysis through action,* as most clearly revealed in *Creating a Role* (from

Chapter 5). This is a process of discussing and *improvising* the text from the first rehearsals, and is also evident in Stanislavski's Opera-Dramatic Studio classes, 1935–8 (see *Stanislavski and the Actor*, J. Benedetti); in Vasili Toporkov's account of Stanislavski directing, *Stanislavski in Rehearsal;* and in *On the Active Analysis of Plays and Roles* by one of his pupils, Maria Knebel.

We should stress that *analysis through action* is a new *rehearsal* method and still links in with all the basic tenets of Stanislavski's approach to actor training and preparation as described in *An Actor's Work, An Actor Prepares* and *Building a Character* – but, as compared to his earlier rehearsal processes, it has a different starting point in physical action and the impulses behind it: a practical psycho-physical approach.

Reading

Actors should come to rehearsal of a play prepared in the ways outlined in Chapter 15, particularly given the frequently brief nature of our rehearsal periods. For the purpose of examining our scene, it would be best if you have colleagues to work with, of course.

Start by reading the scene quietly, simply aiming to connect with each other through a responsive communication; to grasp the literal sense of the lines and a sense of what may lie behind them; and to place yourselves imaginatively in the circumstances of the characters. Don't try to 'act' the whole character and play, to get big emotion, endgame and do a performance, and don't rush – this is a rehearsal, a process, so explore, probe, take your time and discover.

In rehearsals for a full play, an alternative to doing a cast reading of the play is for the director or someone else to read it clearly, intelligently and quite neutrally, but not flatly, while the actors listen and *take it all in* – something that isn't usually possible in a first read-through when nerves and concern for one's own role tend to take over.

Basic analysis of the scene

We can then do what Stanislavski called a *mental reconnaissance* of the scene and play – discussing given circumstances, theme, facts and other elements covered in the last chapter – before tackling improvised explorations of the action of the play, often called *etudes*. Look at how the scene breaks into smaller bits or units according to an event and dynamic occurring between the characters.

Ask: *If* I'm in these circumstances, saying these words, what do I want? What might my range of actions be? What is at stake for me in pursuing my objective? What obstacles are in my way?

Also, be easy and take the time to see how each line or part of a line comes from a new impulse – thought, feeling, response, image. We need to come back to our centre to discover and experience each impulse and give it full and clear expression, psychologically, vocally and physically, through a new action. To warn and to soothe, to implore and to attack may have different energies and tempos, different physical and vocal qualities, and these will only be realized through ease and stillness. Pushing, rushing and endgaming produce a false adrenalized energy and will set us back, blocking organic responses and connection and the development of an inner life and rich expression. Unfortunately, short rehearsals and directors eager for quick results can make that block more likely.

Breakdown of the scene

Here is our suggestion on how the scene might break down into units, character objectives and beats/impulses marked with a **/** :

UNIT 1: Othello searches into Desdemona

Enter DESDEMONA and EMILIA to OTHELLO

E: I want to work out what's happening
D: I want to find out the matter
DESDEMONA   **/**My lord, what is your will?

                              O: I want to uncover her sin in her eyes
OTHELLO   **/**Pray, chuck, come hither.
DESDEMONA   **/**What is your pleasure?
OTHELLO   **/**Let me see your eyes.
              /Look in my face.
DESDEMONA   **/**What horrible fancy's this?

Unit 2: Othello instructs Emilia to keep guard like a brothel-keeper

O: Make her perform her function as a bawd

OTHELLO [To Emilia]

/Some of your function,* mistress: *your job as a brothel-keeper*

/Leave procreants* alone and shut the door;   *copulators*

/Cough or cry 'hem' if anybody come.

/Your mystery, your mystery!* /Nay, dispatch!   *trade, of a*
                                                                                      bawd

Exit Emilia

UNIT 3: Othello tries to make Desdemona confess her guilt and she protests her innocence.

D: Make him say what troubles him

DESDEMONA   /Upon my knees, what doth your speech import?

/I understand a fury in your words,

But not the words.

O: Make her confess she's a whore

OTHELLO   /Why? /What art thou?

DESDEMONA   /Your wife, my lord; /your true and loyal wife.

OTHELLO   /Come, swear it; /damn thyself;

/Lest, being like one of heaven, the devils themselves

Should fear to seize thee. /Therefore be double-damned:

/Swear thou art honest.

D: Convince him of my honesty and innocence

DESDEMONA   /Heaven doth truly know it.

OTHELLO   /Heaven truly knows that thou art false as hell.

DESDEMONA   /To whom, my lord? /With whom? /How am I false?

OTHELLO   /Ah, Desdemon, away, /away, /away!

DESDEMONA   /Alas, the heavy day! /Why do you weep?

/Am I the motive of these tears, my lord?

If haply you my father do suspect

An instrument of this your calling back,

Lay not your blame on me. /If you have lost him,

I have lost him too.

OTHELLO   /Had it pleased heaven

To try me with affliction, had they rained

All kinds of sores and shames on my bare head,
Steeped me in poverty to the very lips,
Given to captivity me and my utmost hopes,
I should have found in some place of my soul
A drop of patience. /But, alas, to make me
The fixed figure for the time of scorn
To point his slow unmoving finger at!
/Yet could I bear that too, well, very well;
/But there where I have garnered* up my heart,   *stored*
Where either I must live or bear no life,
The fountain from the which my current runs
Or else dries up – to be discarded thence
Or keep it as a cistern* for foul toads   *cesspool*
To knot and gender in!* /Turn thy complexion there, *copulate*
                                                   and engender

	Patience, thou young and rose-lipped cherubim;
	/Ay, there look grim as hell!
DESDEMONA	/I hope my noble lord esteems me honest.
OTHELLO	/O ay:/as summer flies are in the shambles,* *slaughter-house*

That quicken even with blowing.*/O, thou weed, *conceive as*
                                               soon as they lay eggs
Who art so lovely fair and smell'st so sweet
That the sense aches at thee, would thou hadst ne'er been
born!

DESDEMONA	/Alas, what ignorant sin have I committed?
OTHELLO	/Was this fair paper, this most goodly book,

Made to write 'whore' upon? /What committed!
/Committed? /O thou public commoner!*   *whore*
/I should make very forges of my cheeks
That would to cinders burn up modesty
Did I but speak thy deeds. /What committed!
/Heaven stops the nose at it, and the moon winks;
The bawdy wind, that kisses all it meets,
Is hushed within the hollow mine of earth
And will not hear it. /What committed?
/Impudent strumpet!

DESDEMONA	/By heaven, you do me wrong.
OTHELLO	/Are not you a strumpet?
DESDEMONA	/No, as I am a Christian.

/If to preserve this vessel for my lord
From any other foul unlawful touch
Be not to be a strumpet, I am none.

OTHELLO	/What, not a whore?
DESDEMONA	/No, as I shall be saved.
OTHELLO	/Is't possible?
DESDEMONA	/O, heaven forgive us!
OTHELLO	/I cry you mercy then:* *ask your pardon*

/I took you for that cunning whore of Venice
That married with Othello.

UNIT 4: Othello pays off Emilia as a brothel-keeper

> **O: Make them acknowledge their corruption**
> **E: Grasp his meaning**
> **D: Gather my senses**

/You, mistress,
That have the office opposite to Saint Peter,
And keeps the gate of hell! /You, you, ay, you!

Enter Emilia

/We have done our course; /there's money for your pains.
/I pray you turn the key, and keep our counsel.*   *keep it secret*

Exit

Improvise the action – creating a dynamic through objectives

Having got an understanding of key elements in the scene, we now get up on our feet and improvise the action, one unit or more at a time.

Using our own words, and whatever of the writer's words come to us naturally, we place ourselves in the circumstances using the 5 Ws and 'if'; play our objective against the other person's objective, trying to change the situation and the other person; and while doing this, we listen, respond and adapt to them and discover a range of actions to achieve what we want and overcome the obstacles.

INTEGRATING VOICE

Although in improvising we explore the circumstances through our own words, we need to breathe in the circumstances in order to experience them and the action and really connect with the other actor/characters. Remind yourself of the receiving and responding process (see Chapter 9), and make sure all the *Vocal Givens* are in place – check the exercises at the beginning of Chapter 15.

Vocally experiencing the Ws

Rather than cerebrally thinking the Ws, involve your breathing so that you enter into the present moment of your imagination and have a sensual response. Breathing in and out fills our every present moment. By linking our imagination to the breath with an umbilical cord, we will stay in the moment. The in-breath receives and the out-breath responds. The psycho–physical energy of the centred and natural deep breath will focus our attention and heighten our experience.

Go through the Ws slowly

For example, root yourself into your 'Me/I' (see Chapter 5, Exercise 2): here it is *you in the circumstances of the character*. Connect with your solar plexus, breath energy and muscular support and find a centred onset for *you as the character*. Remember the *magic if*: use yourself as a basis for transformation and don't describe an external 'character'.

Breathe in images of what's happened beforehand, for example, Desdemona's face when struck by Othello. Create sensory images for your surroundings, their particular epoch, the time of day, and for the content of the dialogue, and find focus points for them in the space. Connect your breath to the focus points as described in Chapter 14, and experience the whole circumstances of the character, allowing the voice to respond freely.

Connect your objectives

You now have to breathe in the person/s you are on stage with and make a psycho-physical connection with them. Receive what they give you and then respond through the out-breath to connect with and change the other, engaging with the pelvic floor, lumbar drive and Elastic Band.

Find a clear onset and optimum pitch (although you don't need to project through the walls at this stage). Allow your pitch range to respond to each impulse and keep the resonance areas open and available. Make sure you express your thoughts and feelings with clarity.

Remind yourself of Chapter 4: Exercise 10 – Shooting the arrow – playing 'I want …', 11 – Strengthening the objective by engaging the Elastic Band; Chapter 11: Objectives, Exercise 1 – 'Come closer …', 2 – Lumbar drive, and 3 – Making your point.

Your support muscles have to respond to the acting impulse in reflex mode. The spine responds to the breathed-in and experienced circumstances and drives the objective and actions through the words.

Let's look at Unit 1 of the scene, as an example. Receive the circumstances as outlined in Chapter 15, and improvise the event, *Othello searches into Desdemona*, through enacting the objectives below.

UNIT 1: Othello searches into Desdemona

Enter DESDEMONA and EMILIA to OTHELLO

E: I want to work out what's happening
D: I want to find out the matter
DESDEMONA   /My lord, what is your will?

                              O: I want to uncover her sin in her eyes
OTHELLO   /Pray, chuck, come hither.
DESDEMONA   /What is your pleasure?
OTHELLO   /Let me see your eyes.
                /Look in my face.
DESDEMONA   /What horrible fancy's this?

Here is how the improvised dialogue may go:

Othello is convinced Cassio is having an affair with Desdemona, and that Emilia is complicit. You've summoned Desdemona and *want to get confirmation that she has whored herself and betrayed me.* Breathe the objective into your solar plexus and pursue it through your lumbar drive. Desdemona is shaken and full of trepidation as she answers his summons, and you *want to find out the matter.*

* You see him and breathe in his persona and question, 'What do you want, my lord?'
* This gives Othello his first objective within the scene, *to uncover her sin in her eyes.* Rooted vocally in your sense of 'Me/I' Othello summons with 'Please come here, dear.'

▶

* Desdemona probes with, 'What can I do for you?', rooting your need to find out the problem in your pelvic floor and spine.
* Othello responds with an order, 'Show me your eyes. Look at me', and you now see into her eyes, breathe them in and what you seek to uncover in them, rooting your need in your spine and support muscles.
* Desdemona responds, breathing in his menace, imploring him with 'What terrible thoughts are you having about me?'

Explore moment by moment, allowing pitch range and resonance to respond to these thoughts, actions and words. This is quite different from just reading lines at each other and thinking about how to say them. In-breath receives and out-breath responds, filling each moment, so that your voice reacts to the circumstances and flows the thoughts and actions through the invented words.

At this stage, the emphasis is on exploring, absorbing and responding and not on producing a final acting or vocal result. Your voice can be quite low-key at this stage, but you still need to be in touch with all the *Vocal Givens* below.

The improvisation creates an organic dynamic between the actor/characters, creating the essential event that occurs in the unit. By using our own words (whether we're doing Shakespeare, Miller or Brecht) we imaginatively connect to the action, rooting ourselves in it, and forming a real bond with the other actors/characters. Without using this process, too often the written text, especially classical text with its dense content and form, remains written text, which we recite and declaim from our left brain without making it our own. Although we are not performing the writer's own lines here, it's *one* stage in the process of trying to connect fully with that work – we should, however, try to keep in the tone and spirit of the specific genre and period of the writing.

Stanislavski might have spent six months on such analysis and improvisation, until gradually the writer's words become more and more present and the whole text is absorbed. Most of us have to work more quickly, but even spending a week or two on this improvisatory part of the process on a play produces more connection between actors and with the action and the text, and a deeper more experienced understanding of the world of the play. It prevents us from starting with a formalistic reading of complex text, so that instead, we go from the text to the action and subtext, then back to the text having found out what imaginative elements give rise to the text from our actor's point of view.

After an initial exploration, we can assess what happened in the improvisation. Did we imaginatively create the circumstances and believe in what we were doing? Did we really connect with each other, psychologically, vocally and physically? Did we play the objectives and uncover a range of actions to achieve them? Did we create the essence of what occurs in each unit? Where did we fail to find the transitions from one thought and action to another? Where were we unclear about the meaning and what did we miss out?

Even if things go wrong and we fail to create the action clearly and truthfully, it's still a learning process. It's not about a final result, it's about play and exploration. So, we can then have another go, actively discovering what we need to do to create the action more fully and to connect with each other and the words. You may have time for more attempts, and as a result the writer's own words will be absorbed more easily and organically.

After a few improvised attempts at some units, we could then go back to the text and read it again on our feet – particularly useful with classical text where the form is different from everyday speech – and allow elements of what has been understood from the improvisation to come through.

The next exercises focus on work on the text itself.

INTEGRATING VOICE

Having connected with the action in your own words, let's now focus on objectives on the actual text.

Objectives on text
Go through the scene unit by unit.
- Imagine the circumstances and your 5 Ws and let the objectives launch you into speaking the text.
- Breathe in each objective through your solar plexus, then play it through the lines, riding the wave of the out-breath: *impulse, breath, action.*
- Commit to the objective and use each new impulse and action to achieve what you want, using the words to express them. Support the out-breath with the

▶

pelvic floor, the lumbar drive and the lengthening of the Elastic Band through the spine (see the exercises from the previous box).

- Let the sense of 'Me/I' in the situation create a clear onset of sound and articulation.

Key words

- Now we focus on *impulse, breath and action,* emphasizing the *key words.*
- Look at Unit 3 below and our suggestions for these. Play the objectives through these lines, accenting these words, and sense how the objectives acquire greater clarity and energy.

UNIT 3: Othello tries to make Desdemona confess her guilt and she protests her innocence.

D: Make him say what troubles him
DESDEMONA / Upon my **knees**, what doth your speech **import**?
              / I understand a **fury** in your **words**,
                 But **not** the **words**.

O: Make her confess she's a whore
OTHELLO   /Why? /What **art** thou**?**
DESDEMONA / Your **wife**, my lord; /your **true** and **loyal** wife.
OTHELLO   / Come, **swear** it; /**damn** thyself;
              / Lest, being like one of **heaven**, the **devils** themselves
                 Should **fear** to **seize** thee/Therefore be **double-damned**:
              / **Swear** thou art **honest**.

- Rooted and connected to your lumbar drive, now respond to your breathed-in circumstances through the key words *alone.* Channel your thoughts and feelings into them; they will clarify the literal sense and help you make your point. Make sure that the key words fill out your entire out-breath movement. Radiate your objective through the words.

- Now go back to speaking the whole lines. Sense how accenting the key words helps to communicate the sense through your whole pitch range.

Remind yourself of Chapter 6, Pitch Range, and stimulate your pitch range by doing Exercise 1 – From relaxing into sirening; 4 – Connecting your pitch range to the balance line of your body; 5 – The responding voice through the vowel energy; and Integration into acting.

Vowels

- The next step is to focus on your response to each acting impulse through the vowel vibrations of the text. This will activate your body resonance, making it spontaneously available, and release emotional experience. You only need do this on a couple of thoughts to get the process going.

For example, 'Your **wife**, my lord; your **true** and **loyal** wife.'

- Connect to Desdemona's objective *to make him say what troubles him*, and start by exploring the vowel vibrations through the key words only.

- Now, as in Chapter 7, Resonance, release *only* the vowels on the wave of your out-breath, and allow them to resonate wherever they want in your body. You will find they open up wider spaces and your body will start to vibrate.

- Now go back to speaking the whole lines and note the difference. Your body resonance should be right behind the text, vibrating your experience as the character within the circumstances, integrating acting impulse and vocal expression.

Move the beats

As with the speeches in Chapter 11, moving the beats will help to give you a psycho-physical connection to the language. Don't try to play the full character but do it as yourself within their given circumstances.

Try moving – walking, stopping, turning, sitting, standing – where each of the forward slashes appears in the text above. Let each new impulse move you psychologically and physically and then prompt you into speech. Allow yourself to be affected by the nature of the thought and feeling, which will determine the type of movement you do spontaneously.

Also, be aware that longer lines/beats may comprise several measures created by the commas and semicolons, and these have to be observed to carry the whole sense of the line – e.g.

Heaven stops the nose at it, and the moon winks;
The bawdy wind, that kisses all it meets,
Is hushed within the hollow mine of earth
And will not hear it.

For example you might do these actions and physical moves:

Desdemona moves to Othello, assuring him with –
  /I hope my noble lord esteems me honest.

Othello walks away, spurning her with –
  /O ay:

He turns in a different direction, besmirching her on –
  /as summer flies are in the shambles
    That quicken even with blowing.

He strides back to her, condemning her –
  /O, thou weed,
    Who art so lovely fair and smell'st so sweet
    That the sense aches at thee, would thou hadst ne'er been born!

Desdemona sits, imploring him with –
  /Alas, what ignorant sin have I committed?

Go through the whole scene in this way, allowing the psychological, physical and verbal actions to come intuitively.

Now try the scene again without feeling you have to do such large physical movements at every change of impulse.

INTEGRATING VOICE

Voicing the beats

Again start by imagining the circumstances through your five Ws and let the objective launch you into the speech.

- Breathe in and receive each impulse through your solar plexus, find and begin the accompanying physical movement, then speak the line with a verbal action, riding the wave of the breath: *impulse, breath, action.*
- Keep still, easy and centred, without extraneous gestures, and keep in the present moment.
- Don't speak automatically at the beginning of each beat so that movement and speech become mechanical and abrupt. Let the lines come through the impulse and movement. This does not mean a *pause* before speaking, but simply a beat.

- Use your own voice with an optimum pitch, making sense of the line with your full vocal identity. Don't recite.
- Commit to the objective and use each new impulse and action to achieve what you want. Support the out-breath with the pelvic floor, the lumbar drive and the lengthening of the Elastic Band through the spine (see Objective exercises in Chapter 11).
- Let the sense of 'Me/I' in the situation create a clear onset of sound and articulation.
- Allow rhythm, intonation, pitch range and resonance to respond spontaneously to situation, objective, impulse and action, and what the other person is doing to you.

Through this process you can *anchor the impulses* in your body, breath and voice, and in time it will quickly become second nature.

Mind, feeling and will

Now let's look at the influence of mind, feeling and will in the scene. For much of it, Othello appears to be torn by his feelings of disgust for Desdemona's perceived betrayal and corruption and his continuing feelings of love for her. His conviction that she is guilty prevents any new rational thought, but occasionally his will for revenge comes through, too; for example:

> /Come, swear it; /damn thyself;
> /Lest, being like one of heaven, the devils themselves
>   Should fear to seize thee. /Therefore be double-damned:
> /Swear thou art honest.

Desdemona is overcome with confusion and has to make sense of Othello's violence and insinuations and is using her mind to achieve this:

> /I understand a fury in your words,
>   But not the words.

Then, perhaps, she is willing things to change later in the scene:

> /By heaven, you do me wrong.

And appealing, with emotion, to Heaven for help when all fails with:

> /O, heaven forgive us!

It's as though Othello's feelings are speaking to his will to spur himself on to take revenge; and Desdemona's head is speaking to her heart to try to keep control over the situation.

Try the whole scene from this perspective, moving on the beats but letting their origin in mind, feeling or will affect the verbal and physical action more specifically, e.g. Desdemona's probing for reasons may cause her to be cautious and steady, while Othello's surging feelings might prompt seething, wringing movements. You will start to connect with different aspects of your psychophysical make-up.

INTEGRATING VOICE

Keep integrating the vocal points from above. Your actions, and your pitch range and intonation may well change – also, your vocal resonance may switch from head to chest to pelvis as the predominant force of mind, feeling or will shifts.

Resonance areas
The work on the vowel sounds we did above will also have encouraged your voice to resonate.

Remind yourself of Exercise 2 – Resonating in different body areas, in Chapter 7, Explore the intellect/head resonance through *YUH, YU-UH-UH, YA, YEH, YEY, YI, YEE.*

Explore the heart/chest resonance through *YAA.*

Explore the will/pelvis/solar plexus resonance through *YOO, YOE, YAW, YOH.*

Once you've stimulated these areas try the scene. Explore the effect of mind, feeling and will on resonance by just allowing it to occur in the body wherever it wants to as a response. Also, your whole pitch range should communicate the objectives and meaning freely and expressively, rather than getting stuck in a certain resonance area or notion of a beautiful sound.

Obstacles

Focus now on how the scene alters when we introduce obstacles.

Othello wants to make Desdemona confess she's a whore. What stands in his way? The romance and innocence of their courtship; her loyalty and bravery towards him in the face of powerful opposition to their marriage; her appearance and unblemished character; his knowledge of his own inexperience in these affairs and his lower social status than hers in Venetian society; his troubled mind, which has led to a recent fit.

Desdemona wants to convince him of her honesty and innocence. Her obstacles might be: her total confusion as to why Othello is acting in this way; his strange, intense and unpredictable moods; her own limited and circumscribed experience of the world; being physically shaken after Othello has struck her in public.

INTEGRATING VOICE

Obstacles comprise a double set of problems: those presented by the other person, and extra ones as outlined above. An internal dynamic is set up within the characters, and this deepens the experience of their conflict with each other. This means the objective has to work in a different way, through a different range of actions, to achieve its ends. For example, Desdemona might humble herself and implore Othello more; he might intensify the violence of his attacks and vilification to compensate.

The result will then be a different vocal response, particularly in pitch range, intonation and resonance. Where the stakes are high and the objective and obstacle strong, we need to employ more rooting and lumbar drive – so we pursue the objective against an extra resistance, and physically against the spine, to create greater grounding. This will open the body's resonators and give strength, conviction and responsiveness to the actor's voice. The in-breath and solar plexus need to absorb awareness of the various obstacles, and our out-breath and spinal movements need to link with our objective to overcome them. Even if the characters are in turmoil and fear and the voice adapts, we can use this struggle combined with physical rooting to keep vocal onset clear and defined, however lacking in power.

Obstacles

Remind yourself of Chapter 4, Breath: Exercises 8, 10 and 11; Chapter 6, Pitch range: Integration into acting; Chapter 8, Articulation: Playing with the articulators, Exercises ▶

6 and 7; and Chapter 11, The Action: Objectives, Exercises 1 and 2. Be sure that you are engaged with a muscular and spinal movement that responds to the impulse of the objective voiced through the out-breath wave.

Choose part of the scene, and go through the vocal process outlined in Voicing the beats above, but this time focus your in-breath energy on the obstacles and, in response, focus the rooted out-breath energy through the objective to overcome them. Make sure you don't shout and strain but ensure that your vocal channels stay open, allowing the vowels to flow on the out-breath wave and the consonants to be rooted into the spine.

- *Against the wall*: Each actor/character should stand against opposite walls with knees bent, lumbar area pressing lightly into the wall and weight rooted in the balls of the feet. Head and neck should be detached from the wall, free and well aligned. The wall will give you extra support and strength as the rooted muscular and spinal response drives the objective through the thoughts, words and actions on your out-breath wave. Breathe in each other, the circumstances and the obstacles, making the umbilical cord connection. Respond with your objectives towards each other by engaging your lumbar drive, pressing the back of the pelvis and lumbar area against the wall, and the feet against the floor. Keep your neck long, the larynx and jaw released and resonators open. The energy of the objective fighting the obstacles should be communicated by breath flowing through open channels rather than through tension.
- *Vowel energy*: Choose a line, and breathing in each other, the circumstances and the obstacles, speak only the vowels and let them resonate freely on your out-breath wave, communicating the feelings that arise in response to overcoming the obstacles. Make sure you don't emote or strain – stay grounded in your objective.
- *Consonantal energy*: Enhance the consonants of key words, glue them to your spine and pelvic floor, then drive them on your out-breath wave to overcome the obstacles with your objective, e.g. Come, **sw**ear it; / **damn** thyself
- *Tonal energy*: With the same aim, engage with the tonal energy by elongating the vowels of key words along the Elastic Band from the floor to the ceiling.
- Go back to the scene and away from the wall. Stay engaged with each other, the circumstances, objectives and obstacles, and with your breath energy and reflexive support muscles, and play the scene, allowing the above elements to come through without concentrating on them.

Images

As in Chapters 10 and 12, we emphasize the importance of creating images in vocal expression. We stressed the need to really see images and draw on our other senses in order to bring to life a character's circumstances, the surroundings, their past, and the words – so that we achieve *'the word made flesh* rather than *the word as symbol'* (*Freeing Shakespeare's Voice*: 35).

Previous circumstances

> Stanislavski referred to the events of the day before entering a scene as the *before-time*, or *the line, or flow, of the day* (*Stanislavski Produces Othello*: 203, and *Stanislavski Directs*: 148). The whole imaginary life of the character before the play begins and between the scenes in which they appear was known as *the second plan* at the Moscow Art Theatre.

Our scene is the last major scene before Othello comes to kill Desdemona in Act 5, Scene 2. In Act 4, Scene 1, we saw Othello have a fit, resolve with Iago that Cassio and Desdemona should be killed, and later strike Desdemona in front of Lodovico. Although, Othello has committed to kill Desdemona, he comes to her again to convince himself he's in the right, to erase any remaining shadow of doubt – and this nagging doubt and inner conflict continues right up to where he kisses her repeatedly while she sleeps before the moment of her murder.

Between Act 4, Scene 1 and 4, Scene 2, there might be three hours. What has Othello been doing? Has he gone to sit alone at the top of a tower in the fortress? Or in a cell underground? Has he considered and worried over Lodovico's instructions to him that he must return to Venice and leave Cassio in his place – Cassio, whom he wants dead for his alleged adultery with his wife? Has he sought out, or been searched for, by Iago, who wants to make sure Othello is resolved to kill? Has time alone renewed his doubts and amazement that Desdemona could be so treacherous and corrupt? Why does he need to question Emilia about Desdemona and Cassio at the start of Act 4, Scene 2, and then see his wife again to make her confess? What drives him into the scene? This is the before-time you as the actor playing Othello need to imagine.

For Desdemona, she has been sent away by Othello after striking her in Act 4, Scene 1. Where did she go? To her lodgings to discuss matters with her only reliable friend, Emilia? To walk alone by the harbour to clear her head? To lock herself away in her own bedroom to think and recover, release her confused feelings, or find escape in sleep? Supper for the Venetian visitors is announced during the scene following Othello's departure, and she is expected at that, and does go; so immediately before Othello enters, perhaps she is preparing herself for that high-level social engagement.

Whatever events you select, you need to create the images which give them imaginary life, so that you believe/imagine you've come from a specific place, to another, with a clear reason, at a particular time, and with an objective to achieve.

INTEGRATING VOICE

Even though you are not onstage, you may *imagine* where you are between scenes, alone or with somebody. What do you speak and in what voice? Consider the character voice elements from Chapter 13.

Surroundings

What is in the room? There will be elements of design and decoration in a production, but what is on the imaginary wall/s facing the audience, the area known as the *fourth wall*? Cyprus had been invaded by Greeks, Romans, Byzantines and Italians at different points in its history, and the Ottomans (Turks) were keen to take possession, which they achieved only after the time of the play, in 1570. So you might imagine a mix of Mediterranean influences in the couches, hangings and ornaments of your lodgings. See the fabrics, the textures, the rich colours; imagine the layout of the building and the number of rooms in it.

INTEGRATING VOICE

Imagining the space fully will affect the voice. You can hear when an actor is not in the right space; for example, in a small room, a castle yard, outside in fields.

Surroundings

Remind yourself of Chapter 10, Awareness, ease and focus: Exercise – Connecting images to language.

You need to breathe the *imaginary* space as well as be aware of the *real* space: the former may sometimes be in conflict with the real stage space, or TV or film set, e.g. a battlefield may be in front of a green screen on a film stage, surrounded by technicians; or you may be on a huge stage in a 2,000-seat theatre, and in an imaginary small apartment in bed with your lover. Finding this imaginary reality within the actual reality will give you the right vocal quality, energy and volume (see Chapter 14).

The past

As the scene progresses, Othello and Desdemona, like any married couple in conflict, may see images of the past before them and projected onto the other. As Othello first asks her to come to him, he might see the image of the young spellbound girl listening to his stories of dangerous adventures; or an image of their wedding, as he urges her 'away, away, away'. Desdemona can only see images of her noble, loving husband, the doppelganger of this vilifying, accusatory stranger – only briefly interrupted by an image of her father, who she thinks might be the cause of her husband's rage. Again, create real images of imaginary events and people, in order to create real impulses for our physical and vocal responses.

Textual images

This scene is full of images suggested by the words, which we need to visualize in order to give full life to the words. For example, as Othello looks into Desdemona and says, 'Let me see your eyes', he might have an image of Cassio and she copulating. While he urges Emilia out, he could see images of a brothel.

Equally, it will help to have images for literal things Othello conjures up: 'devils', 'sores and shames' rained on his head by heaven, scorn pointing 'his slow unmoving finger', 'the fountain from which my current runs', 'a cistern for foul toads', 'thou young and rose-lipped cherubim', 'summer flies' in the abattoir having sex, a sweet-smelling 'weed', a 'goodly book', a 'public commoner', a 'forge' burning up modesty, 'the moon winks', 'the bawdy wind' hushed within caves of the earth.

INTEGRATING VOICE

See the image before and as you speak, so that the intensity and richness of the images gives rise to the words describing them, and your voice responds spontaneously and intuitively in the moment of speaking.

We don't aim to describe and illustrate the words with a preconceived vocal expression, but to experience them, their significance and power, their emotional content and how they convey the will and specific state of mind of the character.

The need for the words will come from the images and metaphors, controlled by the right brain. The intonation and flow of the lines, the pitch range and resonance will be prompted by an inner impulse, not a conscious manipulation for effect. Shakespeare's highly vivid language, in particular, evokes the characters' experiences and emotions.

Images
For example, look at this passage:

Desdemona: I hope my noble lord esteems me honest.

Othello: O ay: as summer flies are in the shambles
             That quicken even with blowing. O, thou weed,
             Who art so lovely fair and smell'st so sweet
             That the sense aches at thee, would thou hadst ne'er been born!

Images and sensory experiences will fine-tune and deepen our vocal responses to the text.

- The same process applies as above:
    - receive through the in-breath energy and respond through the reflexive muscles and spine, keeping that umbilical connection to the images.
    - use the vowel, consonantal and tonal energy exercises we've described before to explore the words and Othello's experience; resonance is particularly important here because it is through the vowel sounds mainly that we vibrate the experience.

- See the images, breathe them in: 'summer flies' copulating in the abattoir, a sweet-smelling but good-for-nothing 'weed'.

- Play Othello's objective through these lines, aware of the obstacle of Desdemona's seeming purity, as you see, hear and smell the images. Let your voice – intonation, pitch range, resonance, articulation – respond to all these influences. See how the images give extra life to the language; and how the vowels communicate Othello's sense of foulness, disgust and despair to the audience.

Sensing

Nothing is given by Shakespeare about the sensory and physical nature of the scene. This has to come from the actors' imagination.

Because of the tense and claustrophobic nature of this scene, it might help to imagine intense heat, which may well occur in Cyprus in the early evening. Othello's head might be aching from his tortured, seething thoughts and emotions, playing chemical and neural havoc on his body. Desdemona might begin in a sleepy, or confused and dazed state.

Certainly, there will be a sensory score to the scene: what I see, hear, smell, taste and touch. Desdemona will see and hear Othello, and possibly smell the sweat from his fear and anger, taste her own dry mouth, and feel the touch of her dress or wedding ring. Imagine such aspects for yourself.

Feeling

The atmosphere of the scene is oppressive. In wanting to make Desdemona confess her guilt, Othello manifests feelings such as fear, disgust and anger. In real life this might create short in-breaths, tension and deep out-breaths – the latter can be for real, but with the first two symptoms we have to act *as if* we are tense and snatching breath, otherwise we'd never get through the whole performance. Desdemona is full of confusion, dismay and fear, and her solar plexus will be working overtime, possibly drawing in the horrifying circumstances with quicker breaths.

INTEGRATING VOICE

Of course, in our theatrical reality the actor has to be easy even if the character is tense, because we may have to deliver long and dense sentences with clarity

▶

for an audience. So we must never get lost in the emotion, there must always be control; but it is only a question of control – sustaining ease, focus and clarity – and not one of dropping into pretending and faking. In terms of breath, we may be experiencing fear or anger, but we need sufficient breath, support and control to deal with the characters' language given us by the playwright.

So, make sure you root the breath and onset of sound into the pelvic floor and spine, while keeping the resonators open, and the breathing movement fluent whatever the emotion. Don't tighten, hold the breath or lock the jaw. Make sure you find a centred note within the new character pitch range, from which you can rise and fall.

We might express Othello's state through the lower resonance areas and a volatile pitch range, with a strong onset and defined articulation. Desdemona's resonance might be concentrated in the upper chest and lower areas, with a limited pitch range and intonation pattern. The sensory elements also will contribute to the experience and vocal quality at any particular point.

Character voice

Look back over Chapter 13. What creates Othello and Desdemona and the nature of their voices?

Othello

Othello is a Moor. This means he came from North Africa and was from Berber, Arabic or black African stock, possibly even from Mauritania, which Iago mentions in the play. What you decide specifically depends on your research and interpretation of references in the play to Othello's appearance. He has been played in the past as both black African and Arabic. These geographical and cultural influences will clearly prompt different accents, which you will need to research.

He was a Muslim but converted to Christianity. He was of royal descent but sold into slavery. He became a general for Venice – Venice liked to use foreign mercenaries to defend their lands – and he was accepted in that role, but not in a personal capacity. The racist language used against him by Brabantio, a leading senator, is testament to that. He fought in wars and experienced many adventures and life-threatening events. He is a commander of men, getting on in years, but, through his stories, he won the heart of a young white woman from a different country and culture. All this is given in the text.

We get a picture of a man of action, a soldier, a foreign outsider, not educated like the Venetian nobles and bourgeois – but who wants to fit in and be accepted fully. This is evident in his dignified and calm handling of the accusations of witchcraft levied against him by Brabantio after he has married Desdemona secretly (another sign of his awareness of prejudice against him).

INTEGRATING VOICE

If I am this man in these circumstances, how has my voice been shaped? I will have a black African or Arabic accent; a voice that can command and reach through outside spaces in the midst of noisy battle, used to interacting with rough men; a centred control that can keep me in balance in socially demanding situations; a poetic use of imagery deriving from extraordinary experiences, mythology, superstition and fear; a voice that seeks to appease rather than confront, and, until my confusion and desperation sets in, to contain rather than express anger.

Othello's Life Superobjective is to find happiness with Desdemona as an accepted part of Venetian society, but his main objective at the end is to take vengeance for her alleged crimes. Try a Psychological Gesture for each of these two opposing objectives. He's led in the beginning by his mind and will, then taken over by his feelings, and at the end, he is willing destruction. He might be centred in his chest at the start, and in his lower gut by the end. The focus of his body might be up and out at the start, and then inwards and down towards the ground by the end. His inner tempo-rhythm begins with quick and steady, and his outer with slow and controlled. He ends with an inner and outer of quick, seething, jagged, contradictory impulses. In terms of Laban's effort actions, he begins with a mixture of glide and press and ends, with a great sense of polarity, as wring and slash. His main qualities at the start might be unworldly but dignified and dutiful, and by the end, jealous, vengeful and ruthless.

INTEGRATING VOICE

So, vocally, in the beginning, we get a sense of a man with an easy, flexible but alert physicality, and an alignment in balance; with deep easy breathing, rising up through the earth to fill his body for action; with a necessarily strong and clear onset, a range that can adapt to different spaces and numbers of people, and a resonance shifting from head, to chest, to pelvis according to the formality of the social situation or emotional experience.

Othello's voice

Try to find your connection to Othello's voice at the beginning of the play. Improvise how he commands his soldiers; how he relaxes with them for a drink; how he is with Desdemona when they are just married; how he is with the nobility of Venice who need him but also see him as an outsider. Receive his success, respect, love, admiration through your in-breath energy and respond in your own words, allowing your voice to find a responsive resonance and range.

You might experience a predominant resonance in the solar plexus or sternum, confident and successful in your official role; which can shift into the head, as you plan your journey to Cyprus; then down into the pelvic area of commanding and will, as you assert control over unruly officers; and up into the heart, as you respond to a loving Desdemona.

Make sure that your resonating areas are responsive (see Chapter 7). Tune into the solar plexus with a *YAW*. Find your centred note (do you like holidays?) and root your onset into the pelvic floor, saying 'This is me, Othello' as a response to someone's comment, e.g. 'Who's there!' Breathe in again and with this connection allow your out-breath wave to resonate through *YAW*.

To ensure that your pitch range is still free and expressive, say straight after this: 'I can speak high and I can speak low.'

Try the same thing on the other possible resonance areas: *YAA* (chest/heart), *YOH* (chest bone), *YOE* (pelvis), and *YUH* (head/mouth), keeping the range flexible.

In the second half, his voice matches his new persona. His physicality becomes wracked by doubt, pain, and desire for violent retribution – though, again, the actor/artist has to keep an easy control. His breathing might produce deeper out-breaths that shake his whole frame. The onset and tone might become gruffer, more animalistic, to fit his imagery. The pitch range may lose some variety, and resonance may lie in the pit of the stomach.

Now find your response to Othello in this part of the play. Breathe in the doubt, the pain and the desire for revenge. Improvise situations such as receiving suspicions from Iago that Desdemona is unfaithful with Cassio; talking to Desdemona alone; responding to Emilia believing her to be complicit; or planning revenge. Keep your breath rooted and free flowing, moment by moment, your resonators open, your jaw released and your pitch centred.

Find out if you use a predominant resonance area here – for example, tune into the gut area with a *YAW* that expresses his pain. The sounds we use here are simply a means of accessing the different resonance areas – how they are expressed depends on character and situation. Follow the earlier steps, keeping the range flexible.

Desdemona

Desdemona could not be more different: a young woman in her teens, brought up in a highly protective nobleman's household in a sophisticated, dynamic and wealthy trading city-state. She is educated and cultured, possibly plays an instrument and sings. In Venice, courtesans abounded and women generally had more economic independence than elsewhere at the time, but they were also expected to be obedient and chaste. Desdemona, though, is not only innocent and inexperienced but independent and feisty as well. She has invited Othello to tell his stories, fallen in love with him, and then eloped in the middle of the night and secretly married: outrage is caused!

INTEGRATING VOICE

She will have the accent of the educated ruling-class nobility. Her interaction will be with other young women, her father, servants and numerous wealthy suitors. Never challenged or put to the test, she and her voice will not have been exerted beyond the drawing room. It will most likely be calm, controlled, easy and confident, fitting to her manner of speech, which is reasonable, clear, simple, to the point.

Desdemona's Life Superobjective is to create a perfect family life with her lord, Othello. Try a Psychological Gesture for this. She is led by her feelings at the start, and then by her mind when Othello begins to act strangely. Throughout the play she is loving, innocent and constant, and we get a sense of her being centred in her chest. Her physicality will be in equilibrium, easy, energized, alert and playful: childlike. Towards the end, she has a centre like a dark cloud weighing on her head and heart, making her body feel closed in on itself inside endless, oppressive time. Her inner tempo-rhythm is quick and receptive, and the outer is a mixture of steady in social situations and lively with Othello. By the end, the inner is racing and the outer may have become quicker from disturbance and restlessness. Her initial effort actions might be glide and dab, which turn into wring and press as she's attacked.

INTEGRATING VOICE

Vocally, what could all this produce? A balanced, energized alignment and natural easy breath at the start, followed by a body that feels like lead and a breath disturbed by emotion into a broken, arrhythmic pattern; clear onset and a flexible, responsive range, which might become unpredictable after Othello begins to accuse her; a head resonance possibly until the emotional traumas begin, when more upper chest and lower resonance take over.

Desdemona's voice
Find out your vocal response by improvising different stages throughout Desdemona's life and the play. What is your vocal response when engaging with your father? How are you with servants? With suitors? When falling in love with Othello? Find out if there is a predominant resonance area – chest/heart (love, joy) or face (innocent, childlike), for example.

Then imagine situations later in the play where she is challenged: confused about what Othello wants from her, threatened by him, insisting on being loyal to him, etc. Her main centre and resonance area here might be the solar plexus (vulnerable, sensitive). Explore possible sounds for these areas: *YAA, YA, YAW,* following the earlier steps and keeping the range flexible.

Of course, there are other interpretations, but this gives you an idea of the many elements that produce our voices and will steer you away from playing a manner or emotional state, from simply using your own voice as it is in everyday life, or reciting.

The space

Space and preparation

Let's imagine the space for this scene is that of an Elizabethan theatre, like the Globe in London's Bankside. Look back to Chapter 14: it's essentially a 'wooden O' with a raised stage, tiered seating and a standing space for 'groundlings', and very likely with a vibrant acoustic.

INTEGRATING VOICE

As actors playing Othello and Desdemona, you will need to keep aware of the audience on three sides. Violent argumentative moments will carry easily, but you must focus on sharing the intimate, quiet ones. The audience will be behind you at some points and you need to keep aware of them as part of your playing space. Reach behind and to the sides, both by breathing in the whole space and by retaining pelvic and spinal support and drive for the voice on the out-breath. Physically and inwardly keep alive and energized so that you always radiate presence and even your backs are expressive, and your articulation and onset stay clear and resonant.

Preparing for the space

In preparation for performing in such a space do the exercises in Chapter 14:

- explore the space
- focus the 'tonal energy' to achieve the pillar of sound along the spine
- let the 'spine speak' to achieve good onset in all positions
- expand the breath and voice into the space
- tune articulation, pitch and resonance to the space
- focus on the audience and how to reach them
- do individual and group warm-ups and energize and synchronize voices together
- sustain thoughts through the breath in the space

Focus

Throughout our scene, the *object of attention* for Othello is Desdemona, and for Desdemona, Othello. Each object, in the tense circumstances, releases the objectives, actions and inner motive forces we've examined, and these determine where the characters apply their focus.

INTEGRATING VOICE

Desdemona's focus may well be totally fixed on Othello at all times, such is her confusion and need to discover what's wrong and defend her innocence.

Othello is fixing on her, probing her for signs of guilt, but there are points where he turns from her in frustration and addresses other focus points in the space.

Focus points
Explore the possibilities in the speech below.

His first focus might literally be upwards towards the heavens, imploring them.

> Had it pleased heaven
> To try me with affliction, had they rained
> All kinds of sores and shames on my bare head,
> Steeped me in poverty to the very lips,
> Given to captivity me and my utmost hopes,
> I should have found in some place of my soul
> A drop of patience.

The focus shifts to a personified figure of scorn pointing at him, possibly from off stage right, as he mocks himself.

> But, alas, to make me
> The fixed figure for the time of scorn
> To point his slow unmoving finger at!

For the next single line he focuses inwards, but assuring Desdemona.

> Yet could I bear that too, well, very well;

Then he returns to Desdemona, but as a contradictory image of life force and foul cesspool, vilifying her.

But there where I have garnered up my heart,
Where either I must live or bear no life,
The fountain from the which my current runs
Or else dries up – to be discarded thence
Or keep it as a cistern for foul toads
To knot and gender in!

Finally, we have another personification in the form of Patience, which he might see out front and direct towards Desdemona, as he condemns her.

Turn thy complexion there,
Patience, thou young and rose-lipped cherubim;
Ay, there look grim as hell!

17
FROM ACTION TO FORM

We now address the form of language, an understanding of which is vital if the content is to be richly and clearly expressed, and we'll explore mainly the *Othello* scene.

Some practitioners focusing on acting classical text *start* with detailed analysis of its formal nature, often to the extent of being formalistic, claiming that the form alone gives you the content: 'it's all in the line, just say the words', 'the rhythm gives you everything', 'Shakespeare is all form', 'there's no subtext in classical drama', etc.

All of these statements sound so authoritative – but they create a mystification of classical theatre and all are wrong. Sometimes, they come from a deep respect for the wonderful language of Shakespeare and a fear of 'naturalistic' monotone and pausing, and also from a misunderstanding of what subtext actually is. As we've explained, subtext for Stanislavski is all the imaginary world of the play that gives rise to the lines for the actor. It doesn't have to mean something that is in contradiction to the stated lines, as may occur in a Pinter or Chekhov play; although even in Shakespeare, where most characters say what they think and feel, some do not in dialogue with others: the manipulative villains like Edmund, Iago and Richard III, for example. To respect the subtext doesn't mean disrespecting the text, quite the opposite: bringing out the subtext will enrich the text. Nor does it mean acting parallel to the text, so that character, situation and action do not connect to the expression of the words. Everything must be channelled through the language, as we've made clear before. Nor is subtext about putting in loads of pauses, but every speech that is spoken without pauses must still be prompted by an experienced impulse. When actors speak without this launching impulse they seem mechanical and often warm up through the first part of the speech, instead of hitting the first words with clarity of thought, feeling and intention.

The *form* is the way in which a script is written: the rules and conventions employed, how it's composed and structured. For example, a modern play may have minimal dialogue with short phrases or sentences in prose; it may adopt a vernacular, naturalistic tone; and be written in two acts. A sixteenth-century play, like *Othello*, will be written in iambic pentameter blank verse and prose; employ numerous figures of speech; and be in five acts. The play's *genre* is the style into which it fits: drama, comedy, farce, tragedy, melodrama, absurd, political, etc.

We've left our analysis of the form until this point because, as we've made clear throughout the book and in the quotes from John Barton's book above, there is a danger that tackling the formal detail too soon in rehearsal will create at best a cerebral, intellectual grasp of the text, and block organic involvement in the action of the play and full connection with the text. Linklater concurs: 'if we had started with the discipline of form, we would have found it hard to persuade the energy of the content to emerge at all' (*Freeing Shakespeare's Voice*: 99).

Our experience is that an imaginative approach to text, by going from the text to subtext and back to the text, produces a fuller grasp of it, involving the imagination, senses, feelings, will and body of the actor, as well as the intellect. All this informs how the lines are interpreted and expressed and, if the job has been done well, the formal detail of the lines should be coming through as we rehearse. We need to analyze fully what is there on the page, though, to make sure we don't miss any important aspect of the text that can help us to communicate the writer's themes and presentation of human life. We shan't attempt an exhaustive analysis of text in all its varied forms – that is not the purpose of this book, and there are several useful books in the bibliography that cover matters at greater length. Nevertheless we aim to cover the basic issues from our perspective.

Rhythm – the flow of meaning

Rhythm and metre

Rhythm is the pattern formed by the number, length and stress of beats of sound, stillness, and movement in a particular bar of music or measure of text. The tempo is the speed of movement, speech or music. For example, J. S. Bach's Gavotte in A minor is in 2:4 time (two beats to the bar) with an andante tempo (moderately slow). A waltz will be in 3:4 time and will often have a slow tempo, or a fast one in, for example, the Viennese form.

The *Othello* scene is written in iambic pentameter blank verse, the metre or rhythmic verse form common to Shakespearean and Jacobean drama. An *iamb* is a foot consisting of an unstressed and stressed, weak and strong, short and long syllable: – /, de-*dum*, as in words like 'alive', 'debate', 'aside'. It has the feel of a heartbeat. Within classical Latin and Greek poetry, it had the meaning of to drive forth and aspire, and so suits a narrative dramatic form (see *Freeing Shakespeare's Voice*: 122). *Pentameter* is a line with five feet and ten syllables. This basic iambic pentameter form was adopted because it was thought to express most naturally the English rhythm and pattern of speech, and it has been used by versifiers from Chaucer through to Seamus Heaney.

The regular iambic pentameter rhythm is more consistently present in Shakespeare's early plays like *Romeo and Juliet,* but irregular rhythmic lines enter more frequently in the later plays such as *The Winter's Tale*, and in the work of Jacobean and Carolinian writers. We hear a *sprung rhythm* where the sense clashes with the regular rhythm to create an improvisation on the main beat: the iambic pattern breaks down, lines become longer, and there may even be more than five beats to the line.

The regular metre establishes a basic template and this will help us to find the right accents in the line. The easier we get with that rhythm, the more easily we'll see where the rhythm becomes *irregular*. But it is the meaning, the character and circumstances and structure of the line that tell us where the irregular lines are, and those vital aspects of content must lead us through the regular lines as well. Otherwise, we may end up either 'de-dumming' emptily on the one hand, or monotonously droning through the verse as if it's TV prose on the other. Content and form are a bit like a rider and horse, or surfer and wave working together.

For example, given modern speech patterns, we might be tempted to say as Desdemona, '**What** is your pleasure?', losing the meaning of the line in a downward inflexion. Or under the influence of Australian soaps, 'What is your plea**sure**?', emptying the line of emotion with a mechanical upward flick. The iambic pentameter indicates a more balanced and rhythmical, 'What **is** your **plea**sure?' On the other hand, we can't say as Othello, 'Look **in** my **face**.' The circumstances, Othello's condition and objective, the use of the verb at the start, all indicate we must say, **Look** in my **face**, which also gives us a different, and stronger and more direct, action on the line.

Look at these lines from the start of the scene:

DESDEMONA   My lord, what is your will?
OTHELLO   Pray, chuck, come hither.
DESDEMONA   What is your pleasure?
OTHELLO   Let me see your eyes.
                       Look in my face.
DESDEMONA   What horrible fancy's this?

OTHELLO [To Emilia]
                       Some of your function, mistress:
                       Leave procreants alone and shut the door;
                       Cough or cry 'hem' if anybody come.
                       Your mystery, your mystery! Nay, dispatch!

One of only two regular lines here is:

> Leave procreants alone and shut the door;

The beats go like this:

> Leave **procreants** a**lone** and **shut** the **door**;

The first three lines are divided between Othello and Desdemona:

> D: My **lord**, what **is** your **will**?
>   O: **Pray**, chuck, **come** hither.

Desdemona starts with a regular rhythm and Othello breaks it abruptly, creating a dramatic jarring.

> D: What **is** your **plea**sure?
>   O: **Let** me **see** your **eyes**.

A regular rhythm on the line, but divided between them.

> O: **Look** in my **face**.
>   D: What **hor**rible **fan**cy's **this**?

An irregular line, with Othello emphasizing the first syllable.

> O: **Some** of your **func**tion, **mis**tress:

Another irregular line with the first syllable stressed, and also a short line with only seven syllables and three beats in it – possibly indicating a pause as Othello weighs up the situation.

> O: Leave **procreants** a**lone** and **shut** the **door**;

A regular line, followed by:

> **Cough** or cry **'hem'** if **any**bo**dy come**.

This again starts with a stressed first syllable.

> Your **mys**tery, your **mys**tery! Nay, dis**patch**!

This begins regularly but ends irregularly – this time, because the line has more than ten syllables, as does:

> O: **Look** in my **face**.
>
>   D: What **hor**rible **fan**cy's **this**?

Longer lines that have a *weak* ending are unfortunately known as a *feminine* ending – the most famous examples of which are the first four lines of Hamlet's 'To be or not to be' (Act 3, Sc. 1), which each have an eleventh unstressed syllable – this actually helps to keep the question alive and full of searching:

> To be, or not to be: that is the question:
> Whether 'tis nobler in the mind to suffer
> The slings and arrows of outrageous fortune,
> Or to take arms against a sea of troubles,
> And by opposing end them.

To create these irregular lines, then, Shakespeare includes elements from classical Greek prosody in addition to the iamb, in the form of fragments rather than whole verses in these forms. A few examples within lines of our scene are:

> *trochee* (/ -, dum-de), as in a whole line, which has *six* beats: **Hea**ven **tru**ly **knows** that **thou** art **false** as **Hell**

> *anapaest* (– – /, de-de-dum) as in, (as summer flies are) in the **sham**bles

A clearer example is the Fairy in Act 2, Scene 1 of *A Midsummer Night's Dream*:

> Over **hill**, over **dale**
> Thorough **bush**, thorough **brier**

> *spondee* (/ /, dum-dum) as in, **Come**, **swear** it

> *dactyl* (/ – -, dum-de-de) as in, **Swear** thou art (honest)

These points may seem technical, even difficult, but the variance in rhythm also affects tempo, and therefore feeling, and sense and intention. We pick up meaning and the writer's intentions from the content and form of the lines as written – but we also *interpret* meaning from our own understanding of life and literature. We should use the rhythm as our guide and start by assuming a regular rhythm, exploring the writer's possible intentions, but ultimately we perceive and define what is regular and irregular from understanding meaning through our research, experience and imaginations, *and actually speaking the lines out loud* – but the rhythm of the lines, once clarified, will help us to convey that meaning.

The actor is the rider, taking in all the aspects of the journey, and the form is the horse enabling the journey to happen.

INTEGRATING VOICE

Sometimes physicalizing the rhythm can help the body to get a feel for the contracting and expanding qualities of the iambic rhythm – but be careful not to fall into endless stepping-out of the rhythm on text. It can fix it and make it sound wooden and clumsy. No stress has the same length. It is rather like a dance.

Physicalize the rhythm
Try dancing the rhythm, jumping it or clicking it with fingers, drumming, clapping or singing it. For example:

Leave **procreants** a**lone** and **shut** the **door**;
Cough or cry **'hem'** if **a**ny**bo**dy **come**.

Taking onboard Othello's debasing actions towards the women, drum the unstressed and stressed syllables with two pens against a table, one for the light and the other for the strong one. The light syllable gives rise to the stressed one. The rhythm should intensify the thought and action. Go back quickly to saying the text, trusting your sense of rhythm. Don't forget the *Vocal Givens* throughout the chapter.

Of course, not all verse is in iambic pentameter. Classical French drama of the seventeenth century – by Corneille and Racine, for example – is in Alexandrine form, *six* beats to the line and rhyming couplets; for example, these lines of Émilie from the beginning of *Cinna* by Pierre Corneille:

Plus **tu** lui **donner**as, plus **il** te **va** don**ner**,
Et **ne** tri**omphe**ra que **pour** te **cou**ron**ner**.

(The more you give him, the more he will give you, and will triumph only to crown you.)

Prose has rhythm, too. Here's a few lines from Act 1 of Jez Butterworth's *Mojo:*

POTTS	He knows why he's here. He's paid to warble and look pretty. He ain't paid to give it large in the backroom.
SWEETS	Has he got the jacket on?
POTTS	Who?
SWEETS	The kid. Has he got the Silver Jacket on?
POTTS	He's took it off. It's on the table.
SWEETS	Hang on. Hang on. He's took it off?
POTTS	It's on the table.
SWEETS	Hang on. Hang on. What the fuck is he doing?
POTTS	What?
SWEETS	What the fuck is going on?
POTTS	What's the problem?
SWEETS	He's supposed to wear the Silver Jacket.
POTTS	Sweets –
SWEETS	He's Silver Johnny. Silver Johnny, Silver Jacket.
POTTS	Sweets –
SWEETS	Silver Johnny, Silver suit. That's the whole point.
POTTS	I know. Relax.

The rhythm here involves some clear rhetorical devices that give the dialogue an edgy, nervy feel: short staccato sentences, successive questions, repetition of words, consonants and vowels. It feels very much in the tradition of Beckett and Pinter. It indicates that it needs to be played without pauses, responsively and rapid-fire; but as with all rhythms, including iambic pentameter, we have to find *the organic human impulse behind it and the pulse within it* in order to make the lines real and not mechanical.

What this piece has in common with classical plays is the need to preserve the rhythm in the mode of vocal expression, so that the meaning, feelings and atmosphere will be conveyed clearly.

INTEGRATING VOICE

Hamlet's advice to the players (Act 3, Scene 2) – not to overgesticulate but to fit the word to the action and the action to the word, neither to 'tear a passion to tatters' nor to be 'too tame neither' – is all good acting advice. He also suggested finding a 'smoothness' and to speak 'trippingly on the tongue', by which he means finding an easy agility, flow and clarity.

Verse tips
- Don't chop up the lines and the sense – play the line not each word separately.
- Flow the thought, objective, image through the line – don't self-consciously listen to yourself or play an intellectual idea or interpretation of the line.
- Don't pause unless one is marked by a line-ending, a caesura, or short line.
- Know where to breathe.
- Be clear where the line endings and beginnings are.
- Keep verse rhythm light and natural, not overemphatic.

Punctuation, pauses and flow

Students and professionals often break the flow of the line by inserting a breath or a pause where there shouldn't be one. We can observe the punctuation given us by the writer, although we don't necessarily need it. Shakespeare's plays were copied down by his actors and then edited. Subsequent editors have added their own punctuation, following their interpretation of what he intended in the meaning, so actually, we should try to interpret for ourselves through the structure of the verse. In modern plays, though, the writer is often giving clear guidelines or instructions.

In Othello's lines below, the offered punctuation clearly aids the sense:

> Had it pleased heaven
> To try me with affliction, had they rained
> All kinds of sores and shames on my bare head,
> Steeped me in poverty to the very lips,
> Given to captivity me and my utmost hopes,
> I should have found in some place of my soul
> A drop of patience.

An example of line-chopping would be:

> O: Given to captivity – *pause* – me and my – *pause* – utmost hopes – *pause*
>   I should have – *pause* – found in some – *pause* – place of my soul

The meaning can only be conveyed by flowing his thought – of retaining some patience even if heaven had punished him harshly – through the lines, fuelled by his objective of wanting to make Desdemona confess she's a whore, and a possible specific action on these lines of shaming her. The only breaks in the lines are where the commas are, *logical* but *small* pauses, and these tend to be at the end of the line where a breath may be taken.

There are examples in lines one and two of the end of the line flowing uninter-ruptedly into the next: this is called an *enjambment*. Usually, we could take a *breath* pause at the end of the line where there is a comma or where the sense ends and is marked by a full stop, also known as an *end-stop*; but it doesn't necessarily make sense to stop after 'heaven' or 'rained' – in fact, that would break the sense if we feel Othello is in full flow. A stop at the end of the lines would only make sense if he is searching for the image and the words. If we flow the sense on, though, it doesn't mean we have to break the line structure of the verse – we can still observe this by following the iambic and pentameter beat, lifting the end of a line and energizing the beginning of the next line.

Conversely, after

> I should have found in some place of my soul

an enjambment is indicated – but the actor/Othello might have a good reason to stop in order to give extra weight to what the previous six lines are leading up to:

> A drop of patience.

It's very much a question of interpretation by the actor – within the structure of the form.

An enjambment can often lead to a punctuated *caesura* in the next line: this is a *short* pause – or *poise*, as Berry terms it – around the middle of the line. The lines below have a dash and an exclamation mark:

> Yet could I bear that too, well, very well;
> But there where I have garnered up my heart,
> Where either I must live or bear no life,
> **The fountain from the which my current runs**
> **Or else dries up –** to be discarded thence
> **Or keep it as a cistern for foul toads**

To knot and gender in! Turn thy complexion there,
Patience, thou young and rose-lipped cherubim;
Ay, there look grim as hell!

The caesuras after 'dries up' and 'gender in!' are logical pauses and one *could* take a breath there (although purists won't like it!) – or surge on into the next thought, *providing the new thought and action are made clear in the line.* Again, it's interpretation. There are no hard-and-fast rules – other than communicating the meaning, using the form of the verse as guide and support.

Meaning, as is clear from the example above, is not always encapsulated within one line; it can run through many lines. Here there is a sentence of over six lines, and there are longer ones in classical plays. The meaning will only be communicated through clarity of thought, keeping each line alive and unresolved through our inflexions at the end of lines, and knowing that the sentence only finishes with 'To knot and gender in!' Even then, the two lines after this, and the first half of the whole speech are about Othello's patience being tested, and this idea has to flow through four whole sentences.

We've mentioned two types of pauses, the logical and the breath; there is also what Stanislavski identified as the *psychological* pause, determined by the character's inner life, but taken only where the verse structure and tempo of a scene allow. Michael Chekhov emphasized that it was never just a pause, but 'always the result of what has just happened, or is the preparation for a coming event' (*Lessons for the Professional Actor*: 63). For example:

OTHELLO   Ay, there look grim as hell!
DESDEMONA   I hope my noble lord esteems me honest.

Othello's is a short line with only three feet in it, so space for a pause is indicated as Othello sees the image of Patience judging the sullied Desdemona and she considers his meaning and how to address his disturbed mood.

Finally, whatever the beat in verse, it shouldn't be hammered. It has to sound natural and easy as though you are making up the lines as you go, riding a wave, rather than plunging and ascending on a roller-coaster! Again, verse drama is to be acted, not recited. An audience comes to the theatre to see actors bring a script to life, create the subtext and imaginary world of the play, connect with other actor/characters, and communicate the language – otherwise they can stay at home and read the text – but the more easily and respectfully we speak verse and prose, the better we will act the plays. Inner life, physical expression and a grasp of external form must be integrated in our psycho-physical technique.

Accent and intonation – making the point

In everyday life, our intonation, the variation and accenting of our voice, is affected by what we're saying, to whom, why, in what circumstances and what we've just heard. We simply respond, as well as speaking with intent. If this process isn't mirrored in performance and if our intonation patterns are consciously worked out by the left brain instead of allowed to develop spontaneously through the musicality of the right brain, we may end up sounding very technical, possibly boring, perhaps impressive – but not organic.

The big danger actors face in our industry is pressure to rush and endgame. People decide how to say the lines very early on, maybe for the first reading, and then frequently get stuck and don't develop through rehearsal. You can only know *how* to say a line – as one option among several – when you know the thought, objective, image, feeling, attitude, circumstances behind the line – when you know more of 'the life and spirit of the given role' (*Stanislavski Directs*: 320). That's why Stanislavski didn't focus on picking out the *key words* of the text until months into rehearsal – we don't have months, but we can still observe a more organic development. There isn't a formally correct way to say the line. Correct in relation to what? A director's concept? A voice teacher's interpretation of verse form or sense of humour? An actor's desire to impress?

Stanislavski believed the way to overcome the danger of fixing things unimaginatively was to raise the stakes, make everything mean more, to recreate what we do in life and allow the subtext to influence us. We need to focus on the other person and changing the situation rather than on how we sound. We need to *speak to the eye* again, conveying all those images we have in our mind so that our partners see them, too. This will free up our intonation, making it receptive to creative impulse.

If this imaginative work isn't leading to a clearly communicated text by itself, if actors have real problems with the language, or even if we just need to sharpen up the detail, then we shall need to focus more on accenting. We would say, don't worry initially about the form but be clear what the character is saying and in what circumstances and just say the lines as if you are there in this moment, make them real for you, see where the accent naturally comes in conveying the meaning of the line and the character's objective. Essentially, we are likely to get the stresses which carry the meaning if we see the lines as real interactive language and not as something forbidding and removed from us called 'classical theatre', 'Beckettian prose', or 'Brechtian alienation'.

Look at the key words in this later section of the scene:

OTHELLO   Was this **fair paper**, this most **goodly book**,
               Made to write **'whore'** upon? What **committed!**

> **Committed?** O thou **public commoner!**
> I should make very **forges** of my **cheeks**
> That would to **cinders burn** up **modesty**
> Did I but **speak** thy **deeds**. What **committed!**
> **Heaven** stops the **nose** at it, and the **moon winks**;
> The **bawdy wind**, that **kisses** all it **meets**,
> Is **hushed** within the **hollow mine** of **earth**
> And will not **hear** it. What **committed?**
> Impudent **strumpet!**

DESDEMONA   By **heaven**, you do me **wrong**.
OTHELLO   Are not you a **strumpet**?
DESDEMONA   No, as I am a **Christian**.

If you had to choose only one key word it would be 'strumpet'.

INTEGRATING VOICE

Key words

Play this section of the scene with an objective, but only communicate the whole thoughts through the *key words* in bold. Make sure you have images behind words such as 'fair paper', 'public commoner', 'moon winks', and so on.

Then do it as written but retaining awareness of the key words.

The words that naturally demand a stress are the nouns and verbs plus a few strong qualifying adjectives – they carry the literal sense and the weight of Othello's objective and feelings.

The block to arriving at these stresses will be failing to understand the meaning of the words and lines, working out accents as if a mental puzzle, following habitual patterns of speaking (e.g. on a monotone, hitting every word, repetitive downward or upward inflexions), or fashionable idiosyncrasies (e.g. stressing 'a,' or prepositions like 'in', 'with', 'to', or imitating characteristics of popular TV actors and comedians), or simply not fully responding to creative impulse within the given circumstances.

Once the key stresses have been discovered, we'll find other varying degrees of lighter accentuation that give movement and life to the line, informed of course by the iamb and five beats in the line, although there are only three regular lines here. Our suggestions are in italics, while the key words remain in bold. Just as certain words need accenting, so particular phrases or sentences may have greater prominence due to their role in developing the storyline, or expressing the character's objective and emotional state and conflict with another person. See the lines underlined below.

OTHELLO   Was *this* **fair paper**, this most **goodly book**,
               Made to *write* **'whore'** upon? *What* **committed!**
               Committed? *O* thou **public commoner!**
               I should *make very* **forges** of my **cheeks**
               That *would* to **cinders burn** up **modesty**
               Did *I* but **speak** thy **deeds**. *What* **committed!**
               Heaven *stops* the **nose** at it, and the **moon winks**;
               The **bawdy wind**, that **kisses** *all* it **meets**,
               Is **hushed** with*in* the **hollow mine** of **earth**
               And *will not* **hear** it. *What* **committed?**
               *Impu*dent **strumpet!**
DESDEMONA   By **heaven**, you *do* me **wrong**.
OTHELLO   Are *not you* a **strumpet**?
DESDEMONA   *No*, as I *am* a **Christian**.

The underlined lines build through repetition to Othello's final challenge and Desdemona's denial and might be given a different tempo and rhythm to the other lines, with more directly challenging actions on them, and a corresponding vocal quality. The last line, divided between the two, interestingly has 13 syllables for maximum emphasis, so six beats may be justified here.

Of course, different people will have different interpretations of elements of the above – and these stresses do not predetermine inflection on individual words, resonance or pitch range through the scene.

INTEGRATING VOICE

Explore the accents
Now speak through this whole section and see how the key words and the suggested rhythm work together to establish the accenting.

Figures of speech – rhetorical colour

These are rhetorical devices used to accentuate the meaning, emotional content, wit and atmosphere of the language and define more specifically the nature of a character.

Shakespeare also builds an argument by placing words and phrases alongside each other – known as *apposition* or *juxtaposition* – to complement and develop an idea, for example:

DESDEMONA: Your wife, my lord; your true and loyal wife

And to counterpoint an idea, for example:

OTHELLO: You, mistress,
                That have the office opposite to Saint Peter,
                And keeps the gate of hell!

The sharpest use of such juxtaposition is in debate, either with self or with others, when Shakespeare uses clear *contradiction,* with one point opposed by another. We see this in the first three examples.

Antithesis: This is very commonly used in classical theatre and clarifies meaning by presenting opposites in close proximity, e.g.

OTHELLO   Lest, being like one of **heaven**, the **devils** themselves
              Should fear to seize thee.

              Heaven truly knows that thou art false as **hell**.

              Was this **fair paper**, this most **goodly book**,
              Made to write **'whore'** upon?

The contrasting opposites also give us the stresses in the line. Othello emphasizes what Desdemona is in his view by pointing to what she's not.

INTEGRATING VOICE

Contradiction
Using the above lines, create the opposing images of the antithesis and imagine them on opposite sides of the room and in specific areas – e.g. heaven up in the left and hell down in the right. Breathe them in through your solar plexus and allow the physical difference into your response.

Do the same with oxymoron and paradox below.

Oxymoron: Contradictory terms are placed in conjunction, e.g.

O, thou weed,
Who art so lovely fair and smell'st so sweet

A more extreme and succinct example would be Iago's 'Divinity of hell!' in Act 2, Scene 3, or his observation in Act 4, Scene 1 that many 'a civil monster' exists. Clearly, a sweet-smelling weed, a godlike hell and a civilized monster are contradictions in terms and heighten the contradictory nature of people's perceptions or behaviour.

Paradox: An apparently contradictory statement or occurrence, e.g. Iago, in Act 3, Scene 3, trying to sow doubt about Desdemona's fidelity, says:

In Venice they do let God see the pranks
They dare not show their husbands.

In response, Othello says a little later:

O curse of marriage,
That we can call these delicate creatures ours,
And not their appetites!

Pun: Or *quibble*, a witty play on a word to suggest different meanings, e.g. Iago, who's rather more playfully witty and vulgar than Othello, puns on 'housewife' in Act 2, Scene 1 when he insults Emilia and Desdemona and all women, calling them 'players in your housewifery, and housewives in your beds': meaning they play at doing the housework but are wanton hussies in bed.

Mercutio, in *Romeo and Juliet,* is stabbed and puns on two meanings of 'grave': 'Ask for me tomorrow, and you shall find me a grave man.'

Metaphor: A term is applied to a person or action in an imaginative and non-literal way. Shakespeare is chock-a-block with this very right-brain imaginative figure, e.g. Othello describes Desdemona as:

> **The fountain** from the which my **current** runs
> Or else dries up – to be discarded thence
> Or keep it as a **cistern** for foul toads
> To knot and gender in!

Metaphor is frequent in Othello's speech because his tormented diseased mind is conjuring up vivid and lurid images, often of a sexual nature, fuelled by his fear, pain and jealousy. Things literally appear to be imagistic versions of their natural reality. They elucidate and heighten the character's state of being. Here, Othello sees Desdemona as the source/fountain from which his own life-force/current flows. She becomes a cesspool for toads to copulate and breed in.

Personification: When a concept is turned into a human being, e.g. in the line after the above, 'Patience' is described by a metaphor and made into a living, albeit heavenly, creature:

> Turn thy complexion there,
> **Patience, thou young and rose-lipped cherubim;**

Simile: One thing is compared to another of a different nature, e.g.

DESDEMONA I hope my noble lord esteems me honest.
OTHELLO O ay: **as summer flies are in the shambles,**
That quicken even with blowing.

So, Desdemona's honesty is sarcastically compared with slaughter-house flies repetitively conceiving.

Imagery: Of course, this scene is full of imagery – the use of sensory conceptual language to convey with greater richness and power the nature of actions, feelings, atmosphere and states of mind, often using the above devices. A further example, also containing *hyperbole* or exaggeration, would be:

> Heaven stops the nose at it, and the moon winks;
> The bawdy wind, that kisses all it meets.

Is hushed within the hollow mine of earth
And will not hear it.

This emphasizes the sheer shock and horror that Othello feels over Desdemona's alleged adultery: even the great forces of God and Nature cannot face her betrayal and corruption.

INTEGRATING VOICE

Images
As we've made clear in earlier chapters, we need to see, hear, smell and experience all the images in the above texts, e.g. fountain, cistern, bawdy wind, and allow the voice to respond to them with imagination and spontaneity as well as muscular and spinal support. Speak the above examples with this focus.

Consonants and vowels
Speak the lines in the next three sections and sense how the repetition of consonants and vowels enhances the intentions, qualities, feelings and images of the speaker. Keep integrating all these elements to avoid speaking sounds mechanically.

Alliteration: Repetition of the same sound, usually a consonant, at the beginning of words placed close together, e.g.

OTHELLO   All kinds of **s**ores and **s**hames on my bare head
                      Steeped me in poverty to the very lips

                      The **fi**xed **fi**gure for the time of scorn

                                    What **c**ommitted!
                      Committed? O thou public **c**ommoner!

The repetition gives extra weight to the indignity Othello feels.

Assonance: The similarity of vowel sounds within words close to each other, e.g.

Ah, Desdemon, away, away, away!

The repetition of the open vowel sounds – 'ah', 'a', 'ay' – reveal the intensity of Othello's grief, and carry the emotion which leads to the tears noted by Desdemona a line later.

> The bawdy wind, that kisses all it meets,
> Is **hu**shed within the **ho**llo**w** mine of earth
> And will not **hea**r

Here, the similarity of the vowels and the alliteration on the 'h's gives the sound of the wind itself.

King Lear's 'Howl! Howl! Howl!' is an example of both alliteration and assonance – and also of *onomatopoeia*, where a word is formed from a sound (crack, woof, miaow). We get a sense of the basic raw human animal, alone and rejected in a wilderness outside of civilization.

Consonance: The similarity of consonant sounds within words. In these lines, we have both alliteration with 'c' and consonance with 'c':

> Some of your fun**c**tion, mistress:
> Leave pro**c**reants alone and shut the door;
> **C**ough or **c**ry 'hem' if anybody **c**ome.

This gives Othello's instruction a cutting edge of scorn.

Words and sounds

We now come to the knotty issue of words and sounds.

Most people would accept that to make ourselves understood we have to speak in phrases and sentences and not just say words: the words have to be linked together by thought to convey a particular meaning. But we have to understand the meaning of every word we choose to use to do that, and every word has a sound, and sounds can help to convey meaning – but where does meaning begin?

Understanding language

In Chapter 1 we make the point that language has developed out of human experience, and although language will partly frame our understanding, as will where we live, who we meet and what we do for a living, our understanding is not limited by it. 'In the beginning was the word', implying a god-given and finite set of rules and words, only applies to religious myths and not human reality. We created, and go on creating, our language through our experience and need to communicate and act together for specific purposes: to hunt and gather, to make farms, houses and cities, to build civilizations, to create art and science, and so on. Look in any dictionary to see how words multiply according to our inventiveness. Listen to how ways of speaking have changed during the last 60 years.

There are those who believe that language determines consciousness and thought. There is clearly a facility in humans, developed over centuries of brain development, to grasp language: young people are often able to learn a language early on in life and quickly – *but* put a child in isolation for years, deprived of human interaction, and they won't automatically develop language skills. These are not an inborn instinct but are culturally transmitted.

Antonio Damasio backs this up: 'Words and sentences translate concepts, and concepts consist of the nonlanguage idea of what things, actions, events, and relationships are', and 'Of necessity, concepts precede words and sentences in both the evolution of the species and the daily experience of each and everyone of us' (*The Feeling of What Happens*: 185). Clearly, thought existed before a verbal language, otherwise language couldn't have developed. We think without words when, for example, we intuitively solve problems, use our creative imaginations or meditate. Our particular language may give shape to our world, but it's a product of that environment, society and culture, and as they change we invent new additions to the language and alter it according to our needs (see *The Master and his Emissary – The Divided Brain and the Making of the Modern World*: 106–10). Our existence in the world determines consciousness and language, not the other way round.

There are two important concepts we'll emphasize here relating to understanding language and dramatic texts like the one above. One is *arbitrariness*. The words we use originated in non-verbal sounds, but their current meaning is not *given* to us by the sound: there is no natural, indicative connection between a word's form and its meaning. Words have an *arbitrary* relationship to what they describe. For example, the sound of 'door' doesn't tell us what a door is, and it's a different sound in different languages: in French, it's 'porte' and in German, 'Tuer'. 'Horse' in French is 'cheval' and in German, 'Pferd'. Different sounds for different words meaning the same thing. Only onomatopoeic words, like cuckoo, plop and crash, tell us their meaning – in English – and they are very rare.

The second concept is *coherence*: it is people who make sense of language; sense isn't always implicit within language. We interpret a play according to our understanding of the world and literature; that's why every production of the same play is different. As Peter Brook says, 'There are a million ways of saying one line' (quoted in Cicely Berry's *From Word to Play*: 40). For example:

Christina:	Package!
John:	I'm on the computer.
Christina:	Papa rang.

There is no clear coherent connection between these lines in themselves. Of course, to approach the meaning we have to start with the words on the page, as opposed to an assumed feeling or manner, but we'll only grasp the meaning when we understand that Christina is expecting a package that has now arrived, that she wants John to fetch it but John is resisting because he's occupied, and that Christina is insisting because she's talking to her father on the phone and hasn't spoken to him for a while. That information offers us a range of actions on the lines, and they will determine the sounds and intonation we use to convey them.

Here's Othello before his fit in Act 4, Scene 1:

Lie with her? Lie on her? We say lie on her when they belie her! Zounds, that's fulsome! Handkerchief – confessions – handkerchief! To confess and be hanged for his labour. First to be hanged and then to confess. I tremble at it. Nature would not invest herself in such shadowing passion without some instruction. It is not words that shakes me thus. Pish! Noses, ears, and lips. Is't possible? – Confess? Handkerchief? O devil!

What Othello says and how he says it is where we start, but that alone doesn't unlock the speech. Only an imaginative grasp of his history and position in Venetian society, of what he fears to have taken place between Cassio and Desdemona, of his altered state of mind and emotions and the intensity of his mental images will bring that about.

So, again, we have to go beyond the lines and words and their sounds to experience how to express them.

Some practitioners like to *start* examination of text with the sounds. This may be technically interesting in a class situation, but for the actor in rehearsal it can encourage an overly conscious and mechanical illustration of the text, which may then block a deeper grasp of it through exploring the inner impulses and their vocal and physical expression. Berry has emphasized that 'it is the meaning that must always dictate the sound, and not the other way round. It is through the words that we will find the possibilities of the sound' (*The Actor and the Text*: 18).

Words and impulse

The words we use, especially in classical text, will be a mixture of short and long, of Anglo-Saxon, French or Latin origin. For example, Othello's speech in Act 1, when justifying his marriage to Desdemona before the Duke and her father, is far more formal and considered than in the imagistic, lurid, intense and frequently monosyllabic words of our scene.

This raises another controversial issue: do we know what we are going to say before we speak? We would say not. We start speaking and discover what we say as we speak, in response to others, and from what thoughts and images come to mind in the moment. **But, we know what we want to achieve by speaking on some level, however subconscious, before we start. We have an impulse, a need to speak, and we must identify what this is and where it's coming from to bring text to life.** The objective is such an impulse – but we don't keep thinking it and our actions as we speak, making the language slow, pausey, and falsely naturalistic: we get the thought and allow that to run through the lines like water through a pipe, adapting and reacting as we go to achieve what we want by speaking. There has to be an initial impulse to drive us into the first lines, otherwise we start speaking mechanically: 'To be or not to be' or Macbeth's 'If it were done when 'tis done' have to come from an impulse created in concrete, albeit imaginary, circumstances. The temptation in our pressured world is to get on and speak and don't pause. Often, actors rush into a speech and then chop it up with pauses, instead of doing the opposite – taking a moment to create the reality out of which the lines come and then flow the objective easily through the lines.

Most soliloquies, whether Macbeth's, Hamlet's, Angelo's or Iago's, involve a process of 'working out': whether it's working out what's happening within me, what I should do, or how to resolve a problem. They are never simply about reporting a set of facts or predetermined ideas. Even when a character – Richard III or Edmund in *King Lear*, for example – directly addresses the audience to inform them of a viewpoint or plan, they are trying to win the audience over, to justify their intentions and actions.

Here's a bit from Iago, Act 1, Scene 3:

Cassio's a proper man: let me see now;
To get his place and to plume up my will
In double knavery. How? How? Let's see.
After some time, to abuse Othello's ear
That he is too familiar with his wife;

He's *working out in the moment* how to get revenge on Othello and Cassio. At the start of the speech he doesn't yet know what to do. He goes through a process. He knows what he *wants*, but only discovers *how* to get it through the speech.

Even when Iago wants to impress us with the devilish ingenuity of his worked out plan, in Act 3, Scene 3, what he actually says is being created in the moment. The actor has to create that impression, and can only do that by absorbing in rehearsal the indicated and imagined life experience of Iago. This enables him to say the lines in italics below:

> I will in Cassio's lodgings lose this napkin
> And let him find it. *Trifles light as air*
> *Are to the jealous confirmations strong*
> *As proofs of holy writ.* This may do something.
> The Moor already changes with my poison:
> *Dangerous conceits are in their natures poisons,*
> *Which at the first are scarce found to distaste*
> *But, with a little act upon the blood,*
> *Burn like the mines of sulphur.* I did say so.

He doesn't know at the start of the speech that he will say these italicized lines. They only come out of his observation and experience of life, which he draws on to justify his resolved actions.

It's often said we need to be 'on the line', but this still implies a technical approach. We think we should be *in* the line, experiencing the line as our thoughts, feelings, responses, images, drives, so that there is no gap between the actor, the character, the circumstances and the text. **Text, meaning, character and action become one.**

Berry quotes Brook again:

> We are ready for another revolution … the purifying of thought. This comes about by a long weighing and tasting of the words and their sequences, that is never separated from – on the contrary, rigorously related to – levels of meaning. Only when the thought pattern gradually becomes clear can a new level of fresh, ever-changing impulses inform the words … It is a natural music, rediscovered each time. (*Word to Play*: 22)

This spontaneity within the structure is to our minds the essence of art: a freedom within a discipline, a flexibility combined with precision.

Traditional representational acting may offer technical skill often lacking in impulse and belief. The Strasberg Method may offer belief and feeling without the discipline of technique and form. Stanislavski's approach suggests both spontaneity and belief, and skill and structure. This integration is essentially the aim of this book.

A free flow of impulses *through* the words will also create the oft-quoted *energizing the line*, energy from word to word, line to line and speech to speech

– but it will be an energy that is not a fake adrenalized energy, or one of technical adroitness, but one coming organically from the situation.

Enriching through sound

So, having considered meaning, circumstances, objectives, images, all the subtext of the imaginary world of the play which gives rise to the lines, we can see how sounds can be experienced to accentuate and enrich, as in the figures of speech section above. For example:

OTHELLO   Cough or cry 'hem' if anybody come.

The alliteration of 'c' can be highlighted to express the abrupt and demeaning instruction to Emilia, likening her to a bawd.

Your mystery, your mystery!

The accusatory scorning will be brought out by savouring the three syllables and sounds in 'mystery'.

DESDEMONA   Your wife, my lord; your true and loyal wife.

Desdemona's need to convince him of her innocence, and her earnestness and genuine feeling will come through more strongly if we fully express the long open sounds in 'wife', 'lord', 'true', and 'loyal': ah-ee, aw, oo.

Similarly, their pain can only be expressed, flowing the thought and feeling *through* the lines, and not parallel to them, if we give full weight to the 'ay' sound in Othello's 'away, away, away', and Desdemona's 'heavy day'. An easy released open expression will lead to greater musicality, pitch range, and resonance. It also engages deep breathing and access to feeling.

OTHELLO   O ay: as summer flies are in the shambles

The sensual sound of the s's will highlight Othello's condemnation of her adulterous lust.

We receive the consonants, vowels and words they define from impulses, but then they can enhance the impulses and create new ones.

It may also be clear from these examples that, although the open vowels may best express emotions, both emotion and meaning can be expressed through vowels *and* consonants. This is as important for the gritty language of Arthur Miller's *The Crucible* and the poetry of Ted Hughes as for the classics.

CONCLUSION

We have talked of the creative state of *I am being*, when actors become one with the character in imaginary circumstances and experience the role moment by moment, able to take off into intuitive flights of action and imagination. When we experience the part like this rather than describe it from the outside, we also feel *I am my character's voice and body*. We become an integrated whole.

The process towards achieving this, and to connect voice teachers and other practitioners with it, has been the central focus of this book. We've looked at how to eradicate the blocks to integration, and how to reconnect with our natural vocal resources and allow them to follow inner creative impulse. We've looked at how these impulses are generated in the creative process as in the natural process of living, and at how they need artistic discipline, clarity of form and connection with audience in order to be communicated fully.

This astonishing voice/body/mind instrument we all possess will find creative fulfilment as long as we use it with care, respect and imagination, and create in performance recognizable human beings with a rich and alive vocal expression. There may be many obstacles to achieving this in an actor's life. We hope our book will help you to find ways to overcome them.

SELECTED BIBLIOGRAPHY

Aderhold, E., *Sprecherziehung des Schauspielers* [*Vocal education of the actor*], Henschel Verlag, Berlin, 1963

Adler, Stella, *The Art of Acting*, Applause Books, New York, 2000

Baggaley, Ann (ed.), *Human Body*, DK, London, 2001

Balk, H. W., *Performing Power*, University of Minnesota Press, Minneapolis, 1985

Barton, John, *Playing Shakespeare,* Methuen Drama, London, 1984

Benedetti, Jean, *Stanislavski and the Actor*, Methuen Drama, London, 1998

—*The Art of the Actor: The Essential History of Acting, from Classical Times to the Present Day*, Methuen, London, 2008

Berry, Cicely, *Voice and the Actor,* Virgin Books, London, 1973

—*The Actor and the Text,* Virgin Books, London, 1993

—*From Word to Play,* Oberon Books, London, 2008

Bogart, Anne and Landau, Tina, *The Viewpoints Book, A Practical Guide to Viewpoints and Composition*, Theatre Communications Group, New York, 2005

Boston, Jane and Cook, Rena, *Breath in Action: The Art of Breath in Vocal and Holistic Practice*, Jessica Kingsley Publishers, London and Philadelphia, 2009

Bunch, Meribeth, *Dynamics of the Singing Voice,* Springer, Wien, 1997

Carey, David and Carey, Rebecca Clark, *vocalartsworkbookanddvd*, Methuen Drama, London, 2008

—theVerbalartsWorkbook, Methuen Drama, London, 2010

Chekhov, Michael, *To the Actor,* Harper & Row, New York; Evanston, London, 1953

—Lessons for the Professional Actor, *Professional Arts Journal Publications*, USA, 1985

—*On the Technique of Acting* (Mel Gordon (ed.), preface and afterword by Mala Powers), Harper Perennial, New York, 1991

—*To the Actor,* London, Routledge, 2002

—*The Path of the Actor* (Andrei Kirillov and Bella Merlin (eds)), London and New York, Routledge, 2005

Cheng, Stephen Chun-Tao, *The Tao of Voice – A New East-West Approach to Transforming the Singing and Speaking Voice*, Destiny Books, Rochester, 1991

Cook, Orlanda, Singing with Your Own Voice, Routledge, New York, 2004

Damasio, Antonio, *The Feeling of What Happens – Body, Emotion and the Making of Consciousness*, Vintage, London, 2000

Dennis, Anne, *The Articulate Body, The Physical Training of the Actor,* Nick Hern Books, London, 2002

Dodin, Lev, *Journey Without End*, trans. Oksana Mamyrin and Anna Karabinska, Tantalus Books, London, 2005

Farhi, Donna, *The Breathing Book – Good Health and Vitality Through Essential Breath Work,* Holt Paperbacks, New York, 1996

—*Yoga Mind, Body and Spirit – A Return to Wholeness*, Newleaf, Dublin, 2000

Gillett, John, *Acting Stanislavski – A Practical Guide to Stanislavski's Approach and Legacy,* Bloomsbury Methuen Drama, London, 2014

Gorchakov, Nikolai M., *Stanislavsky Directs*, Connecticut, 1973

Grotowski, Jerzy, *Towards a Poor Theatre,* Methuen Drama, London, 1991

Hagen, Uta, *Respect for Acting*, Macmillan Publishing Company, New York, 1973

—*A Challenge for the Actor*, Scribner, New York, 1991

Hall, Peter, *Shakespeare's Advice to the Players*, Oberon Books, London, 2003

Hampton, Marion and Acker, Barbara, *The Vocal Vision, Views on Voice*, Applause Books, New York and London, 1997

Hartnoll, Phillis, *The Theatre, A Concise History*, Thames and Hudson, GB, 1985

Herbig, Regine, *Der Atem (The Breath)*, Schulz-Kirchner Verlag, Idstein, 2005

Hodge, Alison, *Twentieth Century Actor Training,* Routledge, Oxon, 2000

Houseman, Barbara, *Finding your Voice, A Step-by-Step Guide for Actors,* Nick Hern Books, London, 2002

—*Tackling Text, A Step-by-Step Guide for Actors*, Nick Hern Books, London, 2008

Hughes, Arthur, Trudgill, Peter and Watt, Dominic, *English Accents and Dialects,* Hodder Arnold, 2005.

Kaiser, Scott, *Mastering Shakespeare, An Acting Class in Seven Scenes,* Allworth Press, New York, 2003

Kaminoff, Leslie, *Yoga Anatomy*, Human Kinetics, USA, 2007

Knebel, Maria, *On the Active Analysis of Plays and Roles,* Isskustva, Moscow, 1982, trans. Mike Pushkin with Bella Merlin in an unpublished version (2002), courtesy of Bella Merlin

Laban, Rudolf, *Principles of Dance and Movement Notation*, Dance Horizons, New York, 1975

—*The Mastery of Movement*, Dance Books, 2011

Lessac, Arthur, *The Use and Training of the Human* Voice – *A Biodynamic Approach to Vocal Life,* Mayfield Publishing Company, California, 1997

Lewis, Dennis, *The Tao of Natural Breathing: For health, Well-Being, and Inner Growth,* Rodmell Press, Berkeley, California, 2006

Linklater, Kristin, *Freeing Shakespeare's Voice, The Actor's Guide to Talking the Text,* Theatre Communications Group, New York, 1992

—*Freeing The Natural Voice, Imagery and Art in the Practice of Voice and Language,* Nick Hern Books, London, 2006

Lowen, Alexander, *The Spirituality of the Body: Bioenergetics for Grace and Harmony,* Macmillan, New York, 1990

McCallion, Michael, *The Voice Book*, Faber and Faber Ltd, London, 1998

McCoy, Scott, *Your Voice: An Inside View*, Inside View Press, Delaware, 2012

McGilchrist, Iain, *The Master and his Emissary – The Divided Brain and the Making of the Modern World,* Yale University Press, New Haven and London, 2010

McNeill, D., *Hand and Mind: What Gestures Reveal about Thought,* University of Chicago Press, Chicago, 1992

Meisner, Sanford and Longwell, Dennis, *Sanford Meisner on Acting*, Vintage, New York, 1987

Middendorf, Ilse, *Der Erfahrbare Atem* [*The Perceptible Breath: A Breathing Science*], Junfermann-Verlag, Paderborn, 1990

Mitchell, G. A. G., *The Essentials of Neuroanatomy,* Churchill Livingstone, Edinburgh, 1971

Morrison, Malcolm, *Clear Speech*, A & C Black, London, 2001

Nachmanovitch, Stephen, *Free Play, Improvisation in Life and Art*, Tarcher/Penguin, New York, 1990

Newlove, Jean and Dalby, John, *Laban for All*, Nick Hern Books, London, 2004

Noble, Adrian, *How To Do Shakespeare,* Routledge, Oxon, 2010

Richards, Thomas, *At Work with Grotowski on Physical Actions,* Routledge, Oxon, 1995

Roach, Peter, *English Phonetics and Phonology,* Cambridge University Press, Cambridge, 1991

Rodenburg, Patsy, *The Actor Speaks,* Methuen Drama, London, 1997

Segalowitz, Sidney J., *Language Functions and Brain Organisation*, Academic Press, 1983

Sellers-Young, Barbara, *Breathing, Movement, Exploration,* Applause Books, New York and London, 2001

Sharpe, Edda and Haydn Rowles, Jan, *HOW TO DO ACCENTS,* Oberon Books, London, 2009

—*HOW TO DO Standard English ACCENTS,* Oberon Books, London, 2012

Shewell, Christina, *Voice Work – Art and Science in Changing Voices,* Wiley-Blackwell, Chichester, 2009

Stanislavski, Constantin, *An Actor Prepares*, translated by Elizabeth Reynolds Hapgood, Bloomsbury, London, 2013

—*Building a Character*, translated by Elizabeth Reynolds Hapgood, Bloomsbury, London, 2013

—*Creating a Role*, translated by Elizabeth Reynolds Hapgood, Bloomsbury, London, 2013

—*My Life in Art*, translated by J. J. Robbins, Methuen Drama, London, 2001

Stanislavski, Konstantin, *An Actor's Work,* trans. Jean Benedetti, Routledge, Oxon, 2008

—*An Actor's Work on a Role,* trans. Jean Benedetti, Routledge, Oxon, 2010

Stanislavsky, Konstantin, *Stanislavsky Produces Othello,* Geoffrey Bles, London, 1948

—*Stanislavsky on the Art of the Stage*, trans. and intro. David Magarshak, Faber and Faber, London, 1960

Steiner, Rudolf, *Speech and Drama*, SteinerBooks, 2007

Toporkov, Vasili, *Stanislavski in Rehearsal*, Methuen, London, 2001

Turner, Clifford, *Voice and Speech in the Theatre,* A & C Black, London, 1976

Walton, J. N., *Essentials of Neurology,* Churchill Livingstone, Edinburgh, 1989

Wright, D. S., Taylor, Ann, et al., *Introducing Psychology*: *An Experimental Approach*, Penguin, London, 1970

Yule, George, *The Study of Language*, Cambridge University Press, Cambridge, 1990

ABOUT THE AUTHORS

Christina Gutekunst trained as an actor in Germany and Britain, and then gained her PG diploma and MA in voice studies at the Central School of Speech and Drama. She has taught voice in numerous acting schools, coached for television and theatre productions, worked on voice-overs as actor and director and co-ran two theatre companies. She has been Head of Voice at East 15 Acting School since 2003.

John Gillett trained as an actor in the approach of Stanislavski and Michael Chekhov, and has worked widely as an actor in repertory, touring, small-scale and London theatre, radio, film and television. He has taught and directed in a number of drama schools, was Head of the Post Graduate Acting Course at East 15, and helped to run two theatre companies and acting training for professional actors. John is the author of *Acting on Impulse – Reclaiming the Stanislavski Approach* (Methuen Drama, 2007), now fully updated and revised as *Acting Stanislavski – A practical guide to Stanislavski's approach and legacy* (Bloomsbury Methuen Drama, 2014). www.gillettweb.co.uk.

INDEX

Page references in italic denotes a figure

PERMISSIONS